SWORD AND SHIELD
The Soviet Intelligence and Security Apparatus

JEFFREY RICHELSON

BALLINGER PUBLISHING COMPANY
Cambridge, Massachusetts
A Subsidiary of Harper & Row, Publishers, Inc.

Copyright © 1986 by Ballinger Publishing Company. All rights reserved.
No part of this publication may be reproduced, stored in a retrieval system, or transmitted in any form or by any means, electronic, mechanical,
photocopy, recording or otherwise, without the prior written consent of
the publisher.

International Standard Book Number: 0-88730-035-9 (C)
0-88730-039-1 (P)

Library of Congress Catalog Card Number: 85-15073

Printed in the United States of America

Library of Congress Cataloging in Publication Data

Richelson, Jeffrey.
  Sword and shield.

  Bibliography: p.
  Includes index.
  1. Intelligence service—Soviet Union. 2. Internal security—
Soviet Union. 3. Soviet Union—National security. I. Title
UB251.S65R53   1986   327.1'2'0947   85-15073
ISBN 0-88730-035-9
ISBN 0-88730-039-1 (pbk.)

CONTENTS

LIST OF FIGURES

LIST OF TABLES

LIST OF ABBREVIATIONS
AND ACRONYMS

AAPSO	Afro-Asian People's Organization
ABM	antiballistic missile
AFB	Air Force Base
AFL-CIO	American Federation of Labor-Congress of Industrial Organizations
AFOSI	Air Force Office of Special Investigations
AGI	Auxiliary-Intelligence Gathering
Amtorg	American Trade Organization
APN	Novosti Press Agency
ASAT	Antisatellite
ASIS	Australian Secret Intelligence Service
ASW	antisubmarine warfare
AVH	*Allavedelmi Hatosag*; State Security Authority (Hungary)
BFV	*Bundesamt für verfassungschutz*; Federal Office for the Protection of the Constitution (W. Germany)
BND	*Bundesnachrichtendienst*; Federal Intelligence Service (W. Germany)
CAD/CAM	computer-aided design/computer-aided manufacture
CC	Central Committee (Soviet Union)
CEDOK	Czechoslovak travel office
CEP	Circle of Equal Probability
CIA	Central Intelligence Agency
CINC	Commander-in-Chief

xiii

COCOM	Coordinating Committee for Multilateral Export Controls
COMINT	Communications Intelligence
COMSEC	Communications Security
CPC	Christian Peace Council
CPUSA	Communist Party of the United States of America
CPSU	Communist Party of the Soviet Union
CSA	Czechoslovak Airlines
CTK	Czechoslovak press office
DA	*Departmento America*; Americas Department (Cuba)
DGI	*Direccion General de Inteligencia*; Directorate General of Intelligence (Cuba)
DGRE	*Departmento General de Relaciones Exteriores*; General Department for Foreign Relations (Cuba)
DIA	Defense Intelligence Agency
DIS	Defense Investigative Service
DOE	*Direccion de Operaciones Especiales*; Directorate of Special Operations (Cuba)
DS	*Durzhavna Sigurnost*; State Security (Bulgaria)
DSE	*Departmento de Seguridad del Estado*; Department of State Security (Cuba)
EEC	European Economic Community
ELINT	Electronic Intelligence
EOB	electronic order of battle
EORSAT	Elint Ocean Reconnaissance Satellite
EPS	Executive Protective Service
FBI	Federal Bureau of Investigation
FIR	International Federation of Resistance Fighters
FSZS	Federal Directorate of Intelligence Services (Czechoslovakia)
FY	Fiscal Year
GAO	General Accounting Office
GLAVLIT	Chief Administration for Safeguarding State Secrets in Print
GCCS	Government Code and Cypher School
GCHQ	Government Communications Headquarters (Britain)
GKNT	State Committee for Science and Technology (Soviet Union)
GLCM	ground-launched cruise missile
GSFG	Group of Soviet Forces in Germany
GOSPLAN	State Planning Agency (Soviet Union)
GPU	*Gosudrarstvennoye Politicheskие Upravleniye*; State Political Administration (Soviet Union)

GRU   *Glavnoye Razvedyvatelnoye Upravleniye*; Chief Intelligence
            Directorate (Soviet Union)

GUGB   *Glavnoye Upravleniye Gosudarstvennoy Bezopasnosti*; Chief
            Administration of State Security (Soviet Union)

HSR   *Hlavni Sprava Rozvedky*; Main Directorate of Intelligence
            (Czechoslovakia)

HUMINT   Human Intelligence

HVA   *Hauptverwaltung Aufklaerung*; Main Administration for
            Intelligence (E. Germany)

IADL   International Association of Democratic Lawyers

ICAP   Cuban Institute for Friendship with People's

ICBM   intercontinental ballistic missile

ID   International Department

IFF   Identification Friend or Foe

IID   International Information Department

IIP   International Institute for Peace

IMEMO   *Institut mirovoj ekonomiki i mezhdunarodnykh otnoshenii*;
            Institute of World Economics and International Relations

INO   *Innostrannoye Otdel*; Foreign Department (Soviet Union)

INU   *Innostrannoye Upravleniye*; Foreign Directorate (First Chief
            Directorate) (Soviet Union)

IOJ   International Organization of Journalists

IREX   International Research and Exchange Board

IUS   International Union of Students

JCS   Joint Chiefs of Staff

JTLS   Joint Technical Language Service

KDS   *Komitet za Durzhavna Sigurnost*; Committee for State Security
            (Bulgaria)

KGB   *Komitet Gosudarstvennoy Bezopasnosti*; Committee for State
            Security (Soviet Union)

KH–11   Keyhole 11 (Satellite)

KI   *Komitet Informatsyia*; Committee of Information (Soviet Union)

LASL   Los Alamos Scientific Laboratory

MAD   *Militärischer Abschirmdienst*; Military Security Service
            (W. Germany)

MAR   Movement of Revolutionary Action

MFA   Ministry of Foreign Affairs

MfS   *Ministerium für Staatssicherheit*; Ministry for State Security
            (E. Germany)

MGB   *Ministerstvo Gosudarstvennoy Bezopasnosti*; Ministry of State
        Security (Soviet Union)

mm   millimeter

MMC   *Glavnyy Voyenyy Sovyet*; Main Military Council

MND   *Militärsche Nachrictendienst*; Military Intelligence Service
        (E. Germany)

MPA   Main Political Administration (of the Soviet Army and Navy)

MPLA   Popular Movement for the Liberation of Angola

MRBM   medium range ballistic missile

MVD   *Ministerstvo Vnutrennikh Del*; Ministry of Internal Affairs
        (Soviet Union)

NAACP   National Association for the Advancement of Colored People

NASA   National Aeronautics and Space Administration

NATO   North Atlantic Treaty Organization

NCASF   National Council of American-Soviet Friendship

NID   Naval Intelligence Division

NIS   Naval Investigative Service

NKGB   *Narodnyy Komissariat Gosudarstvennoy Bezopasnosti*;
        People's Commissariat for State Security (Soviet Union)

NKVD   *Narodnyy Komissariat Vnutrennikh Del*; People's Commissariat for
        Internal Affairs (Soviet Union)

NSA   National Security Agency

NSC   National Security Council

NTIS   National Technical Information Service

NTS   *Narodnyy Trudovoy Soyuz*; People's Labor League

NVOI   National Voice of Iran

OGPU   *Obyedinennoye Gosudarstvennoy Politicheskie Upravleniye*;
        United State Political Administration (Soviet Union)

OIRT   International Radio and TV Organization

OKR   *Otdel Kontrrazvedka*; Counterintelligence Department

O.M.   Operations Memorandum

OOs   *Osobye Otdely*; Special Departments

OPC   Office of Political Coordination

OPSEC   Operations Security

OSNAZ   *Osobogo Naznacheniya*; Detachment of Special Purpose

OTA   Office of Technology Assessment

PACOM   Pacific Command

PLO   Palestinian Liberation Organization

PRM	Presidential Review Memorandum
POW	prisoner of war
PRC	People's Republic of China
PVO	*Voyska Protivovozdushnoy Oborony Strany*; Troops of National Air Defense (Soviet Union)
RCMP	Royal Canadian Mounted Police
RDF	Rapid Deployment Force
RNVR	Royal Navy Volunteer Reserve
RORSAT	Radar Ocean Reconnaissance Satellite
RSFSR	Russian Soviet Federated Socialist Republic
RU	*Razvedyvatelnoye Upravleniye*; Intelligence Directorate
RUMNO	*Razuznavatelno Upravleniye Na Ministerstvoto Na Narodnata Otbrana*; Intelligence Division, Ministry of National Defense (Bulgaria)
SAC	Strategic Air Command
SALT	Strategic Arms Limitation Talks
SB	*Sluzba Bezpieczecstwa*; Security Service (Poland)
SD	*Sicherheitsdienst*; Security Service (of the Nazi party)
SDC	Submarine Defence Commission (Sweden)
SICR	Special Intelligence Collection Requirement
SIGINT	Signals Intelligence
SIS	Secret Intelligence Service (British)
SMERSH	*"Smert Shpionam"*; "Death to Spies"
SOSIAC	Singapore-Soviet Shipping Company
SOE	Special Operations Executive
SSD	*Staatssicherheitsdienst*; State Security Service (E. Germany)
START	Strategic Arms Reduction Talks
SWAPO	Southwest African People's Organization (Namibia)
TASS	*Telegrafnoe Agentstvo Sovetskovo Soyuza*
TERCAS	Terminal and En-Route Control Automated Systems
UB	*Uzrad Bezpieczzestwa*; Security Forces (Poland)
UHF	Ultra High Frequencies
UPDK	Directorate for Servicing the Diplomatic Corps (Soviet Union)
USIA	United States Information Agency
USIS	United States Information Service
VECHERA	*Vserossiyskaya Chrezvychaynaya Komissiya poborbe s Kontr-Revolyutsiyey i Sabotazhem*
VHF	Very High Frequencies

VINITI	All-Union Institute of Scientific and Technical Information (Soviet)
VPK	Military-Industrial Commission (Soviet)
VTsIK	*Vserossiiskii Tsentralnyi Ispolnitelnyi Komitet*; All-Russian Central Executive Committee
WFDY	World Federation of Democratic Youth
WFO	Washington Field Office
WFSW	World Federation of Scientific Workers
WFTU	World Federation of Trade Unions
WIDF	Women's International Democratic Federation
WIN	Freedom and Independence (Polish resistance group)
WPC	World Peace Council
WSW	*Wojska Sluzby Wewnetrznej*; Military Internal Service
ZAPU	Zimbabwe African People's Union
ZSGS	*Zpravodajska Sprava Generalniko Stabu*; Intelligence Directorate of the General Staff (Czechoslovakia)

PREFACE

The ability to turn my notes and files on Soviet Intelligence into a book has been greatly enhanced by the opportunity to teach a course on Soviet Intelligence at American University in the previous two academic years. I would like to express my appreciation to the students of those courses for providing a testing ground.

I would also like to thank several individuals for providing material or helpful suggestions. Included in this category are William Arkin, Scott Armstrong, James Bamford, Richard Fieldhouse, and Amy Knight. Special thanks goes to Desmond Ball for sharing with me the product of his research on Soviet signals intelligence activities.

Finally, a debt of gratitude is owed those at Ballinger—particularly Carol Franco, Dave Barber, and Barbara Roth—for rapidly turning the manuscript into a book.

1 HISTORY

The establishment of the Bolshevik regime in 1917 soon brought with it the establishment of a secret police organization and a military intelligence organization. This was, however, far from the first Russian experience with such organizations. As Russia had always been ruled by dictators, it is not surprising that those dictators felt the need to establish organizations to detect and suppress conspiracies and dissent.

SECURITY AND INTELLIGENCE
BEFORE THE BOLSHEVIKS

The first such organization was the *Oprichnina*, set up in 1565 by Ivan the Terrible, the first Grand Duke of Moscow to be crowned as Tsar. The *Oprichniki* were Horse Guards, completely attired in black, including a cowl. The insignia on their saddles—the twin embroidered device of a broom and a dog's head—symbolized the mission of the *Oprichnina*: to sniff out and sweep out anyone who displeased Ivan.[1]

The *Oprichnina* consisted of about 6,000 men, who, over the organization's seven-year lifetime, killed many times that number of individuals. In 1570 Ivan unleashed this force, along with more conventional forces, on the city of Novgorod, which was suspected of

1

collaborating with the enemy state of Lithuania. In a five-week period, tens of thousands of Novgorodians were killed.[2] A foreigner visiting Russia at the time remarked that "if Satan himself attempted to think of a plan for destroying mankind, he could have invented nothing more devilish."[3]

The *Oprichnina* was abolished in 1572, with the death of Ivan, and for the next 125 years no political police organization existed. In 1697, fifteen years into his reign, Peter the Great established the *Preobrazhensky Office*. The office was authorized to investigate political subversion and was assisted by the "Fiscals," a large network of agents whose original function was to oversee tax collections and prevent financial abuses but who specialized more in informing and denouncing.[4]

The *Preobrazhensky Office* was abolished in 1729, four years after Peter's death. In 1731 Peter's successor, Empress Anne, established its replacement: the Chancellory for Secret Investigations.[5] On February 21, 1762 Anne's successor, Peter the Third, abolished the chancellory. By that time, however, Peter's own secret police organization, the Secret Bureau, had been in existence for two weeks. The bureau continued on till 1801, when it was abolished by Alexander I. Under Alexander's directive, political security was to be handled by the regular police, who were supplemented in their political security work by two special commissions created in 1805 and 1807.[6] According to one account, the second commission, "known as the Committee of January 13, 1807 became the successor to the Secret Bureau and was continued until a few years after Alexander's death."[7]

Alexander's successor, Emperor Nicholas I, first set up a secret police organization in response to the "Decembrist" uprising of December 14, 1825, with the intent of preventing similar occurrences in the future. Hence, the Third Section came into being on July 3, 1826. Its responsibilities were basically limited to the capital; another organization, the Corps de Gendarmie, functioned throughout the rest of Russia.[8]

The Third Section had authorization to inquire into all matters. In 1833 an American envoy reported to the president that "you can scarcely hire a servant who is not a member of the secret police."[9] The omnipresence of the Third Section was apparently limited to the capital and a few other large cities, where "it was quite effective in hamstringing political thought and action, censoring books and publications and eliminating liberals from the educational field."[10] In the provinces, on the other hand, it was much less informed and never exercised complete control, as evidenced by the 700 major uprisings of serfs that plagued Nicholas's regime. Toward the end of his reign, Nicholas stated: "I have no police, I dislike it."[12]

In addition to its domestic activities, the Third Section, beginning in 1832, also maintained agents abroad. Its immediate foreign objective was the surveillance of Polish emigré organizations, subsequently branching out to other areas of intelligence collection.[13]

In August 1880 the section was abolished by Nicholas's successor, Alexander II. Its duties were transferred to the Department of State Police, subordinate to the Ministry of the Interior. The Corps of Gendarmerie was maintained.[14] The Department of State Police created a central special department (*Osobyi Otdel*) and a countrywide network of Protective Sections, the *Okhrannye Otdeleniya*, known as the Okhrana. Initial offices were established in St. Petersburg, Moscow, and Warsaw and then in virtually every city and town of significance.[15]

While formally subordinate to the State Police, the Special Department, commonly referred to as the *Okhrana*, became a law unto itself, exercising almost complete power over the Tsar's subjects. This power stemmed from the Okhrana's right of entry without a warrant, its ability to deport undesired individuals to Siberia without trial, its power to conduct surveillance of anyone, and in important cases the authorization to impose the death penalty without trial.[16]

The Special Department was organized into four agencies: External, Internal, Foreign, and Central. The External Agency performed, within Russia, routine surveillance of suspects and possible suspects. The Internal Agency specialized in deep-cover penetration of revolutionary and suspected revolutionary organizations. The Foreign Agency, operated abroad, mainly in areas such as France, Switzerland, and Britain, where Russian revolutionaries and dissidents congregated. The Central Agency operated under the deepest cover, its mission being to handle double agents.[17]

World War I brought an expansion of the Russian intelligence apparatus. At first the German and Austro–Hungary section of the Russian Army's GHQ (General Headquarters) handled intelligence matters concerning Russia's enemies. Subsequently, two organizations attached to GHQ under the overall responsibility of the quartermaster general were established: *Razvedka* (Intelligence) and *Kontrrazvedka* (Counterintelligence). Before the war, intelligence was collected about Germany and Austro–Hungary chiefly via military attachés, although district posts in Warsaw and Kiev also controlled separate intelligence agents in those countries. When attachés had to be withdrawn from Germany and Austro–Hungary after the war, centers were set up in Sweden, Denmark, Holland, and Switzerland.[18]

In addition to running agents, the intelligence service was also gathering and making use of communications intelligence (COMINT). Thus, according to one participant,

> Following the occupation of Courland (West Latvia) by the German troops, the German Ground Forces Command, which was rushing to seize Riga, requested the Naval Staff to provide support from the sea. COMINT revealed these conversations and established the date of the planned operation. The (Russian) Fleet Commander decided to strengthen the naval forces in the Gulf of Riga by sending the battleship *Slava*. On 31 July 1915 the *Slava* took the enemy completely by surprise by crossing over from the Gulf of Riga. COMINT provided such good information about the enemy's plans that when the German fleet, on the morning of 8 August, approached Irbenskij Strait, our torpedo boats and two gunboats were already waiting for them. By 1000 hours the *Slava* also approached the strait. The German's plan to break through into the Gulf of Riga was thwarted.[19]

Whereas the Okrana was dissolved with the fall of the Tsarist regime in March of 1917, the military intelligence organizations probably survived until at the least the fall of the Provisional Government in November of that year, possibly surviving even longer—until the Bolsheviks took firm control of the Army.

CHEKA AND RU

On November 7, 1917 the Provisional Government of Aleksandr Kerensky was overthrown by a Bolshevik-led coup d'état. Six weeks later Lenin reestablished the political police in the form of the All-Russian Extraordinary Commission for Combatting Counter-revolution and Sabotage (*Vserrossiyskaya Chrezvychaynaya Komissiya poborbe s Kontr-Revolyutsiyey i Sabotazhem*) or Vecheka. The Vecheka was formally established in Petrograd by a Council of People's Commissars (*Sovnarkom*) resolution on December 20, 1917.[20]

The functions of the Vecheka, known commonly simply as the Cheka, were to:

1. ferret out and liquidate all counterrevolution and sabotage attempts and actions;
2. hand over all saboteurs and counterrevolutionaries to the Revolutionary Tribunal and prepare measures for combating them; and
3. carry out preliminary investigations only to the extent necessary for suppression.[21]

Although technically it worked in conjunction with the People's Commissariat for Internal Affairs (NKVD) and People's Commissariat of Justice, it acted without interference from other organizations and officially answered solely to the Council of People's Commissars. In the 1918–1921 period, the Vecheka expanded its powers in several ways. When first created, the Vecheka was not entitled to pass sentences or carry out executions. For its first ten days it even lacked the power of arrest.[22]

Several events contributed to the Vecheka's increase in power: the civil war that began within a few months after the Bolsheviks and Left Social Revolutionaries abolished Russia's only freely elected constituent assembly in January 1918, the collapse of the Brest–Livostok peace negotiations in February 1918, and the abortive uprising staged by the Left Social Revolutionaries in early July 1918. On August 30 the chairman of the Petrograd Cheka, M.S. Uritsky, was assassinated and Lenin himself wounded. In response, Lenin signed a *Sovnarkom* decree entitled "The Socialist Fatherland Is in Danger." The decree stated that "enemy agents, speculators, thugs, hooligans, counter-revolutionary agitators, German spies, are to be shot on the scene of their crime."[23] On the basis of this decree, which was, in effect, a temporary martial law edict, the Vecheka arrogated to itself the right to conduct executions without trial or any proceedings whatsoever.

The Vecheka's authority for the use of terror was further formalized by a decree of the All-Russian Central Executive Committee (VTsIK) of June 20, 1919, which contained a list of crimes for which the Vecheka could exact direct retribution. Included were concealment of traitors and spies, concealment for counter-revolutionary purposes of lethal weapons, participation in arson, deliberate damage to railway and military installations, robbery and armed theft, and illegal plundering. In addition, on October 21 of that year, a Special Revolutionary Tribunal was created under the Vecheka and charged with fighting theft and speculation.[24]

Obviously, the program was to establish complete internal control. Any activities that hindered the attainment of this objective—whether they were of a political, military, economic, or sociological nature— were targets for Vecheka action. Nor was the use of capital punishment a reluctant last resort; it was a central instrument of its program. Thus, in June 1918, Felixs Dzerzhinsky, head of the Vecheka, stated that his organization

> stood for organized terror. . . . Terror is an absolute necessity during times of revolution. . . . We terrorize the enemies of the Soviet Government in order to stop crime at its inception. . . . [T] he Cheka is not a court. The Cheka is the defense of the Revolution as the Red Army is. And just as in the Civil War, the Red Army cannot stop to ask whether or not it may harm individuals. . . . [T] he Cheka is obliged to defend the revolution and conquer the enemy, even if its sword does by chance sometime fall upon the heads of the innocent.[25]

Dzerzhinsky's attitude was not simply that of an overly zealous security chief. At the beginning of the century, Lenin himself had expressed his approval of the use of terror: "We have never rejected terror on principle, nor can we ever do so, for that is one of those military actions which can be very useful and even indispensible in certain moments of battle."[26]

Support for the Vecheka and its employment of terror was not universal. One dissenter was the first People's Commissar of Justice, the Left Social Revolutionary I. Z. Shteynberg. Even under revolutionary conditions he tried to build up a judiciary system and protested against arbitrary acts of the Vecheka. He often ordered the release of people arrested and insisted all such cases be discussed by the Council of People's Commissars. Additionally, he drafted Vecheka statutes in such a way as to limit the mandate, whereas Lenin sought to expand the mandate. Finally, Shteynberg argued that arrest should be made only with the knowledge of the People's Commissariats of Justice and Home Affairs.[27]

The conflict between Shteynberg and Lenin reached its most dramatic point when Shteynberg became exasperated with Lenin's support for the introduction of a harsh police measure with extensive implications of terror. He exclaimed: "Then why do we bother with a Commissariat of Justice? Let's call it frankly the Commissariat for Social Extermination and be done with it!" Lenin's response was probably the most disheartening one Shteynberg could have received. His face lit up and he replied: "Well put . . . that's exactly what it should be . . . but we can't say that."[28]

Opposition to arbitrary Vecheka actions also came from the higher circles of the Bolshevik party in the form of Lev Kamenev. At the Sixth Congress of Soviets, which ran from November 6 to 9, 1918, Kamenev proposed releasing all Vecheka prisoners against whom no concrete charges were made within two weeks of arrest. In January 1919 Kamenev proposed to Lenin a draft resolution calling for the immediate abolition of the Vecheka and all its organs and the transfer of its functions to Revolutionary Tribunals. The Tribunals would be supervised centrally by a special department of the All-Russian Central Executive Committee.[29]

With Lenin's help, the Vecheka survived such challenges. Lenin himself did keep a close watch on the Vecheka. According to one observer, "he regulated its powers, he apportioned praise and occasionally, blame, he from time to time inquired minutely into its investigation of individuals."[30] His interventions on the side of the Vecheka's victims have been interpreted by some not as an evidence of concern for justice or particular individuals but rather as a means of exercising control, of reminding the national and regional organizations that he was aware of their activities in detail.[31]

Nineteen eighteen had seen three events of significance with regard to an expanded mission for the Vecheka. Border Chekas were set up by those Provisional Chekas (while the central organization was formally the Vecheka, subordinate units through Russia were simply Chekas), the territory of which included border areas. Three types of border troops were established: Land Border Troops, Maritime Border Troops, and Aviation Border Regiments. This basic framework still exists. The functions assigned to the border troops were to:

1. repel armed incursions into Soviet territory and protect the frontier population and state and private property;
2. prevent illegal entry or exit and, with the Customs Authorities, of the smuggling of goods, literature, and foreign currency;
3. regulate the movement within the frontier areas and into them from elsewhere in the country in collaboration with the militia;

4. maintain frontier markings; and
5. pursue and detect those infringing frontier regulations.[32]

In light of the attempted assassination of Lenin, increased attention was given to the problem of guarding the Soviet leadership. Two Vecheka components, first created in 1918, were assigned responsibility for guarding the leadership and key installations: the Detachment of Special Purpose (OSNAZ—*Otryad Osobogo Naznacheniya*) and Units of Special Purpose (CHON—*Chasti Osobogo Naznacheniya*).[33] In addition to protecting party leaders, the troops were used in guarding key political, economic, and military installations and suppressing counterrevolutionary risings.[34]

The third event was a resolution of the Council of People's Commissars passed on July 15, 1918 which established an Extraordinary Commission (Cheka) on the Eastern Front. This was followed by the establishment of Cheka organs called Special Departments (*Osobye Otdely*—OOs) at other fronts with the mission of combating counterrevolution, espionage, and criminal activities within the Red Army.[35] A central Special Department was established on January 1, 1919 at Vecheka headquarters and a February directive of the All-Russian Central Executive Committee formally assigned responsibility for security in the Red Army and Navy upon the Special Department of the Vecheka. The importance of the Special Department and its subordinate OOs was such that it accounted for one-third of the Vecheka budget for 1920 (1.5 billion rubles out of 4.5 billion).[36]

In addition to expanding its mission in the security area, the Vecheka also moved well beyond the security function and into any area where it could facilitate the attainment of Party goals. Thus, in a December 1920 interview in *Izvestia*, the head of a special commission created to deal with economic speculation stated that in the future the Vecheka would seek to promote "the development and growth of the economic institutions of the Republic by means of appropriate supervision, and when necessary, by bringing pressure to bear on one or another aspect of their work."[37] According to George Leggett:

> The Vecheka . . . proved itself to be such a well disciplined, efficient and versatile machine, applying its widely deployed manpower resources with ruthless authority, that it became an indispensable all-purpose tool of Party and Government. Even if it lacked the specialized expertise to solve, by itself, the various problems encountered, the Vecheka could be relied upon to mobi-

lize and oversee the manpower needed for any given project. In a country ravaged by Civil War and ruled by decree in the face of widespread opposition, it required application of unrelenting pressure and fear to impose the will of the proletarian dictatorship, and to achieve rapid and positive results; armed with powers of life and death, and preceded by a fearsome reputation, the Vecheka proved to be the ideal, ready-made agency for such purposes.[38]

It was not until the end of the civil war and the consolidation of Soviet power at the end of 1920 that a specific department for foreign operations, the Foreign Department (INO–*Innostrannoye Otdel*), was created.[39] As with the Tsarist political police, its primary foreign mission was the surveillance of emigrés abroad and the disruption of their activities.

In pursuit of this mission, the INO launched one of the most famous of all intelligence operations: the Trust. Using infiltrated Soviet-based opposition (Monarchist) groups to make contact with emigré groups, the INO discouraged activity against the Soviet regime on the grounds that such activity would be counterproductive. Eventually, the operation was able to lure some of the opposition leaders back to the Soviet Union. It also lured back British agent Sidney Reilly.[40]

Nineteen twenty-one marked the beginning of the end for the Vecheka. With the Bolshevik position in Russia secure, Lenin addressed the Ninth Congress of Soviets and stated:

Our failures are sometimes the continuation of our virtues, and that is so in the case of the Cheka. It was heroic when it defended the Revolution against countless foreign enemies, when it was our most effective weapon against innumerable attacks. . . . But now, in present circumstances, it is necessary to restrict the institution, to a purely political sphere. We say emphatically that it is time to reform the Cheka.[41]

"Reform" began with a decree of June 23, 1921. The decree specified that in the future the Cheka could condemn to a maximum of two years' confinement only persons belonging to "anti–Soviet political parties" or to "flagrantly white guard elements." It could carry out shootings only in places under military law and then only for espionage, banditry, or armed rebellion.[42]

Despite its reform and numerous name changes, the Vecheka established the basic framework under which Soviet secret police organizations operated. The Veckeka's insignia was a sword on top of a shield. The Vecheka protected the revolution and Party both by its work in the security area and in areas such as transport and the economy. It also served as a sword in all those areas—meting out punishment to "saboteurs," the lazy, and others who did not conform to the Party's wishes.

The 1918–1921 period also saw the further development of military intelligence. In 1918 the Registration Department of the Red Army was formed. In 1921 it became the Intelligence Directorate (RU) of the General Staff and in 1926 the Chief Intelligence Directorate (GRU).[43]

GPU TO KGB

The ultimate "reform" of the Vecheka was its abolition and replacement by the State Political Administration or GPU (*Gosudarstvennoy Politicheskie Upravleniye*) on February 6, 1922. The GPU's functions were more limited than those of the Vecheka. Specifically, its functions were defined as:

1. suppression of overt counterrevolutionary activity, including banditry;
2. counterespionage;
3. protection of railways and waterways; and
4. guarding of the RSFSR's (Russian Soviet Federated Socialist Republic) frontiers against illegal crossing and smuggling.[44]

The declared intent of the decree was to make the GPU responsible for dealing specifically with politically subversive activities; all other, purely criminal matters such as speculation and misuse of official position were to be the preoccupation of law courts and revolutionary tribunals. Vecheka rights of meting out sentence and punishment were not transferred to the GPU.[45]

However, Lenin still required the isolation or elimination of militant class enemies and political adversaries such as Mensheviks, Social Revolutionaries, and Anarchists. By a decree of the All-Russian Central Executive Committee on August 10, 1922, the GPU was authorized to exile by administrative orders either abroad or to designated locations within the RSFSR for a period of not greater than three years, persons engaging in counterrevolutionary activity, subject to approval of a Special Commission of the People's Commissariat of Internal Affairs. On October 16, 1922 the GPU was authorized in cases of bandit raids and armed robbery to punish by summary process, including execution, any persons caught red-handed on the scene of the crime.[46]

The GPU was renamed the United State Political Administration (OGPU—*Obyedinennoye Gosudarstvennoy Politicheskie Upravleniye*) in November 1923. The name change reflected the creation of the Soviet Union as a "federation" of fifteen socialist republics. In addition to its name change, the power of the new OGPU was increased. Article 61 of the new constitution vested the OGPU with the duty "to unite the revolutionary efforts of the Union Republics in the struggle against political and economic counter-revolution, espionage, and banditism."[47] The constitution also reserved a place for its chairman in the All-Union Council of People's Commissars with a deliberative vote. And while Article 63 gave supervisory powers to the prosecutor of the Supreme Court of the Soviet Union, no legal statutes or procedures were permitted to interfere in the carrying out of the Party leadership's directives.

The most significant aspect of the OGPU's being mentioned in the constitution did not relate to any specification of its powers. Rather, it was the fact that it was mentioned at all. Its inclusion in the constitution represented official recognition that a secret police force was to be a permanent aspect of Soviet rule. Previously, the official view was that the secret police was a transitory, extraordinary institution that would disappear when Soviet power was secure. Thus, Vecheka official Martin Latsis had stated that the

> Cheka is an extraordinary organ created for the period of the Civil War. . . . As an extraordinary and temporary organ the Cheka has no place in our constitutional system. The time of the Civil War, the time of extraordinary conditions of the existence of Soviet power, will pass and the Chekas will become superfluous.[48]

One facet of the OGPU's increased importance was the authorization of its censorship role: It was assigned responsibility for censorship of printed matter, plays, and films. More important, labor camps and the border guards were centralized under the OGPU. By a law of April 7, 1930 the OGPU was authorized to banish individuals to labor camps.[49] In 1932 the OGPU simultaneously gained control over the militia and introduced the internal passport system. A decree of March 14, 1933 stated it had the power to shoot.[50] Thus, by 1934 the OGPU had gained a monopoly of police functions.

This expansion of secret police powers and its subsequent contraction is a theme often repeated in the history of the Soviet intelligence and security apparatus. The subsequent contraction came with a decree of July 10, 1934 when the OGPU was absorbed into the NKVD. The foreign intelligence and internal security/political police functions of the OGPU were now exercised by the Chief Administration of State Security (GUGB–*Glavnoye Upravleniye Gosudarstvennoy Bezopasnosti*). Separate chief administrations supervised the Worker–Peasant Militia, the Border and Internal Guards (GUPVO), and the Corrective Labor Camps (GULAG).[51]

During the latter stages of the OGPU's existence (1930–1934) and the years prior to World War II, the Soviet secret police was involved in several major domestic and foreign operations. Stalin issued a decree on December 27, 1929, which unleashed the OGPU on the peasantry, the only group he believed had the potential for organized opposition. According to Barron, "[d]uring the dispossession and collectivization of some 10 million peasants that followed, at least 3.5 million people perished."[52]

Subsequently, Stalin and the GUGB turned their attention to a more startling target: the Communist Party. Stalin's objectives were to gain complete mastery of the Party and country—to eliminate all possible sources of opposition. The purges that followed consumed millions of Party members, including Politburo members Bukharin and Kamenev.

One consequence of the purge was an expansion of the GUGB foreign apparatus. Stalin gave instructions that the OGPU must be able to "purge" officials in foreign countries (whether Soviet or foreign Communists) who were reluctant to return to the "Socialist Fatherland."[53] For this purpose NKVD Chief Yezhov created, in December 1936, the Administration of Special Tasks.[54]

Soviet intelligence operations in the 1930s also focused on the infiltration of agents into the Western and Fascist countries—an infiltration that still has repercussions to this day. In the early 1930s it recruited several Cambridge undergraduates and dons—among them Anthony Blunt, Kim Philby, Donald MacLean, and Guy Burgess. Blunt served in MI5 (the British Security Service) during the war, MacLean and Burgess in the diplomatic corps until 1951, and Kim Philby in the Special Operations Executive (SOE) and Secret Intelligence Service (SIS).[55]

During the 1930s and early 1940s the GRU established agent networks of great significance, including the Sorge network and the Red Orchestra. Richard Sorge was born in the Caucasus in 1895 and moved to Berlin with his family and earned a Ph.D. in Political Science. On the day of his graduation he joined the Hamburg section of the German Communist Party. He was subsequently selected for political intelligence assignments by the covert apparatus of the Third Communist International.[56] His first assignment was to consolidate and expand the GRU's China network. In 1934 he was reassigned to Tokyo. Prior to leaving for Tokyo, Sorge went to Germany and joined the Nazi party and secured an assignment as the Tokyo correspondent of the influential *Frankfurter Zeitung.* The position gave him access to German diplomatic and business circles—an access he used to cultivate the military attaché and the ambassador.[57]

Among Sorge's agents was Ozaki Hozumi, who had contacts with Premier Prince Konoye and other high-ranking Japanese. Hozumi became a member of Konoye's informal advisers, then a full-time special adviser to the cabinet subcommittee on Sino–Japanese relations and in 1938 principal secretary to the cabinet. When Ozaki lost his cabinet job, he became an intelligence officer in the Tokyo office of the Southern Manchurian Railway, a post where he would be the first, next to the Army Command, to learn of troop movements in the Manchurian Sector that was vital to Moscow.[58]

With Hozumi's aid, Sorge was able to forecast, several weeks ahead of time, the Japanese military mutiny of February 1936 and the Japanese invasion of China in July 1937, and he reassured Soviet decisionmakers that troop movements involved were directed south and not against Siberia. Sorge also forwarded details of the Anti–Comintern Pact to Moscow before details reached either the Japanese Cabinet or the German High Command and a month before its public announcement.[59] Furthermore, Sorge was able to warn Moscow that a German attack on the Soviet Union was coming on June 20 (two days off)—a warning that was ignored by Stalin.

However, subsequent information that Japanese military forces would move south against Southeast Asia and the Pacific and that Japanese forces in Manchuria would be depleted to supply reserves for the southern advance was put to good use. Siberian divisions began rapidly moving west, reinforcing Soviet units defending Moscow, then Stalingrad.[60] Shortly after providing the information, Sorge was arrested and subsequently hung.

The Red Orchestra was a GRU network that covered Germany, France, Belgium, Holland, Switzerland, and Italy. In 1940 its main target was switched to Germany. According to a Central Intelligence Agency (CIA) study, the Red Orchestra "expanded to such a degree and took on such proportions with respect to personnel, technical aspects, and increasingly comprehensive assignments that at the peak of its development in 1942–1943 it had become the principal component of the GRU."[61]

The advent of the war Sorge warned of brought the reversal of a February 1941 change in the structure of Soviet intelligence and security. In that month the GUGB was separated from the NKVD and constituted as its own People's Commissariat: the People's Commissariat for State Security or NKGB (*Narodnyy Komissariat Gosudarstvennoy Bezopasnosti*). Motivation for this change may have been the enormity of the NKVD's nonintelligence and counterintelligence tasks, including managing a large part of Soviet industry and virtually all of Siberia.[62]

The NKGB was reestablished as the GUGB/NKVD upon the German invasion. Thus, at the beginning of the war the Soviet intelligence order of battle consisted of the GUGB/NKVD and the GRU. As the war progressed and turned in Soviet favor, two major changes occurred in the structure of the intelligence and security apparatus. In late 1942 the responsibility for military counterintelligence and countersubversion was placed in an organ separate from the GUGB. The organization was known as SMERSH, a contraction of *Smert Shpionam*—Death to Spies.[63]

In addition to military counterintelligence and countersubversion, SMERSH was also given the following responsibilities:

1. *On Soviet territories:* operative command over Exterminating Detachments, both military and civilian, organized at that time for intercepting enemy paratroopers in the front zone; command of operations of Retreat-blocking Detachments and posts organized for the interception of deserters moving to the rear; investigation of civilians suspected of espionage; arraignment and sentencing in espionage cases in the front zone; and execution of those condemned to death.

2. *In occupied areas beyond the prewar Soviet frontiers:* ferreting out of German intelligence agents left by the retreating Germans; hunting out of leaders and active members of anti-Communist

parties, organizations, and groups and potential enemies of the Soviet regime, as listed by local Communists; investigation of the above cases; and extermination or deportation of persons regarded as potentially dangerous to the Soviet regime.

3. *After the capitulation of Germany:* ferreting out of German intelligence agents and senior SS officers and Nazi officials in the Soviet-occupied territory of Germany; hunting ex-Soviet citizens who served in the ROA, or in German formations or intelligence units, detection of ex-Soviet citizens in the Western Zones of Germany; screening of Soviet repatriates; repressions against Soviet citizens suspected of collaboration with the Germans, disloyalty, espionage, etc.; interrogations, investigations, executions; deportations, or extermination of people regarded as potentially dangerous to the Soviet regime; surveillance over Soviet occupation personnel; and arrest and abduction of German experts.[64]

In April 1943 the GUGB was again removed from the NKVD and reconstituted as the NKGB.

The conclusion of the war brought several changes in the nomenclature and structure of the Soviet intelligence apparatus. In 1946 SMERSH was returned to the security service and retitled OKR (Otdel Kontra-Razvedka-Counterintelligence Department). Also in 1946 the NKGB and NKVD became the Ministry of State Security (MGB) and the Ministry of Internal Affairs (MVD).

In 1947 an attempt was made to merge all foreign intelligence elements—those of the Foreign Ministry, the Foreign Directorate (INU, *Innostrannoye Upravleniye*) of the MGB, and the GRU—into a single organization. This organization, the Committee of Information or KI (*Komitet Informatsyio*) was directed by high-level officials of the Ministry of Foreign Affairs.[65]

The arrangement was not successful. The GRU components were returned to the Ministry of Defense in September 1948. In December 1948 the Emigré, Soviet Colony, and Soviet Advisers Department of the INU were reintegrated into the MGB as a new directorate. In 1951 the remaining INU components were returned to the MGB and the KI dissolved.[66]

During the 1947-1951 period there was also substantial variation in the responsibilities of the MGB internally; originally, its functions were restricted to foreign intelligence (till 1947), countersubversion, and counterintelligence. The border troops were transferred to the

MGB in 1950. The MGB also probably took over control of the internal troops. And as did the OGPU, the MGB administered the internal passport system while the MVD retained control of the forced labor camps (GULAG).[67]

January 1953 saw the MGB lose control of the border and internal troops to the MVD. Immediately after Stalin's death on March 15, 1953, the MGB was absorbed by Beria's MVD. This situation persisted for almost a year, with Beria at first controlling all security and police functions as well as the primary foreign intelligence organization.

Beria thus gathered under his direct control the political police, foreign intelligence operations, the militia, some 300,000 special troops, the concentration camps and their inmates, and a major portion of Soviet industry, including the nuclear and missile weapons program. On June 25, 1953 Beria was arrested—an arrest engineered by Khrushchev, Malenkov, and Molotov.[68] The new leaders proceeded to reorganize the state security apparatus, resulting in the March 13, 1954 creation of the KGB (*Komitet Gosudarstvennoy Bezopasnosti*) or Committee for State Security. In conformity with the pattern discussed above, the KGB's initial responsibilities were limited to foreign intelligence, counterintelligence, and counter-subversion, with the MVD retaining control of the border troops, internal troops, and the GULAG. Administration of the border troops was shifted to the KGB in 1957.[69] Since that time, the importance of the KGB has, if anything, increased. Not only has a KGB Chairman become first a full Politburo member and then the General Secretary of the Communist Party of the Soviet Union (CPSU), but the problems confronting the Soviet leadership—dissidence, economic stagnation, and a technology gap with the West—are problems that to varying degrees the KGB has been called on to alleviate. This is in part reflected in organizational changes in the KGB since 1957—changes discussed in the next chapter.

The military intelligence organization, the GRU, has been plagued by the discovery of several "traitors" in its ranks, such as Colonels Peter Popov and Oleg Penkovskiy in the late 1950s and early 1960s and Colonel Anatoly Filatov more recently. The Penkovskiy episode resulted in the replacement of the GRU chief, General Ivan Serov, with KGB Deputy Chairman and former SMERSH officer, Petr Ivashutin.

Despite the impact of the Penkovskiy, Serov, and Filatov episodes, the GRU remains a major intelligence apparatus, particularly given its control over much of the Soviet technical collection effort. It manages much of the signals intelligence effort and all of the overhead reconnaissance program. Thus, despite the GRU being substantially smaller than the KGB—in terms of budget, personnel, and scope of functions—it cannot be viewed simply as an appendage of the KGB or a junior partner.

NOTES TO CHAPTER 1

1. Peter Deriabin, *Watchdogs of Terror: Russian Bodyguards from the Tsars to the Commissars* (Frederick, Md.: University Publications of America, 1984), p. 105.
2. Ronald Hingley, *The Russian Secret Police* (London: Hutchinson, 1970), pp. 1, 2.
3. Quoted in Deriabin, *Watchdogs of Terror*, p. 36.
4. Ibid., p. 115.
5. Hingley, *The Russian Secret Police*, pp. 5–6.
6. Ibid., pp. 16, 23.
7. Deriabin, *Watchdogs of Terror*, p. 121.
8. Hingley, *The Russian Secret Police*, pp. 28, 34.
9. Ibid., pp. 35–36.
10. Deriabin, *Watchdogs of Terror*, p. 28.
11. Ibid.
12. Ibid.
13. Hingley, *The Russian Secret Police*, pp. 35–36.
14. Ibid.
15. Ibid., p. 72.
16. Deriabin, *Watchdogs of Terror*, p. 133.
17. Ibid., pp. 135–36.
18. J.F.N. Bradley, "The Russian Secret Service in the First World War," *Soviet Studies* 20, no. 2 (1968): 242–48.
19. "Comint in the Russian Navy, WWI," *Cryptolog*, May 1976, pp. 1–4.
20. George Leggett, "Lenin, Terror and the Political Police," *Survey* 21 (1975): 157–87.
21. Boris Levytsky, *The Uses of Terror: The Soviet Secret Police 1917–1920* (New York: Coward, McCann and Geoghegan, 1972), p. 21.
22. Leggett, "Lenin, Terror and the Political Police."
23. Ibid.

24. George Leggett, *The Cheka: Lenin's Political Police* (New York: Oxford University Press, 1981), p. 216.
25. Quoted in Robert Conquest, *The Soviet Police System* (London: The Bodley Head, 1968), p. 15.
26. Quoted in Leggett, "Lenin, Terror and the Political Police."
27. Levytsky, *The Uses of Terror*, p..17.
28. Leggett, "Lenin, Terror and the Political Police."
29. George Leggett, "The Cheka and a Crisis of Communist Conscience," *Survey* 35, no. 3 (1980): 122–37.
30. Leggett, "Lenin, Terror and the Political Police."
31. Michael Heller, "Lenin and the Cheka: The Real Lenin," *Survey* 24 (1979): 175–92.
32. Conquest, *The Soviet Police System*, p. 20.
33. Deriabin, *Watchdogs of Terror*, p. 265.
34. Leggett, *The Cheka*, p. 227.
35. Amy Knight, "The KGB's Special Departments in the Soviet Armed Forces," *Orbis* 28, no. 2 (1984): 257–80.
36. Leggett, *The Cheka*, pp. 205–8.
37. Ibid., p. 217.
38. Ibid., p. 238.
39. Ibid., pp. 231–32.
40. See Edward Van der Rhoer, *Master Spy* (New York: Scribner's 1981); Robin Bruce Lockhart, *Reilly: Ace of Spies* (New York: Penguin, 1984).
41. Quoted in Levystky, *The Uses of Terror*, p. 42.
42. E. H. Carr, "The Origin and Status of the Cheka," *Soviet Studies* 10 (July 1958): 1–11.
43. Barton Whaley, *Soviet Clandestine Communications Nets: Notes for a History of the Structures of the Intelligence Services of the USSR* (Cambridge, Mass.: MIT Center for International Studies, 1968), p. 84.
44. Leggett, "Lenin, Terror and the Political Police."
45. Ibid.
46. Ibid.
47. Quoted in Simon Wolin and Robert M. Slusser, "The Evolution of the Soviet Secret Police," in Wolin and Slusser, eds., *The Soviet Secret Police* (New York: Praeger, 1957), p. 10.
48. Ibid., p. 9.
49. Conquest, *The Soviet Police System*, p. 17.
50. Ibid.
51. Wolin and Slusser, "The Evolution of the Soviet Secret Police," p. 15.
52. John Barron, *KGB: The Secret Work of Soviet Secret Agents* (New York: Reader's Digest, 1974), p. 340.
53. Levytsky, *The Uses of Terror*, p. 71.
54. Whaley, *Soviet Clandestine Communications Nets*, pp. 120ff.

55. Douglas Sutherland, *The Great Betrayal* (New York: Times Books, 1980).
56. Harry Rositzke, *KGB: The Eyes of Russia* (New York: Doubleday, 1981), pp. 6–12.
57. Ibid.
58. Ibid.
59. Ibid.
60. Ibid.
61. Central Intelligence Agency, *The Rote Kappelle: The CIA's History of Soviet Intelligence and Espionage Networks in Western Europe, 1936–1945.* (Frederick, Md.: University Publications of America, 1979), pp. xii–xiii.
62. Barron, *KGB*, p. 340.
63. E.A. Andrevich, "Structure and Functions of the Soviet Secret Police," in Wolin and Slusser, eds., *The Soviet Secret Police*, p. 130.
64. Ibid.
65. Barron, *KGB*, p. 341.
66. Wolin and Slusser, "The Evolution of the Soviet Secret Police," p. 26.
67. Ibid., p. 28.
68. Barron, *KGB*, p. 342.
69. Conquest, *The Soviet Police System*, p. 23.

2 STRUCTURE AND FUNCTIONS OF THE KGB AND GRU

In contrast to the United States, which has over twenty-five distinct intelligence organizations, the Soviet Union basically relies on two organizations—the *Komitet Gosudarstvennoy Bezopasnosti* (KGB) or Committee for State Security and the *Glavnoye Razvedyvatelnoye Upravleniye* (GRU) or Chief Intelligence Directorate of the General Staff—to perform all the services performed by the U.S. intelligence community. Additionally, the KGB performs many functions that in the United States are the responsibility of agencies not considered part of the intelligence community. Furthermore, the KGB has functions that are not performed by any U.S. government agency—for example, supervision of religious affairs. These latter two disparities account, in large part, for the disparities between the size of the U.S. intelligence community and the Soviet intelligence apparatus.

COMMITTEE FOR STATE SECURITY

As indicated in Figure 2-1, the KGB is organized into five chief directorates, six directorates and six departments, which are further divided into directorates, services, departments, and so on. The First Chief Directorate or Foreign Directorate (INU—*Innostrannoye Upravleniye*) is responsible for foreign intelligence collection, analy-

21

Figure 2-1. Organization of the KGB.

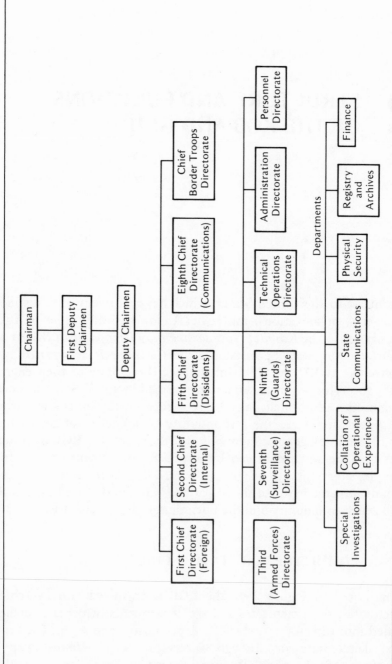

Source: John Barron, *KGB: The Secret Work of Soviet Secret Agents* (New York: Reader's Digest Press, 1974), pp. 70–90; John Barron, *KGB Today: The Hidden Hand* (New York: Reader's Digest Press, 1983), pp. 443–453.

sis, offensive counterintelligence, and active measures. Within the INU are three directorates, three services, and at least sixteen departments.

The largest of the INU directorates is Directorate S, the Illegals Directorate, which selects, trains, and deploys the KGB officers who live in foreign countries under false identities and with no admitted connection to the Soviet Union. Within Directorate S are four divisions. One is responsible for recruiting and training, another for cover and documentation, and a third manages the illegals already deployed.[1] The fourth division administers the Illegal Support Offices stationed in foreign countries—offices that provide "Good Services Assistance" to illegals.[2]

Additionally, Directorate S is now responsible for the formerly independent Department V (Executive Action Department), which it absorbed in the 1970s.[3] The department, renamed Department Eight, is responsible for planning assassinations and sabotage in support of war or crisis activities. The department is strictly a planning activity that does not normally maintain personnel abroad.

A directorate of growing importance is Directorate T, the Scientific and Technical Directorate, which is responsible for the collection of scientific and technical intelligence, including the theft of high technology items.[4] The directorate was created from the former Department 10 in 1963 to intensity acquisition of Western data about nuclear, missile, and space research; strategic sciences; cybernetics; and industrial processes.[5]

In addition to its own collection operations, Directorate T coordinates the scientific, industrial, and technical espionage of all KGB units (e.g., Directorate S). In close cooperation with the State Committee for Science and Technology (GKNT) and Academy of Sciences, it defines national needs and undertakes to fulfill them in accordance with a master collection plan.[6]

Directorate S has an army of co-optees in the various Soviet scientific and technical organizations and places officers among groups of Soviet scientists attending international conventions and conferences for collection purposes.[7] For analytical purposes, it maintains a research institute near the Belyoruski railroad station in Moscow that employs hundreds of scientists, analysts, and translators.[8]

Directorate K, formerly known as the Counterintelligence Service, has as its primary responsibility the penetration of foreign intelligence and security services by recruiting members of those organizations.[9] This is an area where the KGB has had notable success, having recruited several British and West German intelligence and security officials and some lower level U.S. intelligence employees.

To facilitate recruitment, and as a means of disrupting or defeating the activities of foreign intelligence and security services, Directorate K collects information about individuals, organizational structures, operational methods, and tactics.[10] Additionally, it is responsible for the penetration of terrorist organizations as well as controlling merchant seamen, Aeroflot crews, and civilians permitted to travel abroad. Its most secret section, when authorized by the Vice-Chairman of the First Chief Directorate, can investigate any officer in the directorate.[11]

The INU's three services are Service I, Service A, and Service R. Service I is the Information Service, formerly Special Service II, and is responsible for analyzing and disseminating the intelligence collected by the INU. One defector, Stanislav Levchenko, believes that the service makes a "conscientious, scholarly effort to give the Politburo and other clients objective and accurate analyses."[12]

Service A—the *Sluzhba Aktivnykh Meropriyatiyl* or Active Measures Service—evolved in the 1970s from Department A, which had been created in 1958 as the Department of Disinformation.[13] In fact, it always had active measures functions beyond those of pure disinformation. As with the Executive Action Department, it does not maintain a staff or personnel abroad but is a headquarters planning, evaluation, and supervision unit.[14]

Service A works closely with the International Department, the Department of Socialist Countries, and the Propaganda and Information Department of the Central Committee Secretariat. Additionally, an entire section of the Novosti Press Agency is reserved for its personnel, and the Academy of Sciences has a number of Service A personnel in its social science and humanities sections.[15]

Service R was established in 1969 as the Planning and Analysis Unit.[16] By that time the worldwide network of KGB agents had become unwieldy and difficult to control centrally. Service R personnel record and analyze details and results of each officer's meeting with an agent. They submit to the head of the INU statistical reports and analyses of each foreign residency's network, including the level and quality of penetration achieved as well as the number and potential of newly recruited agents.[17]

Just as the operational core of the CIA's Directorate of Operations lies in its area divisions, so the operational core of the INU lies in its eleven geographic departments (numbered one through ten, and seventeen). These departments deploy and run the officers who form the "Political Intelligence" Line (Line PR) in each residency, although their mandate is much broader than pure political intelligence, including both active measures and other forms of intelligence.[18] These departments are as follows:

First Department: United States and Canada
Second Department: Latin America
Third Department: United Kingdom, Australia, New Zealand, and Scandinavia
Fourth Department: Federal Republic of Germany, Austria
Fifth Department: France, Italy, Spain, the Netherlands, Belgium, Luxembourg, and Ireland
Sixth Department: China, Vietnam, Korea, and Kampuchea
Seventh Department: Japan, Indonesia, the Philippines, Thailand, and Singapore
Eighth Department: Arab nations, Turkey, Greece, Iran, Afghanistan, and Albania
Ninth Department: African nations where French is the predominant language
Tenth Department: African nations where English is the predominant language
Seventeenth Department: India, Pakistan, Bangladesh, and Sri Lanka

Each department is further subdivided into desks. Thus, the First Department has a Washington Desk, New York Desk, San Francisco Desk, and Canadian Desk, among others.[19]

One of the INU's most important departments is the Eleventh Department, formerly the Advisers Department, which conducts liaison with and penetrates the intelligence and security services of Soviet satellite nations. In 1974 there were approximately 110 officers at service headquarters in Havana and the Warsaw Pact countries (except Romania).[20] This total has probably grown in the last ten years and also probably now includes advisers to the Vietnamese General Research Service and other Vietnamese intelligence units.

The Twelfth Department, the Cover Organs Department, places KGB personnel in cover positions with other Soviet government agencies and makes arrangements for KGB officers to live or travel abroad as diplomats, journalists, trade representatives, clergymen, tourists, or delegates to international conferences.[21]

As of 1974, the Thirteenth Department was responsible for communications between Moscow Center and overseas residencies and illegals.[22] Presumably, this also includes responsibility for covert Soviet agent communications satellite operations.

The Fourteenth Department develops and supplies the technical tools of clandestine operations—concealment devices, self-destruct containers for the transportation of secret documents and film, disguised audio and radio equipment, and special cameras—as well as providing forged passports, false documents, invisible writing material, and incapacitating chemicals.[23] Specialists from the Fourteenth Department serve in Soviet embassies to monitor police and counterintelligence radio channels as well as provide technical assistance to the residency.[24]

Department Fifteen maintains the INU archives; Department Sixteen directs operations against foreign cryptographic personnel. Additionally, there is a Personnel Department, Party Committee, and Secretariat within the INU.[25] Figure 2–2 illustrates the INU's organizational structure.

The Second Chief Directorate, with responsibility for internal security, is divided into twelve departments, a Political Security Service, Technical Support Group, and Industrial Security Directorate.[26] The first six departments are responsible for monitoring and compromising foreign diplomats. Thus, the First Department, responsible for the United States and Latin America consists of a chief, two deputies, fifty staff officers, recruiters, agent handlers, reservists, and 300 professional surveillants on permanent loan from the Surveillance Directorate. The department's First Section is responsible for the actual recruitment of U.S. embassy personnel, the Second for neutralizing embassy intelligence operations. The Third identifies, investigates, interrogates, and maintains a dossier on each Soviet citizen detected in contact(s) with Americans in the Soviet Union. The Fourth Section attempts to prearrange and stage-manage contacts that Americans may have with Russians while traveling outside of Moscow. Finally, the Fifth Section is responsible for Latin American diplomats with regard to surveillance and possible recruitment.[27]

The remaining six geographical departments are the

Second Department: nations of the British Commonwealth;
Third Department: West Germany, Austria, and Scandinavia;

Figure 2-2. Organization of the First Chief Directorate (INU).

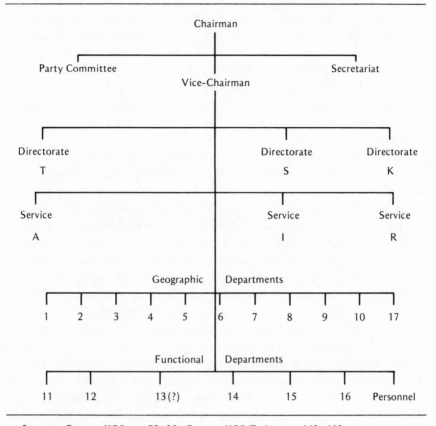

Sources: Barron, *KGB*, pp. 70-90; Barron, *KGB Today*, pp. 443-453.

Fourth Department: all other West European nations;
Fifth Department: non-European nations the KGB considers
  developed; and
Sixth Department: non-European nations the KGB considers
  underdeveloped.

The Seventh Department is responsible for tourists, performing much the same functions with regard to tourists that Departments one through six perform with regard to diplomats. The Seventh Department has 100 staff officers in Moscow, an equal number in the provinces, and 1,600 agents and part-time informers. Its first three sections are responsible for American, British, and Canadian tourists (First Section), other nationalities (Second), and overseeing hotels where foreigners are registered and the restaurants to which they are guided. The Fourth Section runs two travel agencies, Intourist and Sputnik, the latter being a travel agency that offers foreign youth economy trips into the Soviet Union. The Fifth Section arranges contacts between tourists and Soviet citizens and investigates contacts that were not preplanned. The final section in the Seventh Department, the Sixth Section, maintains observation posts at motels, campsites, gasoline stations, and garages along highways traveled by tourists and watches foreigners crossing the Soviet Union by plane or train.[28]

The Eighth Department is responsible for operating the Second Chief Directorate's computers; the Ninth Department handles the surveillance and recruitment of foreign students. To aid it, the department enlists informants among faculties and student bodies of all Soviet universities to which foreign students are admitted. The Tenth Department watches and tries to influence or recruit foreign journalists. It has engaged in conspicuous surveillance and provocations in order to isolate Soviet intellectuals from Western reporters. It also staffs the Directorate for Servicing the Diplomatic Corps (UPDK) in the Foreign Ministry.[29] The directorate provides employees for the embassies—clerks, secretaries, drivers, gardeners, janitors, porters, maids, and governesses—employees who are co-opted by the KGB.[30]

The Eleventh Department approves and regulates the travel abroad of all Soviet citizens, except senior Party members and persons in sensitive positions. It examines the individual's background and the circumstances of each planned trip, looking for any signs of an intention to defect. A staff officer from the Eleventh Department accompanies groups traveling abroad. The Twelfth Department investigates major cases of corruption, graft, and waste in government enterprises.[31]

Much of the KGB's political police work is performed by the Second Chief Directorate's Political Security Service, known simply as the Service or *Sluzhba*. Prior to 1969 it consisted of twelve directions (branches), but in that year the Fifth through Ninth Directions were transferred to the newly created Fifth Chief Directorate.[32]

Of its seven remaining directions, the First through Fourth supervise general investigations and work with local KGB offices in the four geographic sections in which the Soviet Union is secretly partitioned for administrative convenience. The majority of information-gathering networks are run by the local offices which the directions oversee. The Tenth Direction is responsible for detecting and halting economic crime—currency speculation, black market dealings, and proscribed private enterprise. The Eleventh Direction publishes secret manuals and journals for the Service, reporting discontent and dissent. The Twelfth Direction operates against People's Republic of China (PRC) diplomats, seeking to subvert them and to penetrate the PRC embassy.[33]

The Technical Support Group is the directorate's professional burglary unit, responsible for the penetration of foreign embassies as well as Soviet homes and offices. The Industrial Security Directorate conducts surveillance of critical production and research centers through its own network of informants. Departments One through Four of the directorate watch heavy industry, arms factories, nuclear research, and production centers. Officers of the Fifth Department are found throughout the Ministry of Foreign Trade; they supervise commercial exhibitions, monitor foreign exhibitions in the Soviet Union, and spot potential recruits among foreign businessmen. The department also runs various Soviet trade associations. The Sixth Department tries to recruit foreign seamen allowed ashore at Soviet ports.[34]

At present there is no Fourth or Sixth Directorate. In the late 1960s the Fourth through Sixth Directorate (Economic, Secret Political, and Transport) were swallowed up by the Second Chief Directorate.[35] In 1969, however, the Fifth Chief Directorate was established to deal with political, social, and cultural dissent.

The directorate consists of five directions (numbered five through nine) and the Jewish Department. The Fifth Direction is responsible for the control of religion. It seeks to identify all religious believers and to ensure that the Russian Orthodox Church and all other churches serve as instruments of Soviet policy. One means it employs is the placement of KGB officers in the church hierarchy.[36]

One of the most potentially explosive problems facing the Soviet Union is that of ethnicity. The non–Russian segment, particularly the Asiatic non–Russian segment, of the Soviet Union is growing at a faster rate than the Great Russian population and promises to make that segment an increasingly small portion of the total Soviet population. Since the Soviet regime has basically been run by Great Russians for Great Russians, the situation is potentially explosive.[37] Thus, the Sixth Direction is charged with the suppression of nationalism among ethnic minorities.[38]

The Seventh Direction watches Soviet citizens who have relatives living abroad as well as foreigners who come to the Soviet Union to visit relatives. The Eighth Direction is responsible for attempting to negate the influence of Russian emigré groups who slip literature and agents into the Soviet Union. The Ninth Direction suppresses all unauthorized literature, seeks to intimidate heretical writers, and hunts down authors of anonymous books.[39] Created in 1971, the Jewish Department was given the mandate of stopping public protests by Soviet Jews and curbing, if not eliminating, the trends toward increased Jewish emigration.[40]

The Eighth Chief Directorate, the Communications Directorate, has two basic functions: communications security (COMSEC) and signals (or in Soviet parlance, radio and radio-technical) intelligence. In its communications security role the directorate designs ciphers and crypto systems for the KGB and Ministry of Foreign Affairs— both the software and hardware.[41] In its signals intelligence role it intercepts both communications and electronic signals associated with economic, political, and military activities. For communications intelligence purposes it maintains listening posts at a variety of embassy, consular, and other locations throughout the West.

The last of the chief directorates is the Chief Directorate of Border Troops, which is assigned to watch and protect the Soviet frontiers. Divided into Land, Aviation, and Maritime border troops, they number about 300,000 and are equipped with airplanes, tanks, artillery, boats, and armor.[42]

The remaining numbered directorates are the Third, Seventh, and Ninth. The Third (Armed Forces) Directorate—also known as the Directorate of Special Departments—is the present incarnation of SMERSH. Consisting of twelve departments, it is responsible for "overseeing" and detecting subversion or espionage in the Ministry of Defense, General Staff, and the Soviet military services. Third Directorate officers are placed at every level of the Soviet armed forces.[43]

The Surveillance Directorate, or Seventh Directorate, has over 3,000 employees. At one time it functioned strictly as an appendage to other (primarily Second and Fifth) chief directorates. In the 1970s, however, it was granted some autonomy. It was permitted to initiate surveillance on its own as well as establish its own analytical group.[44] The first four of its twelve departments are responsible for surveilling U.S. and Latin American citizens (First); foreign journalists, students, and businessmen (Second) and non-Americans (Third and Fourth). The Fifth Department supervises militia guards posted at each embassy to prevent unauthorized visits by Soviet citizens; the Sixth Department investigates Soviet citizens being considered for KGB employment.[45]

The Seventh Department develops and maintains surveillance equipment for cars and infrared cameras, television cameras, and two-way mirrors.[46] The Ninth Department patrols the streets that members of the Party leadership use in traveling to and from their offices, and the Tenth covers Moscow locales that both foreigners and prominent Soviet citizens are likely to visit. Its targets include parks, museums, theaters, stores, barbershops, stadiums, and air and rail terminals. The Eleventh Department provides disguises—wigs, mustaches, and clothes—and the Twelfth Department consists of a dozen highly mobile surveillance teams which are employed in particularly sensitive operations, such as the entrapment of a foreign dignitary.[47]

The Ninth or Guards Directorate is responsible both for the personal security of the Party leadership and the physical security of important installations.[48] The personnel of this directorate are the most thoroughly and intensively screened of all. They are the only individuals in the Soviet Union permitted to carry loaded weapons in the presence of Party rulers.[49]

The KGB's three unnumbered directorates are the Technical Operations, Administration, and Personnel directorates. Technical Operations develops and produces most of the technical devices used in KGB operations, excluding communications equipment. The Administration Directorate performs routine housekeeping chores such as acquiring and managing property; arranging legal travel; and managing the stores, resorts, and apartment complexes set aside for KGB personnel. The Personnel Directorate is subordinate to the Administrative Organs Department of the Party's Central Committee. It attempts to anticipate and satisfy all personnel requirements, via either recruitment or transfers within the KGB. It must approve all hirings, foreign assignments, and promotions.[50]

The six independent departments of the KGB perform a wide variety of functions. The Special Investigations Department performs sensitive investigations in cases involving suspected treason or espionage, penetrations of the KGB or GRU by foreign intelligence services, and criminality or gross dereliction by important Party members or government officials. It also investigates the circumstances, fixes the responsibility, and assesses the damage of each defection. The Department for Collation of Operational Experience studies the intelligence operations of the Soviet Union and other nations for useful lessons. Its findings are reported in a top secret journal. The Department of State Communications provides signal troops that maintain the telephone and radio systems used by all Soviet government agencies.[51] This makes the KGB responsible for communications throughout the Soviet government. Within the department, most probably, is a special section for crisis communications and for ensuring maintenance of communications in the midst and aftermath of a nuclear war.

The Department of Physical Security provides the guards who patrol KGB offices day and night. They examine every employee every time they enter or leave a headquarters building. They also inspect each office at the end of the workday to make sure all safes, and windows are locked and all classified papers are locked up. The Finance Department manages the payroll and disbursement of and accounting for operational funds and arranges conversion of Soviet currency into foreign currency. The Registry and Archives Department maintains a master index of each file held by the various KGB divisions, the divisions being the repositories for current operational files. The historical files in the archives date back to the Cheka.[52]

Main headquarters of the KGB is located at 2 Dzerzhinsky Square in Moscow. The INU is located in a modern building outside Moscow. Since Yuri Andropov's promotion to the Central Committee Secretariat in 1981, there have been two KGB chairmen. Andropov's first successor, Vitaly V. Fedorchuk, was subsequently appointed Minister of Internal Affairs after Andropov replaced Leonid Brezhnev as General Secretary. Fedorchuk was succeeded by one of his top deputies, Viktor M. Chebrikov.[53]

It should be quite apparent from the discussion of the KGB's structure and functions that it is an immense organization. In terms of personnel, it appears to have between 500,000 and 750,000 employees, including 15,000 at INU headquarters; 25,000 at Fifth Chief directorate headquarters; 100,000 domestic informants; 30 to 50,000 communications troops; and several hundred thousand border guards.[54]

As a means of illustrating the scope of KGB activities and its size, consider Table 2–1. The left column lists KGB directorates, the middle column the functions of the directorate, and the right-hand col-

Table 2-1.   The KGB and U.S. Government Institutions.

KGB Unit	Functions	U.S. Counterpart Units
1. First Chief (Foreign)	HUMINT, active measures, counterintelligence, analysis	Directorate of Operations, CIA Directorate of Intelligence, CIA
2. Second Directorate	domestic counterintelligence countersubversion, industrial security	Intelligence Division, FBI Criminal Investigative Division, FBI Safeguards and Security, DOE
3. Third (Armed Forces) Directorate	counterintelligence and countersubversion, armed forces	Defense Investigative Service, Naval Investigative Service, AF Office of Special Investigations Army Criminal Investigations Division
4. Fifth Chief	suppression of dissent	—
5. Seventh Directorate	surveillance	—
6. Eighth Chief Directorate	COMSEC, SIGINT	National Security Agency (portions)
7. Ninth (Guards) Directorate	leadership protection, protection of sensitive installations	Executive Protective Service, Secret Service Marine Guards
8. Chief Border Guards Directorate	protection of frontiers, preventing smuggling	Border Patrol, Coast Guard, Customs Service

umn the U.S. organizations with similar functions. As we can see, the KGB's mandate extends to areas covered by two different intelligence agencies (CIA, NSA), several security agencies (FBI, DIS, NIS, AFOSI), and several protective and border agencies (EPS, Secret Service, Border Patrol, and Coast Guard) not generally considered parts of the U.S. intelligence community. Yet even this comparison understates the KGB's functions, since its political police role is not duplicated in the United States, and many of its other functions are far more extensive than those performed by counterpart organizations in the United States (e.g., Border Patrol).

CHIEF INTELLIGENCE DIRECTORATE, GENERAL STAFF (GRU)

The GRU is one of eleven departments of the Soviet General Staff. Its responsibilities include conducting and coordinating strategic and tactical intelligence collection and analysis activities for the entire Soviet armed forces. Collection techniques involve gathering of open source data, clandestine human collection, satellite and aircraft photographic reconnaissance, and signals intelligence collection employing a variety of collection platforms (ships, aircraft, satellites, ground stations).

The intelligence collected involves far more than specifically military intelligence. Rather, it is any intelligence relevant to a nation's willingness, capabilities, and intentions of making war. Thus, Marshal V.D. Sokolovskiy has stated that "strategic intelligence, both in peacetime and wartime, systematically procures political, military, economic, scientific and technical data concerning possible enemies and studies their military possibilities."[55]

Figure 2–3 illustrates the present structure of the GRU. The First Deputy Chief of the GRU supervises six directorates concerned with intelligence collection. The First Directorate conducts human collection operations in Europe (not including the United Kingdom) and Morocco and consists of five directions. The Second Directorate covers, again via human agents, North and South America, the United Kingdom, Australia, and New Zealand. The Third and Fourth Directorates perform similar functions for Asia and Africa, respectively. Each directorate has approximately 300 high-ranking officers in the Moscow Center and an equal number abroad.[56]

In addition, there are four directions or branches that report directly to the First Deputy Chief. The First Direction conducts human intelligence operations in the Moscow area and has representatives in Soviet institutions such as the Ministry of Foreign Affairs, the Ministry of External Trade, Aeroflot, the Merchant Navy, the Academy of Sciences, and so forth. The Second Direction conducts human intelligence operations in East and West Berlin, and the Third Direction focuses on national liberation movements and terrorist organizations. The Fourth Direction conducts intelligence activities from Cuba against a variety of countries, including the United States.[57]

Figure 2-3. Organization of the GRU.

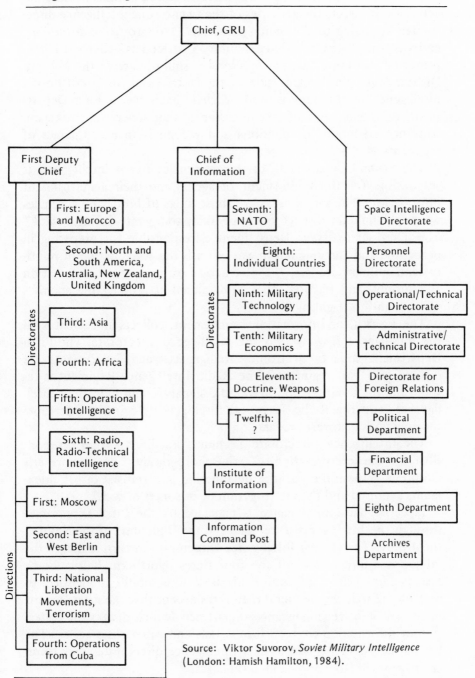

Source: Viktor Suvorov, *Soviet Military Intelligence* (London: Hamish Hamilton, 1984).

The Fifth Directorate does not perform separate human collection activities. It directs the activities of the twenty-one intelligence directorates belonging to the military districts (16), groups of forces (4), and fleet intelligence.[58] Each military district has a Second Directorate or RU (Intelligence Directorate) subordinate to the Military District Staff. The organization of the District and Groups of Forces intelligence directorates is standardized. Each has a First Department, or Department of Reconnaissance, that supervises the reconnaissance battalions of divisions and reconnaissance companies of regiments.[59]

The Second Department, or Department of Agent Intelligence, is responsible for the recruitment of agents and their acquisition of information. The target areas are those areas of bordering countries where the military district would be likely to operate during a war.[60] The Third or *Spetsnaz* Department is responsible for preparing in peacetime and carrying out in war or crisis the assassination of political and military leaders, the destruction of lines of communication and supply, and terrorist operations aimed at eroding the enemy's will to continue fighting.[61]

The Fourth, or Information Department, collects and collates all the intelligence flowing into the intelligence directorate. The Fifth Department collects electronic intelligence. Such departments are divided into two regiments. The Radio Intelligence Regiment is responsible for the interception of radio signals (communications intelligence), and the Radio-Technical Intelligence Regiment intercepts the emissions of foreign radars.[62]

The Intelligence Directorate Technical Facilities Group is reponsible for the interpretation of aerial photography. The Interpreter's Group is responsible for the deciphering and translation of documents acquired and the interrogation of prisoners of war.[63]

Fleet or naval intelligence is managed by the Fifth Directorate through the Intelligence Directorate of the High Staff of the Navy of the USSR. The (Fleet) Intelligence Directorate in turn manages the intelligence directorates of the four fleets (Northern, Baltic, Black Sea, Pacific). The organization of those directorates is identical to that of the military district directorates except that the First Department is a Ship Reconnaissance Department which directs the collection of information from surface vessels and submarines at sea. The Second Departments of the fleet intelligence directorates seek to recruit agents in large ports and naval bases.[64]

In addition to directing the intelligence directorates of the fleets, the Naval Staff Intelligence Directorate also manages Fleet Cosmic Intelligence, which is responsible for the naval intelligence space program—namely, the ocean surveillance satellites.[65]

The Sixth Directorate, the last under the First Deputy, is the Radio-Radio-Technical Intelligence Directorate. Its officers are deployed to embassies and other Soviet installations to intercept communications and electronic transmissions along government, commercial, and military networks. Additionally, regiments responsible to the Sixth Directorate are stationed in the Soviet Union, Eastern Europe, and Vietnam.[66]

Subordinate to the Chief of Information are directorates seven through twelve, the Institute of Information, and the Information Command Post. The Information Command Post is the recipient of all incoming intelligence, whether from agents, illegals, technical collection systems, allied intelligence services, or the intelligence directorates of the military districts, fleets, and groups of Soviet forces abroad. It can request any source to give more precise detail or to double check the information it has transmitted. It carries out preliminary processing of the material and prepares an intelligence summary for Politburo members.[67]

The Seventh Directorate is concerned with all aspects of NATO and consists of six departments, each department being further divided into sections. The departments and sections are functionally divided, each being responsible for the study of individual trends or aspects of NATO activities.[68] The focus of the Eighth Directorate is the study of individual countries throughout the world irrespective of NATO membership. Political structure, the armed forces, and economies of those nations are subject to special emphasis. Particular attention is devoted to the personal activities of political and military leaders.[69]

The Ninth Directorate is concerned with military technology and has close ties with Soviet design bureaus and the arms industry. It is the link between the factories that copy foreign weapons systems and the intelligence officers who obtain the weapons or information that allow copies to be made.[70] The subject of Tenth Directorate studies is military economics. It watches arms sales and studies production and technological development, strategic resources, and vulnerabilities.[71]

The Eleventh Directorate studies the doctrine, targeting policy, and strategic weapons systems of all nuclear-armed nations as well as the nations that may obtain such weapons in the future. It monitors signs of increased activity—in terms of deployments and alert rates—of all nuclear forces.[72] Information on the Twelfth Directorate is not available.

The Institute of Information operates independently of the directorates, is controlled by the Chief of Information, and functions outside of GRU headquarters. In addition to reliance on secret intelligence, the institute also makes extensive use of open source material.[73]

In addition to the directorates, directions, and institutes controlled by the First Deputy Chief and the Chief of Information are several directorates and departments the line of authority of which goes directly to the Chief of the GRU. The most important of these is the Space (or Cosmic) Intelligence Directorate, which manages the space reconnaissance program. It has its own cosmodromes, several research institutes, and a coordinating computer center. It handles the research and development for reconnaissance satellites and constructs them.[74]

The Personnel Directorate is headed by a deputy chief of the GRU and directs the movements of all officers in the GRU as well as those of some Warsaw Pact services and of those in the military district, fleet intelligence, and groups of Soviet forces intelligence directorates.[75] The responsibility of the Operational/Technical Directorate is the development and production of equipment for microphotography, dead-letter boxes, radio appliances, eavesdropping material, armaments, and poisons. To aid it there are several subordinate research institutes.[76]

The Administrative/Technical Directorate manages the GRU's stock of foreign currencies, gold, and diamonds as well as other items of value. The Communications Directorate is responsible for communications, via radio and other means, between the GRU and its overseas units. The directorate controls several transmission centers and can make use of Space Intelligence Directorate satellites for agent communication if necessary.[77] The Directorate for Foreign Relations directs all dealings with foreigners, operating under Ministry of Defense cover.[78]

The Political Department is responsible for the ideological monitoring of all GRU personnel. The Financial Department carries out legal financial operations in the Soviet Union, and the First (Passport) Department studies passport regulations throughout the world. It has amassed a collection of passports; identity cards; driving licenses; military documents; passes; police documents; and railway, air, and sea tickets. Part of its function is to be able to identify the proper set of documents, stamps, and answers to questions that allow passage through any control point in the world. It can also forge documents, whether they be passports, identity cards, or driver's licenses.[79]

The Eighth Department enciphers and deciphers all documents passing into or out of the GRU. The Archives Department controls "millions of personal details and files on illegals, domestic officers, undercover residencies, successful recruitment of foreigners (and unsuccessful ones), material on everyone from statesmen and army heads to prostitutes and homosexuals and designers of rockets and submarines."[80]

The present Chief of the GRU, Petr Ivanovich Ivashutin, was a former deputy chairman of the KGB, appointed in 1963 in the wake of the Penkovskiy fiasco. During the war, Ivashutin was in SMERSH, and from 1944 to 1945 he was Chief of SMERSH on the Third Ukranian front. Subsequently, he became head of the KGB's Third (Armed Forces) Directorate and KGB deputy chairman.[81]

The GRU has been estimated to have a staff of 5,000 at headquarters.[82] However, such a figure seems far too low even for headquarters alone, when one considers the wide range of GRU functions—functions that in the United States are performed by about fifteen different military intelligence units with total personnel over 100,000. When one adds the functions performed outside of Moscow, the 5,000 becomes an even smaller fraction of total GRU strength.

THE ROLES OF THE KGB AND GRU

The role of the KGB and its size are intertwined. The explanation for the KGB's huge size lies not in a Russian or Soviet "penchant" for centralization. Rather, it lies in the nature of the relationship between the CPSU and the Soviet government and the extent to which "security" aspects are perceived to be present in virtually all aspects of Soviet life.

Since the CPSU, and specifically the Politburo, completely rules the Soviet government, it is not unexpected that it would want an organization that can take direct, immediate, and if necessary, brutal action to advance Politburo/Party goals. Since these goals cover all areas of Soviet life, the organization must penetrate into all areas of government activities and Soviet life. Thus, the acquisition of technology that improves productivity and raises the standard of living enhances the position of the Soviet regime. To a leadership that devotes so many resources to military production, the ability to pacify the population with a higher quality of life is a significant accomplishment.

The corollary is that any activities that disrupt normal Soviet life—demonstrations, economic conflict, industrial accidents, poor work attitudes, corruption—may be perceived as threats to the CPSU. Hence, they are activities that "require" investigation by the security organization.

Even more basic than the advancement of Politburo/CPSU goals is the preservation of the Communist party in power—the ultimate rationale for the KGB and its attempts to control all aspects of Soviet life—for example, contacts with foreigners, expression of opinions, and travel within the Soviet Union. This rationale has been emphasized by the "renaming" of the KGB on July 5, 1978 when the KGB's name was changed from "KGB under the Council of Ministers" to "USSR KGB."[83] Thus, even the pro forma designation of the KGB as a government organ has been eliminated.

This relationship is stressed by a basic Soviet text on administrative law, which states that

> The organizing and directing role in the protection of state security have a strikingly pronounced political character. These are political organs executing the line of the Central Committee. . . . Their direction and methods in dealing with the enemies of the Soviet state respond to current requirements and the political aims of the Communist Party. . . . Their organization and activities are carried out under the leadership and unremitting control of the Communist Party.[84]

The role of the KGB and GRU have been contrasted by Suvorov in the following way:

> The basic function of the KGB may be expressed in one guiding phrase, *not to allow the collapse of the Soviet Union from inside.* The function of the GRU may also be stated in one parallel but quite different phrase: *to prevent the collapse of the Soviet Union from an external blow* [emphasis in the original].[85]

The GRU is therefore interested in a wide range of information, although often with different emphasis than the KGB. Military, military-technological, military-political, and military-economic information is of value to the GRU: the structure and capabilities of armed forces (hostile, allied, and neutral), doctrine and target plans, alliances between foreign nations, technology with military or possible military applications, the industrial potential, energy, agriculture, and strategic reserves of other nations.

NOTES TO CHAPTER 2

1. John Barron, *KGB Today: The Hidden Hand* (New York: Reader's Digest Press, 1983), p. 444.
2. Ibid.; Brian Freemantle, *KGB: Inside the World's Largest Intelligence Network* (New York: Holt, Reinhart and Winston, 1982), p. 182.
3. Barron, *KGB Today*, p. 444.
4. Ibid., p. 445.
5. John Barron, *KGB: The Secret Work of Soviet Secret Agents* (New York: Reader's Digest Press, 1974), p. 76.
6. Ibid., p. 76; Barron, *KGB Today*, p. 445.
7. Ibid.
8. Barron, *KGB Today*, p. 445.
9. Ibid., p. 446.
10. Ibid.
11. Ibid.
12. Ibid.
13. Ibid.
14. Ibid.
15. Ibid.
16. Barron, *KGB*, p. 76.
17. Barron, *KGB Today*, p. 448.
18. Ibid.
19. Ibid., pp. 448–49.
20. Ibid.
21. Barron, *KGB*, p. 80.
22. Ibid.
23. Ibid., p. 80; Barron, *KGB Today*, p. 450.
24. Ibid.
25. Barron, *KGB Today*, p. 450.
26. Barron, *KGB*, pp. 80–84.
27. Ibid., p. 81.

28. Ibid., p. 82.
29. Ibid.
30. Bernard Gwertzman, "'Operation Tit for Tat!: Ready for the Russians," *New York Times*, April 1, 1983, p. A14.
31. Barron, *KGB*, p. 82.
32. Ibid., p. 83.
33. Ibid.
34. Ibid., p. 84.
35. Barron, *KGB*, p. 84.
36. Ibid.
37. See Helen Carrere d'Encausse, *Decline of an Empire: The Soviet Socialist Republics in Revolt* (New York: Harper, 1981).
38. Barron, *KGB*, p. 84.
39. Ibid.
40. Ibid., p. 85.
41. Barron, *KGB Today*, p. 452.
42. Barron, *KGB*, p. 85.
43. Ibid.
44. Barron, *KGB Today*, p. 452.
45. Barron, *KGB*, p. 87.
46. Ibid.
47. Ibid.
48. Barron, *KGB Today*, p. 452.
49. Barron, *KGB*, p. 88.
50. Ibid., p. 86.
51. Ibid., p. 88.
52. Ibid., pp. 88–89.
53. John F. Burns, "K.G.B. Chief Is Named to New Post: Move Against Corruption is Seen," *New York Times*, December 18, 1982, pp. 1, 6.
54. "The KGB: Eyes of the Kremlin," *Time*, February 14, 1983, pp. 30ff; "The KGB's Spies in America," *Newsweek*, November 23, 1982, pp. 50ff; Department of Defense, *Soviet Military Power 1984* (Washington, D.C.: U.S. Government Printing Office, 1984), p. 14.
55. Marshal V.D. Sokolovskiy, *Soviet Military Strategy* (New York: Crane, Russak & Company, 1975), p. 318.
56. Viktor Suvorov, *Soviet Military Intelligence* (London: Hamish Hamilton, 1984), p. 56.
57. Ibid., pp. 56–57.
58. Ibid., p. 57.
59. Ibid., p. 139.
60. Ibid., pp. 139–40.
61. Ibid., p. 140.
62. Ibid., pp. 140–41.

63. Ibid., p. 141.
64. Ibid., p. 139.
65. Ibid., p. 61.
66. Ibid., p. 59.
67. Ibid., p. 62.
68. Ibid., p. 63.
69. Ibid.
70. Ibid.
71. Ibid.
72. Ibid.
73. Ibid.
74. Ibid., p. 60.
75. Ibid., p. 69.
76. Ibid., p. 70.
77. Ibid.
78. Cal Carnes, "Soviet Military Intelligence: How Significant?" *Military Intelligence* (January–March, 1981): 6–10.
79. Suvorov, *Soviet Military Intelligence*, pp. 70, 71.
80. Ibid., pp. 70–71.
81. Ibid., p. 181.
82. Freemantle, pp. 60–61.
83. Peter Deriabin with T.H, Bagley, "Fedorchuk, the KGB, and the Soviet Succession," *Orbis* 26, no. 3 (Fall 1982): 611–35.
84. Cited in Ibid.
85. Suvorov, *Soviet Military Intelligence*, pp. 45–46.

3 THE SOVIET NATIONAL SECURITY APPARATUS

As is the case with other nations, the Soviet intelligence and security services represent only a part of the nation's national security apparatus. The activities of the intelligence and security services are directed by portions of this apparatus and their activities are intended to complement and supplement the activities of the entire Soviet state. Thus, understanding the activities of these services requires an appreciation of the entire national security apparatus and its activities.

Additionally, in the case of the Soviet Union, components of the national security apparatus that are not generally considered intelligence units do perform some intelligence functions—usually either intelligence analysis or active measures. Further, the priority placed on intelligence activities in the Soviet Union gives the KGB and GRU the power to co-opt virtually all government institutions.

The Soviet national security apparatus can be divided into the following components: the Politburo, Defense Council, the Central Committee Secretariat, Military, the MVD and MFA, Industrial and Scientific Committees, TASS, and the Research Institutes.

THE POLITBURO

The Politburo (Political Bureau) of the CPSU Central Committee (CC) stands at the apex of the Soviet decisionmaking structure, re-

45

gardless of the subject matter involved—whether it be foreign policy, defense policy, energy, economics, education, or agriculture. Although the Politburo is, in theory, "elected" by the 240-member Central Committee, it is, in reality, the Politburo that chooses the Central Committee and eclipses its functions.[1]

Presently, the Politburo consists of eleven full ("voting") and seven candidate ("non-ranking") members, headed by Central Committee General Secretary, Mikhail Gorbachev. The other full members are the Premier; Council of Ministers (N. A. Tikhonov); the Minister of Foreign Affairs (E. A. Shevardnadze); the President (A. A. Gromyko); two Party secretaries, Yegor K. Ligachev and Nikolai I. Ryzhkov); the Chairman of the KGB (Viktor M. Chebrikov); the Chairman of the Party Control Commission (Mikhail S. Solomentsev); the Premier of the RSFSR (Vitaly I. Vorotnikov); and the first secretaries of the Moscow, Kazakhistan, Azerbaijan, and Ukrainian party organizations (V. V. Grishin, D. A. Kunayev, Geidar Aliyev, and V. V. Scherbitskiy).[2]

There is no fixed number of members for the Politburo and no requirement for individuals (other than the General Secretary) to be elected to the Politburo on an ex officio basis. However, according to one observer, there "was a tendency under Khrushchev, which seems to have continued under Brezhnev, for members of the Politburo to be elected less in their capacity as individuals and more as virtually *ex-officio* representatives of major constituencies."[3] Possible examples of this trend were the promotion in 1973 of the Minister of Foreign Affairs (Gromyko), Minister of Defense (Ustinov), and then Chairman of the KGB (Andropov) to full membership. It remains to be seen the extent to which this trend continues—while the Chairman of the KGB was promoted, in 1985, to full Politburo membership the Minister of Defense was not.

The Politburo, which meets at least once a week (Thursday), operates according to the doctrine of collective responsibility: All major decisions are the responsibility of the Politburo and each of its members. Thus, even though each member has specialized tasks and areas of expertise, they are also free to raise any issue before the Politburo over the head of the responsible Politburo member.[4]

There is a great deal of literature that speaks of consensus as the means of Politburo decisionmaking. Thus, according to Valentin Falin, former international spokesman for the Central Committee, issues or differences are not decided by vote; there must be a consensus.[5] And in a 1973 interview, Brezhnev stated that voting was rarely needed, that "99.9 percent" of the time consensus is reached on the basis of discussion and in other cases a small Politburo subgroup is formed to resolve issues of contention.[6] In the allegedly rare instances in which voting occurs, each full member has one vote, implying the use of majority rule when there are only two alternatives.[7]

On the other hand, even leaving aside specific references in the literature to Politburo voting on the grounds that they might be examples of the 0.1 percent, one might question whether the word consensus is being used in the sense it is normally used—as mutual agreement produced by discussion and compromise—or whether the "consensus" that is often reached is a product of the incipient losing coalition surrendering to the majority will when it is apparent that the votes are not there. Thus, the consensus that results from a Politburo meeting may often be similar to the "nomination by acclamation" that often marks the end of a bitter U.S. presidential nominating convention more than the achievement of true agreement.

Certainly, there is significant evidence in Soviet history of sharp differences in the Politburo concerning issues of major importance— agriculture, economic policy, foreign policy, and defense matters.[8] Such sharp differences may make consensus extremely difficult to attain, especially when the only alternatives are diametrically opposed—for example, to invade or not. The Politburo discussion and resolution concerning the situation in Czechoslovakia in 1968 is one such example of a situation where true consensus appears never to have been attained.[9]

DEFENSE COUNCIL

Whether there exists an elaborate committee structure subordinate to the Politburo is unclear. One author has suggested the existence of committees on internal security and foreign policy; another has suggested subgroups for foreign relations, agriculture, and cultural-ideological affairs.[10]

What is beyond dispute is the existence of a de facto committee for defense—the Defense Council (*Sovyet Orborony*) which formally, under the 1977 constitution, is placed under the Presidium of the Supreme Soviet. In practice, however, it is subordinate to the Politburo if it is subordinate to any group. Like the secret police, the Defense Council has existed under different names and with varying degrees of responsibility, although possibly not continuously, since 1918.[11]

The precise role, membership, and immediate lineage of the Defense Council is a matter of dispute. Soviet sources describe the council as being responsible for the general direction of defense policy and the defense efforts of the country and as playing a major role in the organized development of the armed forces—in sum, with being responsible for "leadership of the country's defense." According to an unclassified Defense Intelligence Agency (DIA) report, the Defense Council's responsibilities include:

- the resolution of major questions relating to the national security, increasing defense capability and the development of national military potential;
- the approval of plans of military development, establishment of the state military system, and principles of Soviet military organization; and
- the coordination of the Soviet state apparatus to ensure that military interests will be considered in all decisions of the state administration.[12]

As noted above, if the Defense Council is subordinate to any institution (other than the Party as a whole) it would be the Politburo. Thus, Jerry Hough notes that, at least in the past, the decisions of the Defense Council seem to have required Politburo approval.[13] There is certainly no dispute that *if* the Defense Council is a subcommittee of any institution then it is a subcommittee of the Politburo. Sergei Friedzon and Michael Checinski, however, suggest that the Defense Council may be the supreme defense decisionmaking authority.[14] Friedzon asserts that "the Defense Council represents the Party leadership in managing the military and hence must possess all plenipotentiary authority given to the highest decisionmaking organ of the country in matters of national security."[15]

A related issue, also the subject of contention, is the exact composition of the council. Announcements following the succession of

Andropov and Chernenko to power clearly establish that the General Secretary automatically becomes Chairman of the Defense Council.[16] Beyond that there are two questions: One is which additional Politburo members are council members, and the second, and more significant, is whether there are any non-Politburo members on the council as full members.

A 1979 account suggested that the members were Brezhnev, Tikhonov, Ustinov, Gromyko, Andropov, L.I. Smirnov (Chairman, Military-Industrial Commission), and possibly the head of the Defense Industry Department of the Central Committee Secretariat.[17] A 1981 version of *Soviet Military Power* listed Brezhnev, Andropov, Tikhonov, Ogarkov, Ustinov, and the chairman of GOSPLAN (State Planning Agency) as permanent members, with other officials attending as required.[18] Hough and Fainsod cite an unidentified Soviet scholar's claim that two First Deputy Ministers of Defense are members.[19]

Such estimates imply a Defense Council membership based on a need to bring together the nation's primary political, military, and military-industrial decisionmakers. Friedzon takes a more "political" or "ideological" approach, suggesting a Defense Council membership of strictly Politburo members—in 1980: Brezhnev, Tikhonov, Ustinov, Gromyko, the Central Committee "Secretary for Ideology" (Suslov), and the Central Committee "Secretary for Commanding Cadres" (Kirilenko).[20]

In any case, the inclusion of the General Secretary and several others of the highest ranking officials in the Defense Council virtually guarantees that its recommendations will be accepted by the Politburo. To do otherwise would be to imply "no confidence" in the judgment of the Party's political-military leadership.[21]

As might be expected, little is known of the inner workings of the Defense Council. Mathew Gallagher suggests the evidence indicates that council meetings "are highly regularized affairs, with agendas set in advance and lists of invitees agreed upon."[22] According to an official in the Central Committee Secretariat, cited by William Jackson, the council does not meet regularly but only as occasions require to deal with topics such as START, production problems, and top military appointments.[23] Additionally, evidence suggests that the council has no independent staff but relies on information provided by the KGB, Ministry of Defense, and relevant Party organizations.[24]

CENTRAL COMMITTEE SECRETARIAT

The Central Committee Secretariat is the link between policy and implementation. The secretaries who direct the work of the Secretariat and its departments are often full or candidate Politburo members and are responsible for the supervision of the various ministries and committees of the Soviet state—ensuring that the will of the Party and Politburo is fulfilled.

Party rules require that the secretaries are elected by the Party Central Committee. The Secretariat as such is a small body with ten to eleven members who generally meet twice a week to discuss the work of the staff. Each secretary is responsible for at least one group of subjects, each of which is the concern of at least one of the twenty-two departments (*otdels*). These departments have a permanent staff of a little over 1,000 persons.[25]

Each department is directed by a department chief and a first deputy chief. In addition to the first deputy chief, each department has several deputy chiefs, the specific number being a function of the size and importance of the department. Each deputy chief heads a Subdepartment or Sector.[26]

The twenty-three departments shown in Table 3–1 constitute the Central Committee departments. The ones with national security responsibilities include Administrative Organs, Cadres Abroad, Defense Industry, Main Political Administration of the Soviet Army and Navy, General, International, International Information, Liaison with Communist and Workers' Parties, and Science and Education.[27]

The Administrative Organs Department is responsible for exercising the Politburo's control over the personnel employed in the Soviet national security apparatus. The department is responsible for approving promotions within the Ministries of Defense and Internal Affairs and the Committee for State Security.[28]

The Defense Industry Department supervises the eight ministries involved in military production—the ministries that produce the rifles, tanks, aircraft, ships, submarines, nuclear weapons, spacecraft, and communications equipment.[29] The department investigates bottlenecks in defense production. The Party secretary responsible for the defense industry often heads special meetings for the review of program proposals and the resolution of production problems.[30] The Foreign Cadres (or Cadres Abroad) Department has, at the very

Table 3-1. Departments of the Central Committee Secretariat.

Administrative Organs	International Information
Agriculture	Light Industry and Food Industry
Chemical Industry	Machine Industry
Construction	Organizational-Partywork
Culture	Planning and Financial Organs
Defense Industry	MPA of the Soviet Army and Navy
Foreign Aid	Propaganda
Foreign Cadres	Science and Education
General	Socialist Countries
Heavy Industry	Trade and Consumers' Services
International	Transportation-Communications

least, a role in personnel decisions with respect to the Ministry of Foreign Affairs, Ministry of Foreign Trade, and State Committee for Foreign Economic Ties.[31]

The Main Political Administration (MPA) of the Soviet Army and Navy is simultaneously a Central Committee Secretariat department and a unit of the Ministry of Defense. The MPA supervises the armed forces to ensure ideological conformity, providing political indoctrination and supervision through the deployment of political officers throughout every level of the armed forces.[32]

The General Department has been described as "the most powerful and most dangerous department of the Secretariat."[33] The General Department was one of the original Central Committee departments. Set up in 1919, immediately after the Eighth Party Congress, it was described as the chancery of the Central Committee. It later became the Secret Department, and was subsequently known as the Special Sector until the end of Stalin's rule. It's original title was restored by Stalin's successors.[34]

According to one account, the functions of the department include the issuance and safekeeping of Party cards, maintenance of the Party archives, handling of complaints, internal security, and being a "secretariat" for the Politburo.[35] In this later respect, the General Department may provide some intelligence analysis services for the Politburo with respect to important issues—synthesizing KGB and GRU reports and placing the information in the broadest policy context.

The International Department (ID) can date its birth at 1943, when it replaced the Comintern, which was abolished by Stalin as a gesture to his Western allies. The department, headed by Boris Ponomarev, is responsible for relations with the Communist countries and provides policy advice toward the United States, Western Europe, Japan, and the Third World.[36] In recent years it has also established links with the Popular Movement for the Liberation of Angola (MPLA), Namibian Southwest African People's Organization (SWAPO), Palestinian Liberation Organization (PLO), and the Patriotic Front of Zimbabwe.[37]

The ID also directs western dialogue activities of such organizations as the Institute for the U.S.A. and Canada. It is also, according to the CIA, heavily involved in attempting to influence Western Europeans on issues of peace and disarmament, maintaining liaison with many foreign organizations that are frequently employed to disseminate Soviet propaganda and views on international affairs as well as managing the front organizations.[38]

Under Politburo direction, the ID serves as an authoritative source of policy guidance for the whole battery of Communist international front organizations and for national revolutionary movements and guerilla groups. It also provides the Politburo with intelligence assessment and policy recommendation as well as being responsible for supervising the execution of large-scale covert action operations, including the covert funding, training, and guidance given to non-ruling Communist parties.[39]

There is also some evidence that indicates that the International Department has representatives in foreign embassies—representatives whose job it is to collect information about political parties and groups, to assess the political situation of the country concerned, and to establish contacts with "progressive" organizations and individuals.[40]

The total staff of the ID is, according to one source, under 100 but growing.[41] Organizationally, it is divided into regional sections with certain special country desks having been established for certain "progressive" Third World states.[42]

The International Information Department (IID) is headed by Leonid Zamyatin, a former director of TASS and presently a full member of the CPSU Central Committee. The IID was created in March 1978 as a direct result of a Central Committee decision to reorganize the foreign propaganda apparatus, improve its effectiveness, and carry on a propaganda offensive against the West.[43] It is presently the directing center of the Soviet propaganda effort, coordinating the activities of TASS, Novosti, and other political propaganda agencies, and it cooperates with the KGB in the implementation of active measures operations.[44]

Until the beginning of 1957 the International Department was responsible for relations between the CPSU and the ruling Communist parties. In that year that responsibility was taken over by the newly created Department for Liaison with Communist Workers' Parties in the Socialist Countries.[45] It is responsible for recommending to the Politburo policy initiatives affecting not only the East European satellites but also the ruling Asian Communist parties, Albania, and Yugoslavia.[46]

The Science and Education Department is responsible for several ministries—Education, Health, Medical Industry—that are not related to national security activities. However, it also supervises the Academy of Sciences and the State Committee for Science and Technology, both of which have national security responsibilities.[47]

THE MILITARY

Clearly, the entire Soviet military is part of the national security structure. The major organs within the Moscow area are the Ministry of Defense, its Main Military Council, the General Staff, and the headquarters organizations of the five armed services: Strategic Rocket Forces, Ground Forces, Troops of National Air Defense, Air Forces, and the Navy. Outside of Moscow are the sixteen military districts, four fleets, and groups of Soviet forces.

Within the Ministry of Defense, the top policymaking body is the Main Military Council (MMC)—*Glavnyy Voyenyy Sovyet* in Russian. Whereas the Defense Council is responsible for the "leadership of the country's defense," the Main Military Council is responsible for the more specific and detailed task of "the leadership of the armed forced."[48]

According to several sources, the Council is chaired by the Minister of Defense and is a collegial body the membership of which also includes the three first deputy ministers—the Chief of the General Staff, the Commander-in-Chief of the Warsaw Pact, and the First Deputy Minister for General Affairs—and the ten deputy ministers of defense.[49] The ten deputy ministers include the commanders-in-chief of the five military services as well as the Inspector General; Chief-of-the-Rear; Chief-of-Civil-Defense; the Commander-in-Chief, Soviet Forces Germany; and the Deputy Minister of Armaments.[50] Additionally, the Chairman of the Defense Council is an ex officio member, although it would be surprising if he attends.

According to the memoirs of Kiril Mertskov, the Council met two or three times a week in the past and is responsible for detailed military policy as well as command and control of the armed forces.[51] It would not be unlikely, then, that the MMC is charged with the detailed implementation of Defense Council decisions—a role that gives it a significant de facto decisionmaking authority with regard to the overall mix of strategic weaponry.

It should be noted that some authors, Michael Sadykiewicz and Friedzon being two, dispute the above standard account. They charge that the Main (or Supreme) Military Council is a policymaking body while there is a separate Collegium of the Ministry of Defense which has little power.[52]

Much of the work in support of proposal development and implementation is the responsibility of the General Staff and its eleven directorates—Operations, Intelligence (GRU), Organization-Mobilization, Military Science, Communications, Topography, Armaments, Cryptography, Strategic Deception, Military Assistance, and Warsaw Pact.[53]

The functions of the GRU have already been discussed. Those of the Chief Directorate of Strategic Deception will be covered in Chapter 8. The Main Operations Directorate is responsible for the formulation of general military strategy as well as setting the direction for future research and development. The directorate may be involved in the development of nuclear targeting plans as well.[54] The Armaments Directorate would be responsible for developing proposals for new weapons systems and coordinating proposals to meet overall requirements.[55] However, the directorate may have been abolished as long ago as 1970, when a ministry-level Armaments Directorate was established.[56] The Cryptography Directorate may well be responsible for the provision of communications security support for space and nuclear weapons systems.

Headquarters management of the Soviet military services is the responsibility of the individual services. The Strategic Rocket Forces (*Raketnyye Voyska Strategicheskovo Naznacheniya*) is responsible for all Soviet land-based missiles with ranges exceeding 1,000 kilometers. The Ground Forces (*Sukhoputnyye Voyska*) is divided into three basic combat branches—motorized rifle troops, rocket troops and artillery, and tank troops. The Troops of National Air Defense (PVO *Strany*) has subordinate to it Fighter Aviation of Air Defense, air defense troops of the ground forces, Zenith Rocket Troops (responsible for the SA-5, SA-10), Radio-Technical Troops (radar), and the antispace defense (PKO) and antirocket defense (PRO) troops. The Air Forces (*Voyenno Vozdushnyye Sily*) consists of Long Range Aviation, Frontal Aviation, and Transport Aviation. Finally, the Navy (*Voyenno-Morskoy Flot*) is responsible for surface ships, submarines, and oceanographic and intelligence collection vessels.[57]

The Soviet Union itself is divided into sixteen military districts as indicated in Figure 3-1. All troops of the Soviet ground forces, except those stationed abroad, are under the control of the military district commanders as well. Thus, military district commanders have under their direct control both ground and air forces capable of waging independent combat action.[58]

Each military district has an Intelligence Directorate controlled by the GRU, as noted earlier. These district staff may conduct intelligence operations up to 100 miles into neighboring countries.

Similar to the military district arrangement are those for the four fleets which manage the Soviet Navy: the Baltic, Black Sea, Pacific Ocean, and Northern. In addition to intelligence units at each fleet headquarters, the fleets may also be responsible for sensitive collection operations involving surface ships as well as submarines.

MVD AND MFA

Just as the military was an obvious part of the Soviet national security apparatus, so are the Ministry of Internal Affairs (MVD) and the Ministry of Foreign Affairs (MFA). They are, however, of far less significance.

The MVD, which once contained the elements of the KGB, is today restricted to more mundane functions, with administrations for Criminal Investigation, Fire Protection, Motor Vehicle Inspection, and the Militia.[59] Its primary national security responsibility stems from control of the 275,000 troops that make up the Internal

Figure 3–1. Soviet Military Districts.

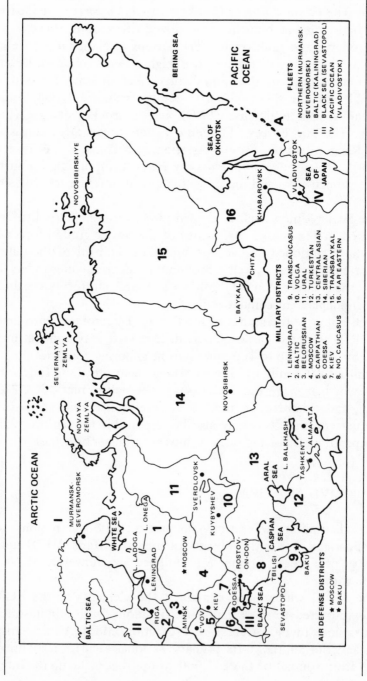

Source: *Air Force Magazine*, March 1975. Compiled by Harriet Fast Scott.

Security Forces. These troops have as their function the maintenance of "domestic order," are used to supress riots, and would be used in a crisis situation to maintain government/CPSU control.

The Ministry of Foreign Affairs, as an institution, plays a distinctly subsidiary role to the Central Committee Secretariat departments in regard to policy formation—although Gromyko, as a full member of the Politburo, may have had more individual influence than any department head. The ministry's role is more that of performing routine foreign affairs functions. In the 1950s, however, there was a Disinformation Department in the ministry. The department was subsequently closed down, with the KGB and Novosti Press Agency (APN) becoming the main vehicles for disinformation.[60]

INDUSTRIAL AND SCIENTIFIC COMMITTEES

Several industrial and scientific committees play a role in the formulation of national security and intelligence policy and requirements. Such committees include the Military-Industrial Commission (VPK), GOSPLAN (State Planning Agency), and the Soviet State Committee for Science and Technology (GKNT).

The VPK is another organization the exact national security role of which is in dispute. According to some, the VPK is charged with the responsibility for the supervision, coordination, and planning of defense research and development; production; and integration of those requirements into the national economy. According to this view, the VPK draws up a specific work program in the form of a "draft VPK decision" for each project. The "draft decision" specifies the tasks assigned to each organization, timetables, financing arrangements, and detailed design specifications. Approval by the VPK leadership is a virtual certainty, at which point the "draft VPK decision" becomes a "VPK decision" binding on all parties.[61]

Arthur Alexander argues that because the VPK provides information, performs technical analysis, and screens recommendations it has earlier approved, it has more than a marginal influence on the type of weapons procured.[62] Hough, on the other hand, suggests that

> the notion that coordination between the military, the defense industry and the scientists is provided by a military industrial commission . . . flies in the face of all bureaucratic logic. . . . [I] t is far more likely that the Military Industrial Commission plays the same production and supply role that it did in the 1930s.[63]

Whatever its broader role in weapons procurement, the VPK does have a very specific intelligence supervisory role. Each year the VPK issues a 500-page "requirements book" to the GRU. The book lists categories of Western technology and defense equipment that are being sought by Soviet industry. The book states the prices the GRU is authorized to spend—for example, $3 million for a British Chieftan tank. Half the contents of the book concern electronics and space technology.[64]

As already noted, the GKNT works with the KGB's Directorate T to identify scientific and technical intelligence heads. It considers first the needs of the Soviet military and then, to a lesser extent, civilian scientific and industrial communities and formulates these needs into acquisition requirements.[65] The GKNT also serves as a cover for GRU officers to collect scientific and technical intelligence via contacts with Western scientists and industrialists, both in the Soviet Union and abroad.[66]

TASS

TASS is the official Soviet news agency. As such it provides stories on its news service for dissemination to the West. It also provides cover for Soviet intelligence officers operating abroad. In addition, it provides internal documents and reports for government and Communist party officials.

Apparently, some reports concern special topics. Thus, in 1983 TASS sent out by mistake, on its English language news service, part of an internal report about U.S. computer technology research.[67] Additionally, it prepares on a regular basis a variety of reports. One classified daily news report for limited use by government and Communist party officials is known as White Tass (for the color of its cover). The material in White Tass closely resembles Western news reports.[68] There are also Green and Red editions.[69]

Other Tass publications for internal use are the *TASS Bulletin of Political Information* and *TASS Atlas*. The former contains fragments of major articles that appeared in Western academic journals, and the latter involves both the description of events and an analysis—comparable, according to one source, to *Newsweek*.[70]

RESEARCH INSTITUTES

Although a great deal is known about Soviet intelligence collection activities, little, indeed almost nothing, has appeared on the public record concerning Soviet intelligence analysis. This dearth of public information is apparently matched by an absence of classified information—an absence due probably to the lack of any Soviet defectors from the analysis branches of the KGB and GRU. Thus, a former CIA officer wrote, in regard to the information collected by the KGB and GRU: "What is done with these 'facts' we do not know. Moscow does not possess the enormous centralized research and analysis capacity we have in our own intelligence community." [71]

As indicated in Chapter 2 and this chapter, analysis functions are performed by Service I of the KGB's First Chief Directorate, various Information Directorates of the GRU, and very probably the International Department of the Central Committee's Secretariat. The types of reports they prepare—in terms of size, whether they prepare estimates rather than simple statements of facts and so on—is largely a mystery.

However, there are several research institutes, outside of the intelligence community per se that appear to have at least a marginal intelligence role. This role involves the assignment of some analysts to the institutes from the KGB and GRU. Others come from university faculties, foreign correspondents, and the military. Included are several social science research institutes—the Institute for the U.S.A. and Canada, the Institute of World Economic and International Relations (IMEMO), and the Institute of the Far East—as well as a scientific research institute.

Such institutes are not intelligence organizations per se. They prepare material for open publication, meet with Westerners (a major function), and have little access to classified information. Nor are they part of the intelligence analysis establishment to the extent of having a formalized and regularized role in the analytic and reporting process. One observer has written that

> there is no doubt that the institutes do perform an intelligence function. Information received or gleaned is passed on, and it is clear that some institute personnel are at times engaged in specific, commissioned intelligence and policy related analysis. But such tasks are commissioned on an ad hoc basis, case by case, and only to certain individual members or sections. There is no

open ended day-to-day type of intelligence analysis. The institutes have facilities for security related work in the sense of relevant experience and clearance, but they are facilities drawn upon as dictated by events. In the intelligence field they serve a reserve rather than a fully integrated function.[72]

The Institute of the U.S.A. and Canada was first organized in 1968, simply as the Institute of the U.S.A. It was given the additional responsibility for the study of Canada in 1974 and at that time its title was changed accordingly.[73] The general research tasks assigned to the institute include the study of:

• the current problems of American capitalism and the scientific-technological revolution;

• the socioeconomic processes occurring in the United States and U.S. ideological trends;

• U.S. foreign and domestic policies;

• Soviet-American relations; and

• contemporary Canadian policies and economy.[74]

The present staff of the institute is over 450, with 50 percent being researchers.[75] As indicated in Figure 3-2, the institute is organized into seven departments—Canada, Economics, U.S. Foreign Policy, U.S. Domestic Policy, U.S. Military, Ideology, and Information—under three deputy directors.

The public activities of the institute include publication of the monthly journal *SSha: Ekonomika, Politika, Ideologiya (U.S.A.: Economics, Politics, Ideology)* as well as numerous books. Among the books have been *U.S.A.: Tariff Protectionism, U.S.A.: The Problems of Domestic Policy*, and *U.S.A.: The Foreign Policy Mechanism.*[76]

Not for public consumption are the reports prepared by institute researchers, of which there are three varieties. The simplest is the *spravka*, a three- to five-page collection of facts with no analysis attached. More detailed is the ten- to fifteen-page *dokladnaya zapiska*, which would include some analysis. The most detailed analysis would be found in the fifteen- to seventy-five-page *analiticheskaya zapiska.*[77]

Some of these reports or other ad hoc studies may include classified information; some may be commissioned by the KGB, International Department, and Ministry of Foreign Affairs—although the commissioning authority will not generally be known to the

Figure 3-2. Organization of the Institute of the U.S.A. and Canada.

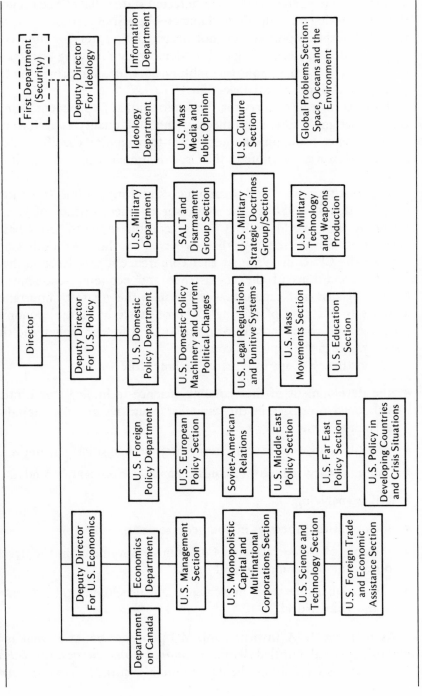

Source: Barbara L. Dash, *A Defector Reports: The Institute of the USA and Canada* (Falls Church, Va.: Delphic Associates, 1982), p. 3b.

analyst.[78] One analyst who since defected stated that the last report she was working on, concerning Japanese-American relations, was for the KGB. Other report topics (not necessarily written for the KGB) have included the weakening of U.S. democracy following Watergate, China after Mao, U.S. political-military doctrine, and projecting the result of a U.S. presidential election.[79]

Analysts writing reports for the International Department, Ministry of Foreign Affairs, and especially the KGB qualify as performing an intelligence function whether or not they employ classified information. However, as noted, this is a marginal aspect of institute activity.

The Institute of World Economics and International Relations was founded in 1956 as the successor to the Institute of World Economy and World Politics.[80] Its creation followed from basic changes in Soviet strategy that occurred at the Twentieth Congress of the CPSU in 1956. At that conference it was declared that: "Under conditions of the coexistence and economic cooperation of the socialist and capitalist world system the greatest importance attaches to the task of making a thorough study of the economic processes, the characteristics of domestic and foreign policy and the class struggle in the capitalist countries."[81]

The institute's scope of research includes forecasting:

- the development of the economy, science-technology, and internal social processes in the capitalist countries and the capitalist system as a whole;
- possible changes in the long-term international situation; and
- contemporary capitalism's conflicts and developmental trends

as well as analyzing:

- sociopolitical processes in bourgeois society;
- the role of democratic and Communist movements in the developed capitalist countries; and
- the national liberation movements and developmental processes in the Third World.[82]

As with the USA Institute, IMEMO publishes books as well as a monthly journal entitled *World Economics and International Relations.* It also publishes the *International Political-Economic An-*

nual.[83] However, its most important work is in support of Soviet strategy—identifying Western vulnerabilities and the opportunities for the Soviet Union. Thus, in 1974 IMEMO's director stated:

We intend to expand our analysis of the new trends in the development of international trade, the investment process, international credit and currency relations, the activities of international monopolies and the integration process. Increasingly great importance attaches to investigation of the problems of international economic cooperation and particularly the problems pertaining to enhancement of the effectiveness of foreign economic relations between the USSR and the capitalist countries.[84]

The Institute of the Far East was established in 1966, primarily to focus on the People's Republic of China. As with the USA Institute and IMEMO, the Institute of the Far East produces books for public consumption as well as reports for government and Party leaders.[85]

It appears that the institute is considered more sensitive than IMEMO and the USA Institute, possibly due to a greater intelligence role. There is virtually no open literature dealing with its organization and functions. Additionally, there is a significantly greater number of militiamen and security guards around and in the institute.[86]

The All-Union Institute of Scientific and Technical Information (VINITI) is charged with monitoring foreign scientific-technical literature, particularly from the United States. VINITI gathers and organizes information to be processed, stored, and disseminated. It is the largest producer of scientific-technical abstracts, and in 1971 it was reported to have processed approximately one million articles, books, and descriptions of inventions. Presently, it processes 25,000 serial publications in sixty-four languages from 118 nations. Its publications include the reference series *Referativnyi Zhurnal*, which contained 975,000 items in 1970, and *Hogi Navki*, which contains reviews of scientific progress.[87]

NOTES TO CHAPTER 3

1.   Arthur J. Alexander, "Decision Making in Soviet Weapons Procurement," *Adelphi Papers* 147–149, 1978, p. 9.
2.   Seth Mydans, "Soviet Chief, Shaping New Rule, Promotes Three to the Politburo," *New York Times*, April 24, 1985, p. A6.

3. Elizabeth Teague, "The Foreign Departments of the Central Committee of the CPSU," *Radio Liberty Research Bulletin*, October 27, 1980, p. 2.
4. Alexander, "Decision Making in Soviet Weapons Procurement," p. 9.
5. Henry Brandon, "How decisions are made in the highest Soviet circles," *Washington Star*, July 15, 1979, p. 3.
6. Theodore Shabad, "Brezhnev, Who Ought to Know, Explains Politburo," *New York Times*, June 15, 1973, p. 3.
7. Ibid.
8. For example, see Sidney Ploss, *Conflict and Decision Making in Soviet Russia: A Case Study of Agricultural Policy 1952-1963* (Princeton: Princeton University Press, 1965); Jiri Valenta, "Soviet Decisionmaking in the Czechoslovak Crisis of 1968," *Studies in Comparative Communism* 8 (1975): 147-73; Jiri Valenta, *Soviet Intervention in Czechoslovakia, 1968* (Baltimore: Johns Hopkins Press, 1979); Michael G. Fry and Condoleeza Rice, "The Hungarian Crisis of 1956: The Soviet Decision," *Studies in Comparative Communism* 16, no. 1-2 (1983): 85-98.
9. Valenta, "Soviet Decisionmaking in the Czechoslovak Crisis of 1968."
10. Michael Sadykiewicz, "Soviet Military Politics," *Survey* 26, no. 1 (1982): 179-210.
11. Alexander, "Decision Making in Soviet Weapons Procurement," pp. 14-15.
12. Ellen Jones, *The Soviet Ministry of Defense and Military Management* (Washington, D.C.: Defense Intelligence Agency, 1979), pp. 4-5.
13. Jerry Hough, "The Historical Legacy in Soviet Weapons Development," in Jiri Valenta and William Potter, eds., *Soviet Decisionmaking for National Security* (Boston: Allen & Unwin, 1984), pp. 87-115.
14. Sergei Freidzon, "The Soviet Defense Council and the Decision Making Process in Military Planning: A Research Note" (UCLA, 1980). (Mimeo.); Michael Checinski, *A Comparison of the Polish and Soviet Armaments Decision Making Systems* (Santa Monica, Calif.: RAND Corporation, 1980).
15. Freidzon, "The Soviet Defense Council and the Decision Making Process in Military Planning."
16. John F. Burns, "A Second Post for Andropov Disclosed," *New York Times*, May 10, 1983, p. A3.
17. Jones, "The Soviet Ministry of Defense and Military Management"; Jack Anderson, "The Gray Haired Dabblers in Doom," *Washington Post*, April 16, 1981, p. 11.
18. Department of Defense, *Soviet Military Power*, 1st ed. (Washington, D.C.: U.S. Government Printing Office, 1981), pp. 16-17.
19. Jerry Hough and Merle Fainsod, *How the Soviet Union Is Governed* (Cambridge, Mass.: Harvard University Press, 1979), p. 384.
20. Friedzon, "The Soviet Defense Council and the Decision Making Process in Military Planning."

21. Douglas Garthoff, "The Soviet Military and Arms Control," *Survival* 19, no. 6 (November–December 1977): 242–50.
22. Mathew P. Gallagher, "The Military Role in Soviet Decision Making," in Michael McGwire, Ken Booth, and John McDonnell, ed., *Soviet Naval Policy: Objectives and Constraints* (New York: Praeger, 1975), pp. 40–58.
23. William D. Jackson, "Leadership and Coordination in Soviet Security Policy," in Duncan Clarke, ed., *Public Policy and Political Institutions, United States Defense and Foreign Policy: Policy Coordination and Integration* (Greenwich, Conn.: JAI Press, forthcoming).
24. Ibid.
25. Teague, "The Foreign Departments of the Central Committee of the CPSU."
26. Ibid.
27. Hough and Fainsod, *How the Soviet Union is Governed*, pp. 412–13.
28. Cord Meyer, *Facing Reality: From World Federalism to the CIA* (New York: Harper & Row, 1980), p. 309.
29. Hough and Fainsod, *How the Soviet Union is Governed*, pp. 412–13.
30. Jackson, "Leadership and Coordination in Soviet Security Policy."
31. Hough and Fainsod, *How the Soviet Union is Governed*, p. 414.
32. Ibid., p. 416.
33. John Lowenhardt, *The Soviet Politburo* (New York: St. Martin's, 1982), p. 113.
34. Leonard Schapiro, "The General Department of the Central Committee of the CPSU," *Survey* 21, no. 3 (1975): 53–65.
35. Ibid.
36. Hough and Fainsod, *How the Soviet Union is Governed*, p. 414; Meyer, *Facing Reality*, p. 307.
37. Teague, "The Foreign Departments of the Central Committee of the CPSU," p. 5.
38. U.S. Congress, House Permanent Select Committee on Intelligence, *Soviet Active Measures* (Washington, D.C.: U.S. Government Printing Office, 1982), p. 6.
39. Meyer, *Facing Reality*, p. 309.
40. Leonard Schapiro, "The International Department of the CPSU: Key to Soviet Policy," *International Journal* 32, no. 1 (1976–77): 41–55.
41. Jackson, "Leadership and Coordination in Soviet Security Policy."
42. Ibid.
43. U.S. Congress, House Permanent Select Committee on Intelligence, *Soviet Active Measures*, p. 5.
44. Ibid.
45. Teague, "The Foreign Departments of the Central Committee of the CPSU," p. 13.
46. Meyer, *Facing Reality*, p. 309.

66   SWORD AND SHIELD

47. Hough and Fainsod, *How the Soviet Union is Governed*, p. 414.
48. Alexander, "Decision Making in Soviet Weapons Procurement," p. 16.
49. Harriet F. Scott and William F. Scott, *The Armed Forces of the USSR* (Boulder, Colorado: Westview, 1979), pp. 99–100.
50. Ibid.
51. Hough, "The Historical Legacy in Soviet Weapons Development."
52. Sadykiewicz, "Soviet Military Politics."
53. Scott and Scott, *The Armed Forces of the USSR*, p. 110; Viktor Suvorov, *Inside the Soviet Army* (New York: Macmillan, 1982), p. 102.
54. Kenneth Currie, "Soviet General Staff's New Role," *Problems of Communism* (March–April 1984): 32–40.
55. Alexander, "Decision Making in Soviet Weapons Procurement," pp. 17–18.
56. Jackson, "Leadership and Coordination in Soviet Security Policy."
57. Scott and Scott, *The Armed Forces of the USSR*, pp. 137-61.
58. Ibid., p. 176.
59. Central Intelligence Agency, *Directory of Soviet Officials* (Washington, D.C.: CIA, 1982), p. 110-13.
60. "Part II – Shevchenko Interview," *Law and National Security Intelligence Report* 2, no. 11 (November 1980).
61. Alexander, "Decision Making in Soviet Weapons Procurement," p. 21.
62. Ibid.
63. Hough, "The Historical Legacy in Soviet Weapons Development."
64. Robert Moss, "Soviets' No. 2 Secret Service a Giant in Shadowy Arena," *Los Angeles Times*, June 28, 1981, pp. 6-7.
65. "Measures Urged to Stem Tide of Soviet Data to Soviets," *Aviation Week and Space Technology*, January 10, 1983, p. 22.
66. Oleg Penkovskiy, *The Penkovskiy Papers* (New York: Doubleday, 1965).
67. Robert Gillette, "Soviet Interest in U.S. Computer Revealed," *Los Angeles Times*, November 20, 1983, p. 32.
68. Ibid.
69. Barbara L. Dash, *A Defector Reports: The Institute of the USA and Canada* (Falls Church, Va.: Delphic Associates, 1982), p. 14.
70. Ibid., p. 50.
71. Harry Rositzke, *Managing Moscow: Guns or Goods?* (New York: William Morrow, 1984), p. 73.
72. Carl G. Jacobsen, "Soviet Thinks Tanks," *Soviet Armed Forces Review Annual* 1 (Fall 1977): 140-52. Also See Tyrus W. Cobb, "National Security Perspectives of Soviet 'Think Tanks,'" *Problems of Communism* (November-December 1981): 51-59.
73. Richard A. Soll, Arthur A. Zuehlke, Jr., and Richard B. Foster, *The Role of Social Science Research Institutes in Formulation and Execution of Soviet Foreign Policy* (Arlington, Va.: SRI International, 1976), p. 23.
74. Ibid., p. 24.

75. Dash, *A Defector Reports*, p. 11.
76. Soll, Zuehlke, and Foster, *The Role of Social Science Research Institutes in Formulation and Execution of Soviet Foreign Policy*, pp. 26-27.
77. Dash, *A Defector Reports*, p. 11.
78. Ibid., p. 126.
79. Ibid., pp. 30, 82-83. For a study of the content of the writings of USA Institute analysts, see Morton Schwartz, *Soviet Perceptions of the United States* (Berkeley: University of California Press, 1978).
80. Soll, Zuehlke, and Foster, *The Role of Social Science Research Institutes*, pp. 18-19.
81. Ibid., p. 20.
82. Ibid., pp. 20-21.
83. Ibid., p. 18.
84. Ibid., p. 21.
85. Ibid., pp. 30-31.
86. Ibid., p. 31.
87. Ibid., p. 78; National Science Foundation, Office of Science Information Service, *The USSR Scientific and Technical Information System: A Report of the U.S. Participants in the US/USSR Symposium on Scientific and Technical Information* (Washington, D.C.: National Science Foundation, 1973), pp. 18-20.

4 HUMINT

Soviet human intelligence (HUMINT) operations are directed against all aspects of a society—political, military, cultural, scientific, and economic—both domestic and foreign. Thus, one KGB document listed the following as priorities for penetration in the United States:

1. the President's Cabinet and National Security Council;
2. the State Department, U.S. Delegation to the United Nations, Passport Office of the State Department;
3. Department of Defense, military intelligence, Permanent Military Group of the NATO staff in Europe;
4. CIA, FBI;
5. National Association of Manufacturers, monopolies, banking houses;
6. scientific centers; and
7. governing organs of the leading political parties in the United States and other influential public and political organizations.[1]

It would be safe to assume similar priorities with respect to other major Soviet intelligence targets, such as Japan, the United Kingdom, and Egypt.

OVERVIEW

The Soviet HUMINT program directed against the U.S. organizations noted above and similar foreign organizations produces a large amount of valuable intelligence, for a variety of reasons. One is the large number of intelligence officers deployed overseas. In general, 30 to 40 percent of an embassy staff and other official missions may actually be employees of the KGB and GRU. Thus, the FBI estimates that of the 280 Soviets assigned to their Washington diplomatic mission, approximately 130 (46 percent) are KGB or GRU agents. Further, the FBI estimates that 35 percent of the 1,300 Soviet personnel stationed in the United States—405—are intelligence officers.[2] In West Germany there are 408 Soviet officials. Of those officials, 109 (27 percent) are confirmed intelligence officers; another 77 (19 percent) are suspected.[3]

A second reason is the rather aggressive nature of these intelligence officers, whether deployed in the United States, Western Europe, or the Third World. A relentless search for agents is, on occasion, bound to be rewarded with a prize catch. At the same time, such aggressive behavior is also likely to lead to frequent instances of intelligence officers being caught and expelled (when under diplomatic cover) or jailed. Thus, as indicated in Table 4-1, in the period 1974 through 1982, a total of 196 Soviet "diplomats" were expelled for intelligence activities. Of the 196, 16 were expelled from the United States, 23 from Canada, 11 from France, 17 from Egypt, 12 from Norway, 13 from Spain, and 14 from Switzerland.[4]

In 1983 alone, 135 expulsions took place, almost three times as many as the previous year and almost twice as many as occurred in 1981 and 1982 combined.[5] Countries expelling Soviet representatives included Australia, Belgium, Canada, Denmark, West Germany, the United Kingdom (4), Ireland, Italy, Jamaica, Japan, Liberia, the Netherlands, Norway, Spain, Sweden, Switzerland, Thailand, and the United States (3). Among those expelled from the United States was Major General Vasily I. Chitov, a member of the GRU and the highest ranking military officer at the embassy.[6]

Additionally, mass expulsions occurred from France (47), Bangladesh (18), and Iran (18). The action by the French government represented the third-largest expulsion of Soviet officials, the two larger being the British expulsion of 105 officials in 1971 and the Bolivian

Table 4-1. Expulsions by Country, 1974-1982.

Country	KGB	GRU
Bangladesh	3	1
Brazil	1	0
Canada	17	6
Costa Rica	2	0
China	2	1
Denmark	7	1
Egypt	14	3
Equatorial Guinea	1	0
France	4	7
Ghana	2	2
India	4	1
Indonesia	0	2
Iran	5	0
Italy	4	1
Japan	1	0
Liberia	3	0
Malaysia	4	1
Mexico	1	0
Netherlands	3	4
New Zealand	1	0
Norway	9	3
North Yemen	1	0
Nigeria	1	0
Pakistan	1	0
Portugal	4	5
Spain	10	3
Singapore	3	0
Sudan	3	0
Sweden	1	2
Switzerland	7	7
United Kingdom	2	2
United States	14	2
West Germany	4	2
Yugoslavia	1	0
	140	56

Source: Barron, *KGB Today*, pp. 442-453.

Figure 4-1. Expulsions by Year, 1974–1983.

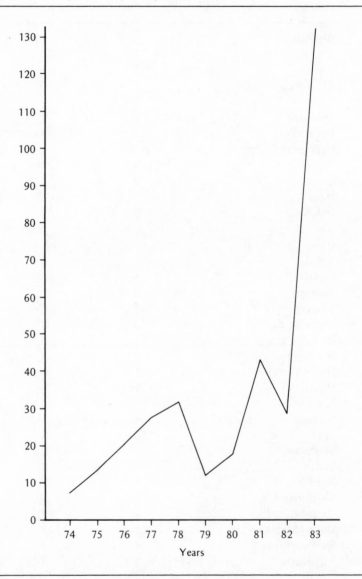

Source: Barron, *KGB Today*, pp. 437–442.

expulsion of 60 officials in 1972.[7] Not all the expulsions can be linked exclusively or primarily to intelligence collection activities as is the case with the officials expelled by Britain in 1971 and by France in 1983. The Bolivian government's expulsion of Soviet officials was related to their financing of leftist rebel movements; the 1983 expulsions from Liberia and Bangladesh were due to Soviet complicity in a Liberian coup attempt and the passing of money to Bangladesh opposition movements.[8]

The general upward trend in expulsions since 1974 is illustrated in Figure 4-1. Although the increase is by no means an uninterrupted trend, the "moving average" indicates a trend toward increased numbers of expulsions. The increase is probably due to both increased Soviet activity, particularly with respect to scientific and technical intelligence, and a decreased tolerance by some countries (such as France) for such activities.

A third explanation for the Soviet acquisition of valuable material via human sources is the nature of the societies in which their intelligence officers operate. Although restricted in their travel areas in the United States and often surveilled by the FBI, the officers still operate in a far looser environment and among a far less suspicious populace than that faced by Western intelligence officers in the Soviet Union. In other Western countries the restrictions are even fewer and the surveillance not as extensive.

OFFICERS AND AGENTS

An important distinction with respect to human intelligence operations is that between the intelligence officer and the intelligence agent. Officers are invariably citizens of the country for the intelligence service of which they work. As a matter of course, they will be trained in their country, spend time at headquarters, and return home at intervals. Agents are generally nationals of the country they spy upon. They may never see Moscow or any other part of the Soviet Union.

As indicated in Chapter 2, the KGB and GRU have two distinct types of officers: legals and illegals. Legals operate from an embassy, consulate, trade mission, or some other official Soviet installation. Thus, though their intelligence activities may not be legal, their presence in the country is legal, and if they are caught they may often be in a position to claim diplomatic immunity.

In addition to diplomatic immunity, the employment of legals offers several other advantages. Under this system each officer operates under the supervision of a superior; thus, a secure training ground exists and less experienced agents can benefit from the knowledge of more experienced agents. The legal framework also provides for secure communications with headquarters, both via radio and the diplomatic pouch. The pouch can be employed for the secret shipping of bulky espionage-related items, such as cameras and communications gear. Additionally, location in an embassy or other diplomatic/commercial installation allows for the co-optation of nonintelligence personnel when required.[9]

Furthermore, diplomatic cover offers a natural circle of contacts, many of whom would be "prize catches." A political officer would expect to be in touch with foreign ministry officials; a defense attaché would be in touch with defense ministry officials; a TASS representative could easily explain contacts with native journalists. Aside from cover professional duties, officers can engage in normal social activities—receptions, Soviet events, club memberships—which can serve as a source of new contacts as well as a cover for intelligence activities.[10]

At the same time, the legal operates under several handicaps, such as those of being identifiable, locatable, and restricted. Every new diplomat is known to the authorities, and the question of any intelligence affiliation is one of the first questions to arise. Although even the most efficient Western security services are by no means able to sort out with perfect accuracy intelligence officers from true diplomats, they are able to identify a large portion of those with intelligence responsibilities, either on the basis of previously acquired information or present surveillance.

Second, the officers are locatable. Their places of work and residence are known and can be watched. The officer who evades surveillance one day can be located at the beginning of the next. Third, activities, specifically travel, may be sharply restricted, as in the United States.

Hence, in many countries the Soviet Union maintains a network of illegal officers, officers who are Soviet citizens and who have been infiltrated into the country under false cover—an elaborate "legend" created for them by the KGB or GRU. These officers operate without diplomatic cover and are in contact with the residency's illegal support officers only in emergency situations.

As documented citizens, illegals have freedom of movement throughout the country without (unless detected) being subject to surveillance. They can therefore service dead drops and provide a variety of assistance to other illegals. More importantly, they can operate against targets that are off limits to legals—either by gaining employment at a sensitive location or by maintaining contact with an agent in the immediate vicinity of a location such as a strategic airbase, radar or warning site, or other sensitive location. Thus, Soviet illegals provided information from the British Naval Underwater Weapons Establishment concerning submarine and other underwater military activities.[11] Finally, in the event of war or massive expulsion, the illegals network can provide a stay-behind human intelligence capability.

At the same time, illegals do have certain handicaps—most prominently an inability to gain access to the same high-level circles freely accessible to diplomats. Thus, as photographer Emil Goldfus, Colonel Rudolf Abel had no natural contact with anyone with access to classified information. Further, there seems to be no evidence that Abel ever accomplished anything with respect to gathering intelligence.[12]

As noted earlier, one must distinguish between agents and officers. Agents are recruited by officers and are generally citizens of the country they are spying on. They may be recruited on the basis of a sensitive position they already hold or with the expectation that they will obtain such a position. Third country agents may be employed when their occupation—for example, businessman or journalist— allows travel and contacts with respect to the target country.

Agents may be recruited by a variety of means—friendship, ideology, money, coercion, or blackmail—and for long- or short-term purposes. A significant portion of Soviet intelligence gathering is devoted to the development of information concerning potential agents, such as identifying those with access to useful information and their financial and personal situations, vulnerabilities, or weaknesses.

GRU instructions concerning possible military recruitment targets call for information:

1. To clarify the basic data
   a. Present position, where did he work previously;

    b. Prospects for remaining in the service;

    c. From what year in the service; does he like it?

    d. His relations with his immediate superiors.

2. To elucidate biographical data
   a. Age, parents, family conditions;
   b. Education, principal speciality, special technical or other knowledge:
   c. Attitude toward politics;
   d. Financial conditions: inclination toward establishing financial security for his family and what hinders the fulfillment of such plans;
   e. Attitude toward the Soviet Union;
   f. Wherein does he see prosperity of his country (e.g., in friendship with the United States)?

3. Personal positive and negative characteristics
   a. Inclination to drink, women friends—or good family man;
   b. Lover of good things—or inclination to solitude and quietness;
   c. Influence of his wife on his actions—or independence in making his own decisions;
   d. Circle of acquaintances and brief character sketches of them.[13]

In other cases, an attempt will be made to create a compromising situation, either personal or professional. In 1981 the KGB made an attempt to compromise the Assistant Military Attaché at the U.S. embassy in Moscow: The attaché was scheduled to join the staff of Vice President Bush. Similarly, the KGB attempted to use compromising pictures to recruit the French ambassador to Moscow, Maurice Dejean—a plan derailed by the defection of a KGB officer. Apparently, the KGB was more successful in exploiting the homosexuality of a Canadian ambassador, who died under questioning by the Royal Canadian Mounted Police (RCMP) Security Service.[14]

On occasion, certain favors may be offered in exchange for information. In 1972 the Reuters correspondent in Peking tried to get a cut-rate ticket to Europe from Aeroflot, the Peking manager of which worked out of the Soviet embassy. "Problems" soon arose with the provision of the ticket. At a meeting to resolve the problems, the correspondent was informed that he could have the ticket in exchange for gathering some information in China. He declined.[15]

In other cases money may be the key ingredient in obtaining information on classified matters. Thus, a Northrop Corporation engineer plagued by debts attempted to sell information on stealth technology to the Soviet Union for $25,000. The engineer had removed classified technical manuals, blueprints, drawings and a list of subcontractors before he was arrested by the FBI.[16]

In some instances a "false flag" recruitment may occur in which the officer tells the prospective agent that he is gathering information for his own country or for the United States, Britain, and so forth. Thus, a pro-American citizen of a "troublesome" U.S. ally (e.g., Greece) might be approached to provide the "United States" with information. Likewise, a Turkish citizen employed at one of the U.S. bases in Turkey might be asked by a "Turkish government representative" to provide information on U.S. activities at the bases so that the "Turkish government" can check to determine that the Americans are living up to the agreements governing activities at the base.

EMBASSY OPERATIONS

The central core of Soviet intelligence operations in any given country is located in the embassy. The chief of the KGB apparatus in each embassy is known as the Resident. As indicated in Figure 4–2, subordinate to the Resident are the Deputy Resident, several staff elements, three "lines," and the illegal support officers.

The Resident is usually the highest ranking KGB official in a Soviet embassy and is in charge of all KGB personnel under whatever forms of cover they may be serving. He is responsible directly to KGB headquarters in Moscow and conducts liaison with the Soviet ambassador and the chief of the GRU unit in the embassy. Additionally, he is responsible for liaison with the chiefs of the representatives of the East European and Cuban intelligence services operating under diplomatic cover—providing them with advice and guidance. The resident also reads and releases all cables and dispatch traffic. Normally only the resident is aware of the true identity of all agents operating in his area of responsibility, excluding those deep-cover illegals who are run directly from Moscow.[17]

The staff elements include the Technical Support Group, the Reports Officer, Residence Secretary, and the Drivers and Cleaning

Figure 4-2. Organizational Structure of a Typical KGB Residence.

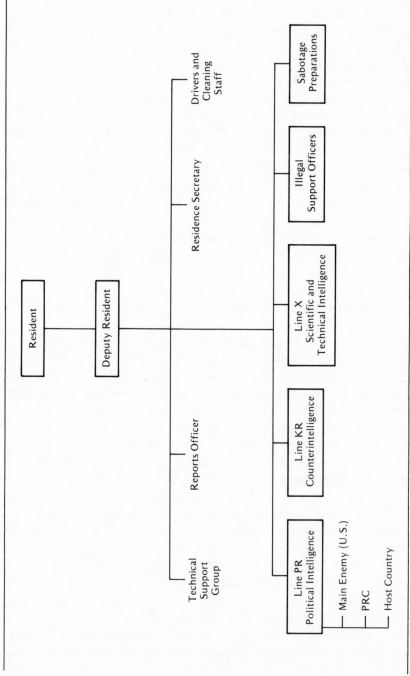

Source: Cord Meyer, *Facing Reality: From World Federalism to the CIA* (New York: Harper & Row, 1974), p. 316.

Staff. The Technical Support Group provides trained technicians and advanced equipment required to conduct electronic and photographic surveillance, including phone tapping, placement of audio devices, and secret photography. The group is also responsible for monitoring the communications of the police and security service as well as ensuring that there is no audio penetration of Soviet installations.[18]

The Reports Officer helps to prepare the information obtained by agents for transmission to Moscow Center. In smaller residencies there is no separate Reports Officer, and the operational offices do the final editing. The Residence Secretary is responsible for the secure vault area and for the maintenance and security of the files kept there. All classified intelligence reports have to be prepared in this area, and documents or files cannot be removed.[19]

Intelligence and counterintelligence operations are the responsibility of the three lines: Line PR, Line KR, and Line X. Line PR — Political Intelligence — is responsible for political, military, and economic intelligence collection as well as active measures operations. Line PR is usually divided into three subsections. The first and most heavily staffed subsection is the "Main Enemy" or U.S. subsection. Line PR's recruitment efforts are directed against both American citizens and foreigners who could conceivably have or gain access to classified U.S. information.[20]

In countries where there is People's Republic of China representation, the second subunit is targeted against Chinese officials and foreigners who have any type of access to them. One technique employed is the penetration of "Maoist" splinter groups in the host country in order to obtain information on local political strategy as well as for the purpose of disruption.[21]

It is the third subunit that is directed against the country in which the KGB residency is located. If the country is an ally of the United States, agent recruitments within that country's government can provide information on combined military and economic planning and the joint development of new weapons systems.[22] This subsection also appears to be responsible for the day-to-day liaison conducted with illegal Communist party organizations that are loyal to the Soviet Union.[23]

Line KR — Counterintelligence — will be discussed in more detail in Chapter 8. Its functions include maintaining the security of Soviet personnel and institutions in the host country, operations against foreign intelligence and security services, and operations against emigrés.

Scientific and technical intelligence acquisition is the responsibility of Line X. Officers of Line X are technically trained and tasked to collect intelligence on advanced Western technology. Much of their time is devoted to the overt acquisition of information and hardware through the collection of unclassified documents and the purchase of unrestricted machinery. The portions of Western technology considered classified or not for export to East Bloc countries represents the highest priority targets of Line X.[24]

A fourth embassy section consists of the illegals support officers. Contact between these officers and illegals is likely to occur only in emergency situations—whether from the view of KGB Headquarters or of the illegal. The fifth section is responsible for establishing an agent network to be held in reserve for the implementation of sabotage plans in case of war. The section collects detailed plans on critical military and industrial facilities.[25]

In addition to the KGB residency there will also be a GRU residence in each embassy, although it will be much smaller than its KGB counterpart. The GRU residency is primarily responsible for recruiting agents within the host country's military forces and defense-related institutions. The GRU also operates the antennae that can often be observed on the roofs of Soviet embassies and consulates.[26]

A strained relationship also exists between the GRU and KGB residents in an embassy. While the GRU is required to clear all agent recruitment attempts with the KGB in advance so as to prevent competing approaches to the same individual, the KGB does not appear to be similarly obligated. In addition, GRU officers "deeply resent the security overview that the KGB maintains over their private lives and the intrusive activity of KGB informants."[27]

COVER

In conducting intelligence collection operations abroad (and within the Soviet Union) the Soviet intelligence services employ a wide range of cover positions. Indeed, no Soviet institution with representatives abroad, either on a permanent or a temporary basis, is immune from having some positions assigned to the KGB and GRU or its employees co-opted to perform intelligence work.

Soviet institutions that are represented around the world and provide cover to KGB and GRU personnel include TASS, the Novosti Press Agency, trade missions, Aeroflot, Morflot (Soviet shipping), Sovexport film, and New Times. Additionally, institutions specific to a particular nation—such as Amtorg (American Trade Organization) and SOCIAC (Singapore-Soviet Shipping Company)—are also employed as covers.[28]

Additionally, Soviet employees of international organizations or attached to Soviet missions to such organizations—for example, the World Health Organization in Geneva or the United Nations—are often KGB or GRU agents. Thus, the Soviet head of the United Nations Information Center, Vassili V. Vakhrushev, is a KGB agent.[29]

Several of the Soviet officers caught and expelled for intelligence activities have operated under cover positions such as those described above. In 1982 two Aeroflot officials were expelled from Spain on espionage charges; another was charged with military espionage in Italy in early 1983. That officer was caught with NATO documents and plans for the twin-engine all-weather Tornado fighter.[30] According to one recent KGB defector, as much as 50 percent of the personnel in the Tokyo Aeroflot office may be involved in scientific and technical intelligence collection.[31]

Soviet trade and shipping officials have been expelled from Spain, Denmark (where they were accused of spying on Dutch and NATO military facilities), and Germany.[32] In the latter case, the Soviet official was caught in the act of purchasing information pertaining to a coding machine used by West German intelligence.[33] New Times (*Novaye Vremya*) was founded by the CPSU in 1943 for the sole purpose of providing cover for intelligence officers abroad. By Politburo decree, twelve of its fourteen foreign bureaus were to be reserved exclusively for KGB occupancy.[34]

In September 1978 two former Soviet employees of the United Nations were convicted of conspiracy and espionage. They were caught attempting to buy U.S. Navy data on the Grumman F-14 fighter and the Navy's LAMPS undersea intelligence system.[35]

KGB and GRU officers assigned cover positions in the embassy and other offices perform their cover jobs as well as their intelligence functions, often complaining that they are not sufficiently trained for their jobs to perform them in a credibly competent manner. In addition, they often complain that their true functions are often widely known within the embassy. Identification is easy because of late working hours necessitated by the frequency of night meetings with agents. Identification also results from the special privileges they receive, which include exemption from attendance at the lengthy and tedious lectures given by the CPSU representative.[36]

In New York and Washington, and other similar cities, Soviet intelligence operatives operate under a variety of covers. Although some nondiplomatic (e.g., trade) cover positions are located in the embassy, others are not and may be located in several different parts of the city. Thus, in Washington eight Soviet installations are spread throughout the city: (1) the Soviet embassy, (2) the Office of the Military, Air, and Naval Attachés, (3) Aeroflot, (4) Office of the Agricultural Counselor, Information Counselor, and Irrigation Counselor, (5) Office of Fisheries, (6) Trade Representative of the USSR, (7) Office of the Consular Division, and (8) TASS.[37] Similarly, there are, in New York, separate Soviet installations for the Soviet Permanent Mission to the United Nations, Amtorg, TASS, and Aeroflot.[38]

In addition to such permanent cover installations, the KGB and GRU exploit the scientific and cultural delegations sent abroad to provide cover for Soviet intelligence officers. The use of the Soviet State Committee for Science and Technology (GKNT) in providing cover for GRU agents is detailed in *The Penkovskiy Papers.*[39] Several years ago a group of Soviet aircraft specialists visited the Boeing Corporation, Lockheed, and McDonnell-Douglas factories under the sponsorship of the State Department. They were able to observe 747s, DC-10s and L-1011s under construction. In 1981 a defector reported that the visitors wore special shoes that picked up metal shavings from the factory floors. Analysis of these particles may have helped identify the alloys needed to produce troop transport planes.[40]

Soviet intelligence also employs less prestigious Soviet travelers for intelligence collection purposes, including Soviet truckers and merchant seamen. Trucks from the Soviet Union (and Eastern Europe) have been observed systematically gathering information, particularly surveying the road network that would be used in any invasion of Western Europe.[41] Some of the truckers may, in fact, be Soviet army tank officers being familiarized with the roads. Suspicions first arose when Dutch officials discovered that some Soviet trucks were taking up to four days to travel the few hundred miles between West Germany and the port of Rotterdam. Additionally, among the listed cargo items were several that were apparently uneconomical for long-distance truck transport.[42]

The truckers' mission apparently involved the systematic reconnaissance of roads and observations in areas off limits to military attachés—for example, Western strategic installations—as well as delivery of material and people to and from Soviet illegals. The truckers also engage in intelligence collection during NATO exercises and troop movements and the interception of official communications.[43]

Likewise, Soviet seamen are employed to collect intelligence concerning alterations in foreign port facilities, new cranes, unusual wharf activities, concentrations of warships, new high-tension lines, or radar screens near the harbor mouth. It is expected that, when feasible, reports will be accompanied by sketches and in some cases photographs.[44]

MATERIAL ACQUIRED

The two most significant questions concerning Soviet human intelligence operations are: What material is acquired by such operations and what is its value? It would be impossible to make a comprehensive assessment. However, it is possible to indicate some of the areas of success, the types of information acquired, and the value involved.

One area where both the KGB and GRU have successfully recruited agents is in the military officer corps of Allied and neutral European nations. Among those who have subsequently been detected was West German Rear Admiral Hermann Lüdke, who retired because of ill health in September 1968. Up until January of that year Lüdke had been the Soviet's senior agent within NATO, serving as the deputy chief of NATO's logistics division.[45] As such, Lüdke would have been able to provide the Soviet Union with information concerning weapons and equipment inventories, the location of such stocks in peacetime, and plans for disbursement in wartime.

In 1977 Brigadier General Jean-Louis Jeanmaire, the retired commander of the Swiss Air Protection Service, was convicted of spying for the Soviet Union.[46] Given his position, it is likely that Jeanmaire provided the Soviets with information on Swiss aircraft capabilities, air defense plans, and early warning systems. In Iran, Major General

Ahmad Moghrarrabi first passed information to Soviet intelligence in the early 1950s while a major. Subsequently, his future cooperation was ensured by showing him photographs of material he had previously turned over and telling him that if he refused to collaborate the evidence would be turned over to SAVAK, the Iranian secret police. Between 1967 and 1978 he thus served as a Soviet agent in the Iranian High Command, serving as deputy chief of Army planning during that period.[47]

One of the best-known Soviet recruitments of a military officer was that of Swedish Colonel Stig Wennerstrom, who was arrested in June 1963 after a fifteen-year career as a GRU agent. During those fifteen years he had served as an attaché at the Moscow embassy (1948–1952) and air attaché to the United States (1952–1957), in the Air Section of the Command Office of the Swedish Ministry of Defense (1957–1961), and as an adviser to the Swedish Foreign Office on disarmament problems (1961–1963).[48]

During his service Wennerstrom passed on information concerning U.S. military aviation; crisis planning regarding Berlin and Cuba; and information on the Bomarc, HM–55, Sidewinder (air-to-air), and Hawk (ground-to-air) missiles.[49] Wennerstrom also passed on information concerning the Swiss air defense system and was tasked to provide information concerning U.S.-NATO war planning against the Soviet Union, British air defenses, and Swedish-U.S. military contacts.[50]

The highest ranking U.S. military officer known to be compromised by the Soviets is Lt. Colonel William Whalen, whose last assignment had been with the Joint Chiefs of Staff (JCS).[51] More important than his rank was Whalen's assignment to the JCS, which is intimately involved in the development of nuclear weapons deployment plans and weapons systems development as well as developing contingency plans for both conventional and nuclear conflict.

Soviet intelligence has also had some success in the recuitment of NATO civilian officials. George Pacques, who served as deputy director of press and information services of NATO from 1962 to 1963, had been recruited by the KGB at the end of World War II.[52] In mid-1956 a Canadian economics professor, Hugh George Hambleton, joined NATO's Economic Directorate. In 1957 he began providing the KGB with NATO Secret and NATO Top Secret documents on nuclear strategy, the balance of military power, weapons systems, and information on political conflicts among NATO members.[53]

Some of the most damaging penetrations regarding the United States involved the recruitment of low-level military personnel. A sergeant at the Armed Forces Courier Center at Orly Airport, Paris was able to provide detailed planning documents concerning nuclear weapons employment policy in the event of a war in Europe. Included was the *Handbook of Nuclear Weapon Yield Requirements* as well as *USCINCEUR Operation Plan NR-100-6* of June 15, 1964.[54]

In addition to its penetration of the British intelligence and security services, Soviet intelligence, both directly and via East Bloc intelligence services, has penetrated British defense establishments via recruited British nationals and Soviet illegals. Thus, John Vassall, a British Moscow embassy employee beginning in 1954, was caught in a KGB homosexual honey trap and submitted to the resulting Soviet blackmail. In 1956 he returned to London and began abstracting secret documents, handing some over to his KGB controllers and photographing others. It was not until 1961 that his activities were discovered.[55] During the same period, the British Underwater Weapons Establishment at Portland, Dorset was penetrated by Harry Houghton, who reported to a Soviet illegal, Konon Molody, operating under the name of Gordon Lonsdale. Houghton passed on information concerning antisubmarine warfare and nuclear submarines.[56]

More recently, Soviet agents have been uncovered in Belgium, Norway, and South Africa. In May of 1984 two Soviets were arrested in Belgium while trying to obtain classified documents from NATO officials. In addition to information on NATO civilian and military headquarters activities, Soviet intelligence in Belgium also has as its targets the European Economic Community (EEC) and Belgian military facilities and industry.[57]

Earlier in 1984 the head of the foreign press section of the Norwegian Foreign Ministry, Arne Treholt, was arrested at Oslo Airport on his way to Vienna, where he was allegedly going to turn over classified documents.[58] Treholt had held a number of important posts in the Norwegian Foreign Ministry since 1973 and had been at the United Nations between early 1979 and late 1982, during which time he "had conspiratorial meetings with a Soviet diplomat at the United Nations headquarters and in small N.Y. restaurants."[59] Before being assigned to the press job in the Foreign Ministry, he was allowed to go through a one-year course at the Norwegian defense college that included access to classified military information and tours of a top secret NATO command post deep inside a mountain outside Oslo.[60] According to Norwegian prosecutors, Treholt, who had apparently been blackmailed into serving as a Soviet agent, provided the Soviets with information about NATO nuclear weapons and their possible use in wartime and military arrangements in NATO's northern frontier with the Soviet Union and provided confidential accounts of meetings between Norwegian officials and Secretary of State Henry Kissinger, Chancellor Helmut Schmidt of West Germany, and the British Foreign Secretary, Lord Carrington.[61]

In 1983 the commandant of the Simonstown Naval Station in South Africa, Commodore Dieter Felix Gerhardt, was arrested and charged with working for the KGB since 1965. According to various accounts, he passed on information about Western naval weapons systems (the French Exocet air-to-surface missile, the British Seacat missile, and the Tigerfish and Stingray torpedoes), British naval movements during the 1982 Falklands crisis, and possibly, Western plans to use Simonstown in the event of a war with the Soviet Union.[62]

NOTES TO CHAPTER 4

1. John Barron, *KGB: The Secret Work of Soviet Secret Agents* (New York: Reader's Digest Press, 1974), p. 348.

2. Carlyle Murphy and Alison Muscatine, "Polite War: Soviet Spies in Our Midst," *Washington Post*, n.d.

3. John Vinocur, "The KGB Goes on the Offensive and the West Begins Striking Back," *New York Times*, July 24, 1983, pp. 1ff.

4. John Barron, *KGB Today: The Hidden Hand* (New York: Reader's Digest Press, 1983), pp. 438–42.

5. Dana Priest, "Number of Soviets Expelled Doubled in 1983," *Washington Post*, July 23, 1984, p. A18.

6. Charles Babcock, "Soviet General Caught in Trap Laid by the FBI," *Washington Post*, February 6, 1982, p. A14.

7. Priest, "Number of Soviets Expelled Doubled in 1983."

8. Ibid.

9. Harry Rositzke, *The KGB: The Eyes of Russia* (New York: Doubleday, 1981), p. 52.

10. Ibid.

11. Brian Freemantle, *KGB: Inside the World's Largest Intelligence Network* (New York: Holt, Reinhart & Winston, 1983), p. 76.

12. Louise Berkinow, *Abel* (New York: Ballantine, 1981); Rostzke, pp. 57–59.
13. Rositzke, *The KGB*, pp. 47–48.
14. Ibid., pp. 91–93; John Sawatsky, *For Services Rendered: Leslie James Bennett and the RCMP Security Service* (New York: Doubleday, 1982), pp. 254–56.
15. "KGB in Asia," *Far East Economic Review*, January 3, 1975, pp. 20–29.
16. "FBI Charges 'Stealth' Theft By Engineer," *Washington Post*, December 19, 1984, p. A18; Judith Commings, "Suspect Held in Scheme to Sell Secrets to Russians," *New York Times*, December 19, 1984, p. A17.
17. Cord Meyer, *Facing Reality: World Federalism to the CIA* (New York: Simon & Schuster, 1980), p. 317.
18. Ibid.
19. Ibid.
20. Testimony of John Stein, CIA Deputy Director for Operations, in U.S. Congress, House Permanent Select Committee on Intelligence, *Soviet Active Measures* (Washington, D.C.: U.S. Government Printing Office, 1982), p. 23.
21. Meyer, *Facing Reality*, p. 319.
22. Ibid.
23. Ibid.
24. Testimony of John Stein, p. 23.
25. Meyer, *Facing Reality*, p. 330.
26. Ibid., p. 327.
27. Ibid.
28. Barron, *KGB Today*, p. 81; "KGB in Asia."
29. Rositzke, *The KGB*, pp. 180–81; Joe Trento and Dave Roman, "KGB in New York: The United Nations Soviet Spy Base," *Penthouse*, n.d.
30. "Crop of Soviet Agents Rounded Up in Europe," *Toronto Globe & Mail*, March 7, 1983, pp. 1, 2.
31. Testimony of Stanislav Levchenko, in U.S. Congress, House Permanent Select Committee on Intelligence, *Soviet Active Measures*, p. 147.
32. Ibid.
33. "Throwing Out Moscow's Spies," *Newsweek*, April 18, 1983, pp. 36–39.
34. Barron, *KGB Today*, p. 81.
35. John K. Cooley, "How U.S., Soviets Compete in Electronic Espionage," *Christian Science Monitor*, December 8, 1978, p. 4.
36. Meyer, *Facing Reality*, p. 329.
37. Murphy and Muscatine, "Polite War."
38. "New York City: Hotbed of Spies," *U.S. News and World Report*, January 18, 1982, pp. 30–31.
39. Oleg Penkovskiy, *The Penkovskiy Papers* (Garden City, N.Y.: Doubleday, 1965).

40. U.S. Congress, Senate Committee on the Judiciary, *Communist Bloc Intelligence Gathering Activities on Capitol Hill* (Washington, D.C.: U.S. Government Printing Office, 1982), p. 9.

41. "Soviet Block Truckers Suspected of Spying," *Los Angeles Times*, January 1, 1983, p. 8.

42. Ibid.

43. Ibid.

44. Thomas Sharpe, "Morflot and the KGB," in National Strategy Information Center, *The Challenge of Soviet Shipping* (New York: NSIC, 1983).

45. Rositzke, *The KGB*, p. 49.

46. "Recent Espionage Trials Conducted," *Aviation Week and Space Technology*, November 27, 1978, p. 21.

47. Robert Moss, "The Campaign to Destabilize Iran," *Conflict Studies* 101 (1978): 1-17.

48. Thomas Whiteside, *An Agent in Place* (New York: Ballantine, 1966).

49. Ibid., p. 72.

50. Ibid.

51. Barron, *KGB*, p. 189.

52. Rositzke, *The KGB*, p. 158.

53, Barron, *KGB Today*, pp. 182, 373-80.

54. Barron, *KGB*, p. 229.

55. Chapman Pincher, *Inside Story: A Documentary of the Pursuit of Power* (New York: Stein & Day, 1978), p. 65.

56. Chapman Pincher, *Their Trade Is Treachery* (London: Sidgwick & Jackson, 1981), pp. 56-57.

57. "2 Soviet Agents Held in Bid for NATO Files," *Toronto Globe & Mail*, May 22, 1984, p. 5.

58. Jon Nordheimer, "Portrait of Spy as a Golden Young Man," *New York Times*, January 29, 1984, p. 10.

59. "Norwegian Diplomat Jailed as Spy Was Trailed by FBI 3½ Years," *New York Times*, January 28, 1984, p. 4.

60. Nordheimer, "Portrait of Spy as a Golden Young Man."

61. "Soviets Blackmailed Diplomat for NATO Data, Norway Says," *Washington Times*, February 26, 1985, pp. 1A, 8A; Barnaby J. Feder, "Norwegian Diplomat Faces Trial Today in Spying Case," *New York Times*, February 25, 1985, p. A9; "Trial Starts for a Norwegian Diplomat Accused of Spying for Soviet," *New York Times*, February 26, 1985, p. A3.

62. Thomas O'Toole, "South Africa's Spying Seen as Painful Blow to West," *Washington Post*, June 11, 1984, p. A10; "South African Officer Guilty of Spying," *New York Times*, October 30, 1983, p. A3.

5 TECHNICAL COLLECTION

For both the United States and the Soviet Union, technical collection systems represent the most significant and valuable source of intelligence, particularly with respect to assessing weapons performance, developing a target base for war plans, and monitoring arms control agreements.

At the same time, there are substantial differences in the relative value and distribution of assets for such activity. The relative value to the Soviet Union of technical collection vis-á-vis human intelligence is less than for the United States—both because of inferior Soviet technology and superior access to information about U.S. military and political activities by other means. Thus, though the Soviet Union has trailed the United States in the development of reconnaissance technology, it has been able to partially compensate by tapping the immense source of freely available data in congressional hearings, trade publications, and newspapers as well as through its human clandestine collection programs.

The Soviet Union deploys the same types of assets as the United States—satellites, aircraft, ships, land-based intercept stations, and submarines—but distribution is sharply different. Although the United States effectively discontinued the use of surface ships for intelligence collection in the aftermath of the Pueblo and Liberty incidents and has only recently begun to use such vessels again, the

Soviet Union has continually maintained a large fleet of intelligence collection ships.

At the same time, the Soviet Union makes relatively little, albeit not negligible, use of ground sites in foreign countries—in stark contrast to the United States, with its worldwide network of tracking, signals intelligence, and seismic detection stations. The failure of the Soviet Union to emulate the United States in this regard can be explained by their differing geographic situations and Soviet uncertainty over the long-term relations with certain Third World countries.

As with the United States, the Soviet Union deploys its technical collection systems in an effort to obtain one of five different types of intelligence: imagery, signals intelligence, ocean surveillance, space surveillance, and nuclear detection.

IMAGERY

Soviet systems employed to obtain imagery include satellites and aircraft. Imagery includes pictures obtained by photography as well as picturelike representations using other sensors. Such representations can be obtained by infrared photography as well as by imaging radar.[1] It is not clear whether Soviet imaging satellites have any capability beyond that of conventional photography.

Soviet use of satellites for imaging began in April 1962 with the launch of *Cosmos 4.*[2] Since then the use of such satellites has grown markedly. Between 1962 and 1980, photographic reconnaissance satellites accounted for 82 percent of all satellite launches for intelligence and early warning purposes. Within the entire Soviet space program, it is the largest single element, representing 39 percent of all launches in 1980 and 38 percent in 1981.[3]

The product of these launches provides the Soviet Union with information concerning war targets, troop deployments, military exercises, and ongoing wars. Such satellites also allow Soviet monitoring of U.S. compliance with arms control agreements such as the ABM Treaty and SALT II.

At present the Soviet Union is operating five types of imaging spacecraft—three varieties of the third generation, one fourth generation and one fifth generation. The least used of the third generation, launched at the rate of about one per year, is a low-resolution film return craft. This spacecraft, of which *Cosmos 1309* of 1981 is an example, has a 82.3 degree inclination, is nonmaneuverable, and may have a global mapping mission. Launched from Plesetsk in northern Russia, it has a twenty-eight-day lifetime and operates with a perigee of approximately 130 miles and an apogee of 160 miles.[4]

The medium-resolution third generation craft is maneuvered within twenty-four hours after launch to an orbit of approximately 225 by 265 miles. These spacecraft have been launched at inclinations of 62.8 degrees, 72.9 degrees, and 82.3 degrees from Plesetsk and 70.4 degrees from Tyuratam.[5] Lifetime for the medium-resolution craft is about half that of the low-resolution craft—approximately fourteen days.[6]

The high-resolution third generation craft are launched from both Tyuratam (at inclinations of 65 and 70.4 degrees) and Plesetsk (at inclinations of 67.1, 72.9, and 82.3 degrees). As with the medium-resolution versions, they are maneuverable, although they have twenty-eight-day lifetimes and fly in no standard orbit.[7]

The third generation satellites consist of three modules. The instrument module carries the chemical batteries and propulsion system; the descent module is beehive shaped and carries the film canisters and other material back to Earth at the conclusion of the mission. The forward module carries the cameras (and other sensors) needed to collect the intelligence. The forward module and any small package attached to the exterior of the descent module are ejected before retrofire and allowed to decay naturally.[8]

The recovery procedure involves the detaching of the spherical payload from the service (instrument) module, followed by ballistic reentry with the transmitter in the service module continuing to transmit until the module is incinerated in the lower layers of the atmosphere. Within six or seven minutes, the recovery capsule is five to six miles above the surface of the earth. At this point a pressure-operated device deploys the parachute system and turns on a recovery beacon to assist ground crews in determining its location.[9]

There is only one variety of fourth generation craft, introduced in 1975. Unlike the third generation craft, it has four small film return capsules which can be ejected at various times during the spacecraft's forty-four-day lifetime.[10] A high-resolution, maneuverable craft, its elliptical orbit takes it as low as 97 miles above the earth as it passes between 35 and 55 degrees North latitude—a range that includes most of the United States and parts of Canada.[11] Its perigee lies in the 200- to 220-mile range, and its inclination has varied between 62.8 and 70.4 degrees.[12]

In 1984 the Soviets began to employ fifth generation photographic reconnaissance spacecraft. The most notable aspect of these spacecraft is their real-time capability; the picture obtained by the spacecraft's cameras is transmitted via digital electronic signals to a geosynchronous relay satellite and then retransmitted back to the Soviet Union. Such a capability will enhance Soviet crisis-monitoring capabilities. Along with the real-time capability comes a longer lifetime as the problem of film exhaustion for such craft is eliminated. Thus, one fifth generation craft operated for 173 days.[13]

The satellites repeat their ground tracks every eight days—allowing reexamination of particular areas—and can photograph 100-square-mile swaths. In contrast with U.S. Keyhole satellites, the Soviet satellites are not placed in sun synchronous orbits which allow viewing at the same sun angle every day. The increase in lifetime of the satellites—from eight days to fourteen, twenty-eight, or forty-four days—allowed ever greater coverage. Thus, from coverage for 40 percent of the year in the mid-1960s to coverage for 75 percent of the year in the early 1970s, the Soviet program now achieves continuous coverage.[14] Table 5-1 shows the evolution in days with some coverage from 1962 to 1983.

In 1983 there were thirty-seven launches which matched the record launch rate set in 1981 and produced 830 mission days. *Cosmos 1504*, launched in the fall, became the Soviet imaging satellite with the longest lifetime—53 days—a lifetime exceeded by the fifth generation satellites *Cosmos 1426* (67 days) and *Cosmos 1552* (173 days).[15]

Such lifetimes represent only a small fraction of the lifetime of U.S. satellites such as the KH–9 (over 200 days) and the KH–11 (about two years) and thus require a much higher launch rate. At the same time, it introduces a certain flexibility: Imaging satellites can be launched in response to a particular crisis, maneuvered without fear of drastically reducing lifetimes, and deorbited after short periods of time without putting a significant dent in Soviet satellite reconnaissance capabilities. Thus, the Soviet Union has made significant use of these satellites to cover particular crises and conflicts.

During the October 1962 Cuban missile crisis, Soviet photographic satellites probably monitored the southern United States to see if U.S. troops were massing for an invasion of Cuba.[16] In 1967 the

Table 5-1. Days with Some Soviet Photographic Reconnaissance Satellite Coverage.

Year	Days with Some Coverage
1962	22
1963	54
1964	77
1965	122
1966	160
1967	168
1968	198
1969	212
1970	249
1971	244
1972	255
1973	285
1974	258
1975	296
1976	306
1977	279
1978	302
1979	303
1980	344
1981	354
1982	341
1983	346

Source: SIPRI Yearbooks, various years.

Soviets monitored the Arab-Israeli war from space and in 1968-69 provided the first unambiguous demonstration of the ability to increase reconnaissance activities in response to specific crises: the invasion of Czechoslovakia and the border hostilities with China in 1969. The Soviets demonstrated a "surge capability to launch and retrieve an extra number of satellites in response to border clashes in March, June and August 1969." [17]

During the Indo-Pakistani war of 1971 the Soviet Union employed both *Cosmos 463* and *Cosmos 464*, third generation craft, to cover the conflict. Both were maneuvered to reduce the westward drift of their ground tracks and increase the number of passes made over the conflict zone. Additionally, they were both recovered before the end of their standard operational lifetime.[18] The NATO naval exercise of September 1972, nicknamed Strong Express, was covered in a similar fashion.[19]

The most extensive use of Soviet imaging satellites took place in October 1973, during the Middle East war. Seven Cosmos reconnaissance satellites were launched between October 3 and 27, for the specific purpose of photographing the hostilities. Some of the satellites were maneuvered to stabilize their ground tracks over the Sinai and Golan Heights at critical moments during the war.[20] On October 9 a Cosmos satellite was returned to earth six to eight days ahead of schedule, possibly indicating the extent of Israeli activities on the Golan Heights.[21] According to Anwar el-Sadat, however, none of the photography was made available to Egypt.[22]

In 1977 Soviet reconnaissance satellites apparently spotted South African preparations for a nuclear test in the summer of that year. The United States and other nations, once informed, protested to South Africa, resulting in that test's cancellation.[23] From November 12, 1980 to November 28, 1980 the newly organized U.S. Rapid Deployment Force (RDF) conducted a joint exercise with the Egyptian armed forces. On November 12 the Soviet Union launched two satellites within twenty-four hours, the latter passing twenty-five miles east of Cairo.[24]

Events in 1982 that were targets of Soviet photographic reconnaissance satellites included flights of the Space Transportation System, further RDF exercises, and renewed fighting between Iran and Iraq. In late March, *Cosmos 1343*, a third generation high-resolution satellite, was in a position to survey two important areas in the western United States. *Cosmos 1343* passed over White Sands, New Mexico fifteen minutes before the expected touchdown of the space shuttle *Columbia* on March 29 just as *Cosmos 1262* had passed over the landing site for *STS-1* just before touchdown. However, Mission 3 was warned off due to high winds and the landing rescheduled for the next day. Subsequently, *Cosmos 1343* lowered its orbit so as to allow it to close in on the landing site about forty minutes before *STS-3* finally touched down. The maneuver also allowed the satellite to pass near the RDF Gallant Eagle war game in California just twelve hours after a massive drop of men and material from around the country. *Cosmos 1343* was recovered in the Soviet Union three hours later.[25]

On November 1, 1982 Iran launched a new offensive against Iraqi territory along a fifty-mile front from Basra to Mandali. On November 2 *Cosmos 1419* was launched and eighteen hours later maneuvered to a 145-by-175-mile orbit with a 70.3 degree inclination. The spacecraft passed to the east of Basra on November 5 and continued up through western Iran. Several hours later the spacecraft lowered its apogee to retard the shift of its ground track over the Iranian-Iraqi battlefield. On the eighteenth *Cosmos 1421* was launched from Tyuratam on a global surveillance mission. On the twenty-second it departed from its normal operations and was maneuvered into a lower orbit, permitting improved coverage between Basra and Baghdad for the succeeding two days.[26]

In 1983 Soviet satellites devoted special attention to events in the Caribbean and Central America. Thus, for the first few days of its lifetime, *Cosmos 1471*, launched from Plesetsk on June 28, appeared to be on a normal worldwide reconnaissance mission. However, early on July 3 it lowered its orbit and retarded the shift of its ground track. As a result, it passed over El Salvador for four successive days.[27]

On October 25, when U.S. forces invaded Grenada, the Soviet Union had only two orbiting imaging spacecraft. One, *Cosmos 1504*, was capable of high-resolution photography; the other, *Cosmos 1505*, was a medium-resolution satellite on a global mission. *Cosmos 1505* would naturally pass near Grenada on October 27, 29, and 31; the ground track of the high-resolution satellite was approximately 100 miles to the east of Grenada on October 25. On October 26 the orbit of *Cosmos 1504* was raised, accelerating the westward movement of its ground tracks. On the twenty-eighth it was maneuvered into a lower orbit, resulting in passes near Grenada at an altitude of 125 miles for the following five days. Subsequently, on November 1, it was boosted to a higher orbit and resumed its normal mission.[28]

A variety of aircraft are employed by the Soviet Union for intelligence collection purposes, including the collection of imagery concerning land-based targets. The most prominent of these aircraft is the TU-95D Bear, one of several variants of the TU-95.

The TU-95D is used for both land and ocean reconnaissance. It has a 147-foot length and a wingspan of 165 feet. It weighs 356,000 pounds and is driven by four turboprop engines. Its unrefueled range is approximately 8,000 nautical miles, and its maximum speed is approximately 500 knots.[29] The Bear E variant is flown by Soviet Long Range Aviation and has six camera windows in the bomber bays in pairs in line with the wing flaps, sometimes with a seventh window to the rear on the starboard side.[30] TU-95 land reconnaissance operations are conducted from a variety of locations including Danang and Tan Son Nhut, from where they overfly Asia on constant reconnaissance missions.[31] In 1968 TU-95Ds overflew Iran, Afghanistan, and India from bases in the Soviet Union at the time of *Luna* spacecraft recovery operations in the Indian Ocean.[32]

According to a 1982 report, the Soviet Union is also developing and testing a high-altitude reconnaissance aircraft which has been assigned the NATO codename Ram-M. The plane is believed to be similar to the Lockheed U-2.[33]

In addition to military aircraft, Soviet intelligence also employs Aeroflot, the civilian national airline, in an intelligence collection role, particularly in the United States and Western Europe. This use has involved missions inadvertently permitted by aviation authorities as well as planes that have gotten "lost" over sensitive locations. Probably both photographic and signals intelligence collection is involved.

In the United States from 1981 through 1982 Aeroflot's once-a-week flights went off course sixteen times. In one case, it filed flight plans, mistakenly approved, that took it over the Air Force base near Plattsburgh, N.Y.; a FB-111 base in New Hampshire; Otis Air Force Base in Massachusetts, where a Pave Paws SLBM (Submarine Launched Ballistic Missile) warning radar is located; and the Groton, Connecticut shipyard, where Trident submarines are constructed.[34] Aeroflot has also attempted to obtain transcontinental flights that would have coincided with missile firings, troop maneuvers, and Strategic Air Command (SAC) practice alerts.[35]

In Western Europe, Aeroflot flights have "accidentally" veered off course to monitor troop movements and maneuvers as well as NATO naval exercises.[36] In April of 1984 an Aeroflot TU-134 strayed into prohibited airspace over the French naval base at Toulon, where France's first nuclear attack submarine, Rubis, and the aircraft carrier Foch were docked. On the flight from Moscow to Marseilles via Budapest, the pilot ignored several warnings from civilian air traffic controllers that it had departed from its approved flight path and entered a restricted area.[37] The French prime minister shortly afterward stated, "investigations have led us to conclude that this infraction did not correspond to a deliberate objective."[38] However, according to a French television report, the aircraft strayed thirty miles off course and a senior air traffic controller stated that in view of ground radio navigation in the area and the equipment on board modern commercial planes, it was unlikely to have been an error.[39]

SIGNALS INTELLIGENCE

Both Soviet intelligence organizations—the KGB and GRU—devote a significant amount of effort to signals intelligence collection. This effort involves the interception of U.S., European, and Third World communications concerning diplomatic, military, economic, and scientific matters as well as the interceptions of the signals or electronic emanations of missiles undergoing flight tests, radars, aircraft, and computers.

The Soviet Union is believed to have had since 1970 a constellation of heavy electronic intelligence (ELINT) satellites the purpose of which is to detect and monitor the emissions of foreign (principally U.S.) radars, such as the Pave Paws SLBM warning radars and the Cobra Dane spacetracking and intelligence radar.[40] Analysis of the intercepted signals provides information concerning radar characteristics, including limitations and potential countermeasure options. Additionally, detection of mobile radars by the ELINT satellites can also provide a modest electronic order of battle (EOB).[41] They also have been able to monitor SAC and NATO exercises during their normal operations.[42]

Until about 1980 the Soviets maintained a constellation of six ELINT satellites at any time. The satellites, with 600-day lifetimes, orbited in six orbital planes spaced 60 degrees apart and inclined 81.2 degrees to the equator.[43] Subsequently, this pattern began to deteriorate, so that by the beginning of 1983 only two were in orbit— Cosmos 1345 of March 31, 1982 and Cosmos 1356 of May 5, 1982 with inclinations of 74 and 81 degrees respectively and orbits of 310 by 335 and 395 by 410 miles respectively.[44]

In 1978 a new type of ELINT satellite apparently emerged in similar orbits to the heavy ELINT satellites, although with a different inclination (82.5 degrees) and launched by a new booster. Three of these satellites—Cosmos 1455, 1470, and 1515—were launched in 1983 and four in 1984. In September 1984 the Soviet Union launched *Cosmos 1603*, the first of a new generation of electronic intelligence satellites. The satellite, launched on September 28, constituted the largest single military satellite in the history of the Soviet space program. It operates in a 530-mile circular orbit with a 71 degree inclination, the latter ensuring that the satellite passes frequently over the United States. Its orbit guarantees that its ground track repeats every twenty-four hours—hence it covers every target in its path once a day—and is also, on every pass, within monitoring range of some of the territory covered on the previous pass.[45]

SIGINT (signals intelligence) collection against land-based targets is also conducted by aircraft, possibly including TU–95Ds that also perform photographic missions. One aircraft with a primary ELINT mission is the II–18 Coot A, an Electronic Countermeasure/ELINT plane. Under its fuselage it carries a container about 33 feet 7.5 inches long and 3 feet 9 inches deep which is believed to house a side-looking radar. A second container apparently holds a camera or other sensor. Additionally, there are several other antennae under the surface of the center and rear fuselage.[46]

In addition to photographic missions, Aeroflot collection activities may also involve the monitoring of VHF and UHF bands at certain points along their European flight paths.[47]

One major difference between U.S. and Soviet technical intelligence collection activities is, as noted earlier, the reliance of the latter on surface ships. According to Department of Defense estimates, the Soviet Union maintains sixty-one intelligence collection ships—known as AGIs (Auxilliary-Intelligence Gathering). Included in the sixty-one are two *Balzam* class, six *Primorye* class, three *Nikolai Zubov* class, two Modified *Pamir* class, nine *Moma* class, fifteen *Okean* class, two *Dnepr* class, four *Mirny* class, eight *Mayak*, three *Alpinist*, and seven *Lentra*.[48] In addition to the AGIs proper, other Soviet vessels have signals intelligence capabilities, including naval survey, naval research, and depot ships.[49]

The two *Balzam*-class ships are the first of a class completed in 1980. In addition to the twin radomes, each ship is armed with a 30 mm Gatling gun and two SA-N-5 Grail missiles, making them the first armed AGIs. The *Primorye*-class ships may possess a built-in processing and analysis capability. Many of the other AGIs have been in service for twenty years or more. Thus, the modified *Pamir* ships were built in Sweden in 1959–60, and the fifteen *Okean*-class ships were built in East Germany from 1959 to the mid-1960s.[50]

AGIs perform both SIGINT and ocean surveillance functions— functions that at times overlap since they monitor naval activities around particular bases as well as the communications going to and from many naval bases. Such activities will be considered in the next section.

The pure signals intelligence activities of the AGIs include telemetry interception as well as ELINT and COMINT collection against a variety of land targets. Thus, on January 17, 1982 a Soviet AGI of the *Moma* class closely monitored the successful launch of a Trident missile from the first operational Trident missile submarine. The Soviet ship initially refused to move away from the launch area and at one point came within 1,500 feet of the telemetry mast of the submerged U.S. submarine. It eventually moved to a distance of 6,000 feet and the launch was conducted forty-one minutes late. Likewise, on December 4, 1984 an AGI monitored a Trident I missile launch from the U.S.S. *Henry M. Jackson* off Cape Canaveral.[51] When the United States conducted an antiballistic missile test in June 1984 the radioed flight data from the experiment were enciphered so that the Soviet AGI loitering in the Pacific would pick up unintelligible signals.[52]

When the H.M.S. *Revenge*, a British Polaris submarine, launched two test missiles off Cape Canaveral on June 9, 1983 it was shadowed by the AGI *Kavkaz*. Until requested to move away by a U.S. instrumentation ship, the *Kavkaz* came to within 1,700 yards.[53] While the *Kavkaz* was monitoring the British missile test, the AGI *Kilden*—a 1,700-ton *Moma*-class ship—was stationed off Lebanon and Israel. The *Kilden*'s electronic eavesdropping equipment was tuned to Israeli radio frequencies along the coastal highway toward the Lebanese frontier, the main Israeli supply route to Beirut.[54]

Previously, Soviet AGIs have monitored or attempted to monitor land and naval communications in Athens (November 1975), Madrid (June 1976), Ottawa (February 1976), and London (1976). Thus, the Soviet AGI *Elva*, disguised as a tramp steamer (but with elaborate antennae) slipped into Piraeus, where she could monitor communications in the Athens area. Likewise, AGIs monitored radio frequencies on both Canadian coasts in February 1976.[55]

As has been evidenced by recent events, the Soviet Union, as does the United States, assigns a significant intelligence collection responsibility to its submarines. Thus, the Swedish Submarine Defence Commission (SDC) noted that it "is virtually a truism to observe that alien submarines violating Swedish territory are motivated in part by military intelligence-gathering."[56]

In 1981 such a submarine ran aground in Swedish waters. In October 1982 there appeared to be the use of an unmanned reconnaissance submarine to collect intelligence near a top secret Swedish naval base on Musko Island.[57] The Swedish SDC concluded that six Soviet subs had been in the Stockholm Archipelago—three submarines and three midget submarines. The midget submarines were about fifty feet long with two- to five-man crews and capable of remaining submerged for long periods. Both were described as having a "bottom crawling capacity of a hitherto unknown character"—with one having tanklike treads while the other scoured out a channel as it moved.[58]

Submarines can be employed for telemetry collection, ocean floor mapping, monitoring of port and base areas, tapping into lines, and emplacement of sensing and directional equipment. Thus, part of the Soviet submarine operations in Swedish waters may be SIGINT related and other parts may be concerned with preparations for sabotage in the event of war or ocean surveillance.

As noted earlier, unlike the United States, the Soviet Union places less reliance on land-based strategic technical collection activities outside the Soviet Union, particularly outside Soviet embassies and missions. The Soviet Union does, however, maintain some such facilities, including those at Lourdes, Cuba; Cam Ranh Bay, Vietnam; Ethiopia (2); Yemen; Syria; and Afghanistan (4). In addition, it is highly likely that the Soviets operate ground stations in Libya and Iraq.[59]

The Soviet communications intelligence facility at Lourdes is the largest such non-American installation in the Western Hemisphere. The facility is run and operated by about 2,000 Soviet personnel and, in addition to the Soviet headquarters, consists of an antenna field; satellite receiver; and about fifty buildings that contain the monitoring, processing, and analysis equipment. The facility targets the eastern United States and intercepts civilian and military U.S. communications, including transatlantic telephone calls as well as communications to and from Cape Canaveral, especially as they relate to shuttle and military space missions. Additionally, it is said to target signals transmitted by U.S. B-52 bombers during practice flights from Florida to Louisiana and Virginia, signals transmitted by Army units on maneuvers at Fort Benning, Georgia, and radio traffic to and from Atlantic Fleet Headquarters in Norfolk, Virginia. The Lourdes facility, along with a similar facility in the Soviet Union, gives complete coverage of the global beams of all U.S. geosynchronous communications satellites.[60]

The Soviet Union has also set up a major station at Cam Ranh Bay, apparently with both land-based and ocean electronic intelligence functions. The station gives the Soviet Union a long-range intercept capability. Additionally, there are two high-frequency/direction-finding sites that provide a capability to gain locational data on U.S. and allied naval units operating in the vicinity.[61] According to an Australian journalist, the Cam Ranh Bay facility

> rivals the Russian electronic eavesdropping installation in Cuba, long considered the largest and most important of its kind operated overseas by Moscow.... In the same way that Russia's Cuban facility tunes into military frequencies throughout the North American continent on a 24-hour basis, the new equipment set up in Cam Ranh Bay will soon be closely monitoring U.S. bases in the Philippines—less than 1,600 km away across the South China Sea—and all U.S. associated naval and air traffic.... A key target will also be military monitoring of southern China, especially in the Hainan Island area.[62]

The four sites in Afghanistan include one just north of Kabul, another about five hundred miles from Kabul and near the Chinese border, and sites in the northwest and southwest corners of the country.[63] The site 500 miles from Kabul is used to intercept Chinese and Pakistani military communications and radar signals. The station in southwest Afghanistan is reported to be targeted on Iran and the Persian Gulf.[64]

In the Soviet Union itself there are hundreds of SIGINT sites, a very large number of which are on the border and coastal areas and probably have a tactical mission. A major complex has been established near the Mongolian border at Chita, the headquarters of the Transbaykal Military District as well as a theater headquarters for the control of the Soviet Pacific Fleet and the Far East and Transbaykal Military Districts. The reported target of this facility is Northeast Asia communications traffic.[65]

Within the United States the GRU conducts signals intelligence collection operations from a number of legal Soviet residencies, employing antennae on top of the Soviet mission to the United Nations; the Soviet embassy; the Soviet consulate in San Francisco; and Soviet residential complexes on Chesapeake Bay and in Riverdale, N.Y. and Glen Cove, Long Island. Each installation's antennae intercept and record, on a daily basis, hundreds of thousands of telephone conversations that are transmitted by microwave. Particular telephone exchanges can be monitored, such as the CIA's 351 exchange or exchanges in the Silicon Valley.[66]

In the Washington area there is one giant (18 by 15 foot) high-frequency antenna atop the old Soviet embassy on 16th Street pointed toward the Pentagon and State Department. Another antenna is focused on a CIA communications facility in Virginia. Additional antennae are capable of monitoring telephone conversations, police and FBI transmissions, and government limousine communications. Likewise, a Soviet residential complex on Chesapeake Bay is close to a major microwave relay site, a large military communications facility in Annapolis, and the National Security Agency's (NSA's) Kent Island research facility.[67] To protect against Soviet interception of electronic emanations from NSA headquarters, the agency is seeking funds for construction of an "electronic envelope" around its headquarters.[68]

A new Soviet embassy is being constructed on top of a hill, called Mt. Alto, 350 feet above sea level which has a commanding view of the entire Washington area and thus is a perfect location for a SIGINT complex. According to intelligence officials, exotic antennae and dish-shaped receivers will be located in the buildings that will make up the ten-acre estate. Some of the equipment may already be in operation.[69]

Interception activity in the Washington area is not directed exclusively at military and foreign policy institutions. Also of great value may be the intercepts of conversations passing through the phone lines of the Departments of Commerce, Agriculture, and Treasury. In the early 1970s the Soviets monitored all telephone calls to the Department of Agriculture so as to be as well informed as possible about the state of the U.S. grain market. They used this information to negotiate a grain deal in 1974 that is referred to by U.S. farmers as the "great grain robbery."[70]

In the New York area the Soviet residential complex in Riverdale contains numerous antennae on its roof. Its location on one of the highest points in the metropolitan area permits interception of calls throughout the northeast corridor.[71] According to a defector from the Soviet U.N. mission, Arkady Shevchenko, all the top floors of the Soviet residence at Glen Cove, Long Island are full of sophisticated equipment to collect communications intelligence. Managed by fifteen to seventeen technicians, the equipment can intercept calls from New Jersey, New York, Connecticut, Long Island, and possibly Massachusetts. This would include communications involving military bases (Griffiss AFB), defense contractors (Grumann, General Dynamics), and naval yards (Groton).[72]

The intercept post in San Francisco is apparently located in the Soviet consulate at 2790 Green Street, located on a steep hill. On December 25, 1982 the consulate received a new addition: a ten-foot-square gray plywood shack on the roof, the type of structure often used to conceal dishlike microwave antennae. The antennae could be used to pick up the conversations of computer firms in the Silicon Valley (to the south) or the Navy installations in San Francisco Bay, to the north and east.[73]

Such activities are, of course, not restricted to the United States. The Soviet embassy in Kensington Palace Gardens is used to intercept microwave-transmitted telephone calls routed through London's Post Office Tower, three miles to the east. Likewise, a listening post exists on the eleventh floor of the Soviet embassy in Tokyo. According to a defector, the post intercepted communications from U.S. satellites and military installations as well as intercepting phone conversations transmitted via microwave. Similarly, the Soviets maintain monitoring facilities in Australia, Canada, and a variety of other countries both for monitoring the activities of the counterintelligence services and collecting a variety of communications intelligence.[74]

OCEAN SURVEILLANCE

Soviet Fleet Cosmic Intelligence operates two types of ocean surveillance/reconnaissance satellites: EORSATs and RORSATs. Soviet Elint Ocean Reconnaissance Satellites (EORSATs) first appeared at the end of 1974, with the primary purpose of monitoring the U.S. fleet. EORSATs are passive collection systems that intercept the signals emitted by ships and locate the ships by interferometry. The satellites are equipped with microthrusters to overcome drag and perform numerous small maneuvers to maintain their 93.3-minute period in circular orbit at 65-degree inclinations. Generally, EORSATs are operated in pairs with carefully chosen ground tracks lying precisely midway between those of their partners.[75]

Radar Ocean Reconnaissance Satellites (RORSATs) are launched from Tyuratam by a variant of the SS–9 ICBM. These Cosmos satellites have a 65-degree inclination and a period of 89.6 minutes.[76] The satellites are equipped with side-looking radar and provide microwave imagery similar to black and white photography, even in the presence of cloud cover.[77]

These satellites have also operated in pairs since 1974—for example, *Cosmos 651* and *Cosmos 654* launched in 1974 and *Cosmos 723* and *724* launched in 1975. They perform their ocean surveillance mission while in orbits with respective perigees and apogees of 155 and 162 miles, almost a quarter of those of U.S. ocean surveillance satellites.[78] After operating for several weeks, the RORSATs are maneuvered into their parking orbits of 545 by 580 miles. The higher orbit is intended to allow the satellite to remain aloft until after the half-life of the 100 pounds of enriched uranium that fuels the RORSAT's nuclear reactor has passed.[79] When RORSATs *Cosmos 954* (in 1978) and *Cosmos 1402* (in 1982) failed to attain and hold this orbit, their premature reentry created fear of nuclear contamination.[80] Fortunately, *Cosmos 954* fell in a sparsely populated area of northern Canada about 200 miles east of Yellowknife on January 24, 1978, and *Cosmos 1402* made an ocean landing.[81]

Both EORSATs and RORSATs provide detection and tracking data in real time to Soviet surface vessels and submarines equipped with antiship weapons as well as to ground control stations. According to a General Accounting Office report, Soviet RORSATs can probably, in good weather, detect destroyer-size ships. In rough seas, the report states, the satellites can detect aircraft-carrier-size ships or smaller ships that are close together. EORSATs are thought to be capable of locating, with two-kilometer accuracy, naval vessels in open and coastal waters. It could also be employed to detect airborne warning and control systems, radar sites, and operating airfields. It has also been reported that RORSATs can provide the same information to Backfire bombers.[82] They have been employed to watch U.S. fleet maneuvers, the Australian Kangaroo naval exercises, and British ships headed toward the Falklands.

EORSATs and RORSATs can work in a complementary fashion. The EORSAT can be employed to establish the presence of a vessel and its signal pattern and the RORSAT can then be used to determine the specifics.

The Soviet Union employs ocean surveillance satellites in crisis situations much as it does imaging satellites. Thus, in addition to the two ocean reconnaissance satellites launched on March 31 (*Cosmos 1345*, a RORSAT, and *Cosmos 1346*, a EORSAT), two days prior to the Argentine seizure of the islands, *Cosmos 1347*, a RORSAT, was launched April 21. Presumably, its mission was the radar imaging of the British fleet moving through the South Atlantic.[83] Likewise, the launch of *Cosmos 1507*, an EORSAT, four days after the Grenada invasion may have been linked both to U.S. naval activity in the Caribbean and the Iranian threat to close the Strait of Hormuz if Iraq employed Super-Etendard planes against Iran. The latter, along with events in Lebanon, led to a buildup of U.S. naval forces in the Persian Gulf.[84]

It is the Soviet RORSATs that have been cited as a primary justification for the U.S. Anti-Satellite program, as the RORSATs can provide information to Soviet naval forces that can be applied directly against U.S. naval forces. Thus, according to the Department of the Air Force:

> The Soviets' Radar Ocean Reconnaissance Satellite (RORSAT) ... would pose a problem to the Navy in time of conflict. ... Therefore, the Navy fully supports the acquisition of an ASAT system as a hedge against RORSAT. ... Without an ASAT capability, a Fleet Commander would lose some flexibility and option for defense against the Soviet long-range cruise missile threat.[85]

Until 1984 both RORSATs and EORSATs were used sparingly. After 1981 and 1982, when six and seven ORSATs were flown, only two were orbited in 1983—both EORSATs.[86] It is highly likely that the use of RORSATs were temporarily suspended given the failures of *Cosmos 1402* and *Cosmos 954*. In 1984 a total of four ocean surveillance satellites were orbited—two EORSATs and two RORSATs. By the end of 1984 one RORSAT and two EORSATs were still in orbit. However, an early 1985 EORSAT launch failed to place the spacecraft in its proper orbit, and the spacecraft reentered the atmosphere the next day, breaking up over Romania.[87]

Soviet reconnaissance aircraft appear to have their greatest role as ocean surveillance aircraft. Assignment of TU-95Ds to the Soviet Navy in 1965 marked the first time the Navy had a specialized long-range reconnaissance aircraft. Prior to that time, maritime reconnaissance was conducted by the Soviet Air Force's Long Range Aviation, which in 1962 conducted the first reconnaissance of a U.S. aircraft carrier transiting the Atlantic.[88]

In April 1970 the Soviets began deployment of TU-95D (Bear D) aircraft for short periods to Cuba. From Cuban airfields they were employed in reconnaissance missions over the northeastern and central Atlantic. Reconnaissance of the southern Atlantic became possible in 1973, when similar deployments to Guinea began. October 1976 saw the deployment of one TU-95D to Somalia; by February of 1977 there was one TU-95D deployed at Luanda, Angola. Bear Ds have also flown from Vietnam on ocean surveillance missions.[89]

The TU-95D has flown from bases in the Murmansk area around the North Cape, down the Norwegian sea, and across the Atlantic Ocean, finally landing in either Cuba or Guinea.[90] In January 1982, two TU-95Ds from Cuba penetrated into the U.S. air defense zone, which extends out 200 miles from the U.S. coast, and closely inspected a new aircraft carrier undergoing sea trials 42 miles off the Virginia coast.[91] In 1981 the Soviets began using Cuba's San Antonio de los Banos military airfield as a permanent facility for TU-95Ds, and, since early 1983, for TU-142 Bear Fs.[92] The Bear Fs, which are antisubmarine warfare (ASW) aircraft, track U.S. submarines. Under Project Bear Trap, specially equipped U.S. P-3C aircraft monitor the Bear Fs electronic emissions, allowing U.S. analysts to assess Bear F performance by using the known locations of U.S. submarines.[93]

Also employed in an ocean surveillance role are the twin-engine TU-22 Blinder C and TU-16 Badger. The TU-122 is 133 feet in length, with an 80-foot wingspan, and is capable of a maximum speed of 1,000 knots.[94] The TU-16 is 125 feet in length, with a wingspan of 110 feet. The twin turbojet plane is capable of a maximum speed of 540 knots. Approximately seventy TU-16s are employed in reconnaissance and electronic warfare roles.[95]

As noted earlier, Soviet AGIs perform both ocean surveillance and signals intelligence roles. Within the ocean surveillance category, Soviet AGI activity is directed at (1) surveillance of U.S. nuclear submarine bases and other major naval facilities, (2) gatekeeping at entrances into critical seas or other maritime "choke points," and (3) combatant surveillance of Western operations occurring within the Soviet maritime defense perimeter.[96]

Since the first deployment of Polaris submarines in the early 1960s, AGIs have conducted surveillance in the immediate vicinity or within easy reach of the bases. AGI surveillance off the East Coast bases began in 1961; surveillance off the West Coast began in 1963. Similar patrols were established off the Polaris bases at Rota, Spain and Apra Harbor, Guam in 1964, and 1965 saw the beginning of similar surveillance of the Holy Loch, Scotland base. The Guam, Rota, and Holy Loch patrol stations are manned continuously due to their proximity to likely SSBN patrol areas, whereas the U.S. East Coast AGI has supplementary responsibilities.[97] The AGI patrols monitor arrivals and departures, permitting the GRU to make estimates of deployment rates and sea time. In addition, by monitoring communications within and to and from the bases, additional intelligence on deployment schedules and readiness can be acquired.[98]

Major naval stations from New England to Puerto Rico also come under AGI surveillance. An annual AGI cruise to the West Coast involves surveillance duties off Alaska, California, and Hawaii.[99] In the Indian Ocean area AGI activity has been taking place regularly since 1975. A particular target is the U.S. Naval Facility at Diego Garcia which is subject to surveillance by AGIs entering the Indian Ocean. In the early 1970s one AGI continuously monitored U.S. aircraft operations in the Gulf of Tonkin; another monitored U.S. carriers moving in and out of Athens.[100]

AGIs also monitor the passage of Western shipping into enclosed seas adjacent to or in the near vicinity of the Soviet Union. Such ships are maintained on station in the Straits of Gibraltar and near Sicily and Tsushima almost constantly. Others are stationed at the Skaw and in the La Perouse and Tsugaru Straits during the spring, summer, and early fall. These stations are manned intermittently or when situations warrant—such as during exercises or periods of heightened international tension.[101]

AGI activities also include the trailing or shadowing of Western forces. The extent of surveillance is a function of the capabilities of the target forces, their proximity to the Soviet Union, and the international atmosphere. Carrier strike groups within 1,500 nautical miles of the Soviet Union are trailed continuously—from the British Islands northward, east of Sicily in the Mediterranean, and in the northeast quadrant of the Indian Ocean.[102]

The ocean surveillance role of the Soviet facility at Cam Rahn Bay has already been noted. It can be assumed that the Lourdes, Cuba facility also has an ocean surveillance role along with the Yemen facility.

SPACE SURVEILLANCE

Just as space surveillance has been an increasingly important aspect of U.S. intelligence activities given increased Soviet dependence on space for military missions, so has it for the Soviet Union. Given U.S. dependence on satellites for photographic reconnaissance, navigation, early warning, communications, and so on as well as introduction of the space shuttle and testing of an ASAT system monitoring of U.S. space activities is of major importance to Soviet intelligence.[103] Further, U.S. efforts to develop a space-based defensive system will focus even greater Soviet attention on space. In surveying Soviet space surveillance capabilities it is harder than for the United States to distinguish military from "civilian" assets and further to distinguish between military assets for support of Soviet space activities and those directed at acquiring information about U.S. space activities.

Soviet space surveillance assets include ground stations (both foreign and domestic), radars, and specially equipped surface ships and other sensors. Thus, there is a network of at least twelve sites within the Soviet Union equipped with receivers to measure Doppler shifts in radio signals, tracking radars, and photo theodolites and which transmit data to a central computation center. The network includes stations at Yevpatoria, Tbilisi, Bear Lake, Dzuhsaly, Izopashevo, Novosibirsk, Ulan Ude, Irkutsk, Ussuriysk, Simferopol, Tomsk, Novokazalmsk, and Petropavlovsk-Kamchatka.[104]

In addition to tracking stations dedicated to space surveillance, any ABM-associated radar—such as the Pushkino, Hen House, Try Add, and Dog House radars—has spacetracking capabilities. Any system that tracks strategic missiles also tracks space objects crossing Soviet territory or its near approaches.[105] Thus, the Soviets assert that the radar discovered to be under construction at Abalakova in 1983 and feared to be an ABM radar is intended for spacetracking.[106] The new radar "closes the final gap in the combined Hen House and new large-phased array radar early warning and tracking network. Together, this radar and five others like it form an arc of coverage from the Kola Peninsula in the northwest, around Siberia, to Caucasus in the southwest. Hen House coverage completes the circle."[107]

Outside of Soviet borders, Soviet spacetracking is accomplished both by tracking stations on foreign soil and ship-based equipment.

References to such stations began in December 1967 with a TASS report referring to stations in the United Arab Republic (presumably Helwan), Mali, and other unspecified countries. This was followed by references to stations in Guinea (April 1968); Cuba (October 1968); Aswan, Egypt (February 1970); and Fort Lamy, Chad (1971).[108]

In 1977 a Czechoslovakian broadcast referred to a laser tracking program named Great Arc. The report stated that Czechoslovakian scientists and technicians had participated in the development and production of laser radars that operate in several East Bloc nations as well as Egypt, Bolivia, and India. Later in 1977 a Cuban broadcast claimed that a powerful laser tracking station built by Soviet and other experts was being constructed at the satellite observation station near Santiago de Cuba, the clear skies over Cuba for almost the entire year being given as the reason for the choice of the site for the station.[109]

In 1980 a Latvian station was added to the set of stations making regular observations of artificial satellites with a laser rangefinder. An accuracy of one or two meters in the distance of satellites several thousand miles from the earth was claimed.[110]

The Soviet Union has placed a significant emphasis on sea-based support of its space program, possibly due to Soviet reluctance to become dependent on foreign-based stations or foreign reluctance to host Soviet stations. Presumably, just as such U.S. ships can be employed to monitor Soviet missile launches and space activity, so can Soviet ships be directed at U.S. targets.

The sea support system consists of ships. One group, which operates in the mid-Pacific, operates under military control. The ships are loaded down with radomes, a variety of specialized antennae, and theodolites. They can record missile tests in the area where the dummy warhead is to splash down or follow the orbital path of a satellite overflying the Pacific in its initial revolution.[111]

Ships operating in the Atlantic and Mediterranean along the path of orbital flights appear to be both less well equipped and under control of the Academy of Sciences. One tracking ship, the *Chumikan*, was in a remote part of the South Pacific, not near known Soviet test areas, during the recovery of the aborted *Apollo 13* flight. The reason for its presence was undoubtedly to collect intelligence concerning the Apollo reentry ablation phase.[112]

NUCLEAR DETECTION MONITORING

There are large gaps in Western knowledge concerning the specifics of the Soviet nuclear detonation detection monitoring program. It is not known, at least on an unclassified basis, whether any Soviet satellites (including early warning satellites) are equipped with nuclear detection packages, as are U.S. Defense Support Program, Global Positioning System, Vela, and other satellites. Also, the extent to which reconnaissance aircraft are outfitted with filters and other sensors for detection of nuclear particles in the atmosphere is not known.

Prior to the signing of the Limited Test Ban Treaty in 1963, ships were employed as one means of monitoring nuclear tests. Thus, a 1962 U.S. government report noted that:

> Three Soviet ships have appeared within a few miles of the area set aside in the Pacific for U.S. nuclear testing. They reportedly are heavily equipped to monitor U.S. activities in progress and have been actively engaged in obtaining what information is possible on our tests.
>
> The largest of these ships is the modern 3,600 ton hydrometeorological research ship SHOKAL'SKIY which is extensively outfitted with scientific instrumentation and is equipped with 16 laboratories for researchers. It has a pad for launching meteorological rockets which the Soviets report can reach the ionsphere for study of the effects on the upper atmosphere by nuclear explosions. Additionally, from its present location, SHOKAL'SKIY can obtain radio-chemical analysis of the debris from explosions which will provide information on bomb design, yield and similar data which have significant military implications. Time and approximate location of nuclear explosions can be determined from electro-magnetic pulses received. Other data can be derived from optical observations of high attitude bursts and from hydro acoustic devices measuring sound waves and from the bursts.[113]

Although there are no U.S. above-ground tests to monitor, Soviet ships may still be employed to monitor French and Chinese nuclear tests. Monitoring of U.S. underground nuclear tests will be the primary responsibility of Soviet seismic instruments. No information appears to be available concerning explicitly military stations and management. It is known that the Soviets do have a seismographic station network known as the Unified Seismic Observation System. The system consists of base, regional, and expeditionary stations. Base stations record earthquakes having surface wave magnitudes

M > 4 and acquire data on world seismicity and on the internal structure of the earth. Regional stations are responsible for recording weak local and near earthquakes not recorded by base stations. Expeditionary stations are semipermanent and perform the same function and are equipped with the same types of seismographs as the regional stations.[114]

All Soviet seismographic stations are equipped with standard instruments and follow the same operating procedures. There are 168 stations, 114 of which are regional, which are managed by institutes within each zone.[115]

In an attempt to introduce some uncertainty into the minds of Soviet intelligence officials who monitor U.S. nuclear tests, the Reagan administration adopted the practice of not announcing some explosions of less than five kilotons, those being the explosions that would be most difficult to detect. However, according to one official at Lawrence Livermore Laboratory, each test at the Nevada site requires the movement of hundreds of technicians and many vans of monitoring equipment, so the Soviet Union can probably detect such activities by satellite.[116]

NOTES TO CHAPTER 5

1. See Richard D. Hudson, Jr. and Jacqueline W. Hudson, "The Military Applications of Remote Sensing by Infrared," *Proceedings of the IEEE* 63, no. 1 (1975): 104–28; Charles Elachi et al., "Shuttle Imaging Radar Experiment," *Science*, December 8, 1982, pp. 996–1003.

2. Philip S. Clark, "Aspects of the Soviet Photoreconnaissance Satellite Programme," *Journal of the British Interplanetary Society (JBIS)* 36 (1983): 169–84.

3. Philip S. Clark, "The Soviet Year in Space of 1981," *JBIS* 35, no. 6 (1982): 261–71.

4. Clark, "The Soviet Year in Space of 1981"; Clark, "Aspects of the Soviet Photoreconnaissance Satellite Programme."

5. Clark, "The Soviet Year in Space of 1981."

6. Clark, "Aspects of the Soviet Photoreconnaissance Satellite Program."

7. Ibid.

8. Ibid.

9. "The Soviet Military Space Program," *International Defense Review* 2 (1982): 149–52; Geoffrey Perry, "Surveillance is the Key Soviet Space Mission," *Military Electronics/Countermeasures*, April 1983, pp. 18–21.

10. Clark, "Aspects of the Soviet Photoreconnaissance Satellite Program."

11. "The Soviet Military Space Program."

12. Ibid.; Clark, "The Soviet Space Year of 1981."

13. Saunders B. Kramer, "Soviet Satellites," *Aviation Week and Space Technology*, October 8, 1984, p. 104; "USSR Boosts Reconnaissance Capabilities," *Aviation Week and Space Technology*, January 21, 1985, p. 15; "Soviets Develop Heavy Boosters Amid Massive Military Space Buildup," *Aviation Week and Space Technology*, March 18, 1985, pp. 120–21.

14. Robert P. Berman and John C. Baker, *Soviet Strategic Forces: Requirements and Responses* (Washington, D.C.: Brookings Institution, 1982), p. 155.

15. Nicholas L. Johnson, *The Soviet Year in Space: 1983* (Colorado Springs, Co.: Teledyne Brown Engineering, 1984), p. 10; Kramer, "Soviet Satellites."

16. Berman and Baker, *Soviet Strategic Forces*, p. 155.

17. Paul Stares, *Space Weapons and U.S. Strategy: Organization and Development* (London: Croon Helm, forthcoming). Also see Philip Klass, "USSR Accelerates Recon Satellite Race," *Aviation Week and Space Technology*, April 6, 1970, pp. 72ff.

18. Stares, *Space Weapons and U.S. Strategy*.

19. "New Soviet Satellite Observes NATO Work from Unusual Orbit," *Aviation Week and Space Technology*, September 25, 1972, p. 19.

20. Stares, *Space Weapons and U.S. Strategy*; "Soviets Launch Five Spy Satellites in Two Weeks," *New Scientist*, October 25, 1973, p. 260.

21. Galia Golan, "Soviet Decisionmaking in the Yom Kippur War, 1973," in Jiri Valenta and William Potter, eds., *Soviet Decisionmaking for National Security* (Boston: Allen & Unwin, 1984), pp. 185–217.

22. Anwar el-Sadat, *In Search of Identity: An Autobiography* (New York: Harper & Row, 1977), p. 260.

23. Berman and Baker, *Soviet Strategic Forces*, p. 156.

24. Nicholas Johnson, "Soviet Satellite Reconnaissance and Trends," *Air Force Magazine*, March 1981, pp. 90–94.

25. "Soviets Integrating Space in Strategic War Planning," *Aviation Week and Space Technology*, March 14, 1983, pp. 110–11.

26. "International Intelligence," *Military Electronics/Countermeasures*, February 1983, p. 18.

27. Johnson, *Soviet Year in Space 1983*, p. 13.

28. Nicholas L. Johnson, "Soviet Satellites Eye Grenada and the Persian Gulf," *Defense Systems Review*, January 1984, p. 42.

29. Norman Polmar, ed., *Soviet Naval Developments* (Annapolis, Md.: The Nautical and Aviation Publishing Company of America, 1979), p. 104.

30. *Jane's All the World's Aircraft 1982–1983* (London: Jane's Publishing, 1982), p. 297.

31. Brian Freemantle, *KGB: Inside the World's Largest Intelligence Network* (New York: Holt, Reinhart and Winston, 1982), p. 119.

32. Bradford Dismukes and James McConnell, *Soviet Naval Diplomacy* (New York: Pergamon, 1979), p. 57.

33. "Industry Observer," *Aviation Week and Space Technology*, May 24, 1982, p. 13.

34. Penny Pagano, "U.S. Moves to Suspend Aeroflot Flights," *Los Angeles Times*, November 17, 1981, p. 28.

35. "Aeroflot's Intelligence Activities," *Armed Forces Journal International*, May 1981, pp. 54–55.

36. "Aeroflot's Intelligence Activities."

37. "Soviet Jet Overflies French Base," *Washington Post*, April 16, 1984, p. A15.

38. "Paris Calls Soviet Flight over Base Unintentional," *New York Times*, April 17, 1984, p. A11.

39. "Soviet Jet Overflies French Base."

40. Johnson, *The Soviet Year in Space 1983*, p. 31.

41. Ibid.

42. Berman and Baker, *Soviet Strategic Forces*, p. 156.

43. Johnson, *The Soviet Year in Space 1983*, p. 31.

44. Geoffrey Perry, "Soviet ELINT Satellites Cover the Globe," *Military Electronics/Countermeasures*, January 1983, pp. 38ff.; *The RAE Table of Earth Satellites 1981-1982* (Farnborough: Royal Aircraft Establishment, 1983), pp. 684, 688.

45. Johnson, *The Soviet Year in Space 1983*, p. 31; "Soviets Orbit Large New Military Electronic Intelligence Satellite," *Aviation Week and Space Technology*, January 14, 1985, pp. 19–20.

46. *Jane's All the World's Aircraft 1982-1983*, p. 297.

47. "Aeroflot's Intelligence Activities."

48. *Jane's Fighting Ships 1983-1984* (London: Jane's Publishing, 1983), pp. 552–55.

49. Ibid.

50. Ibid.

51. Edward H. Kolcum, "Soviet Intelligence Ship Intrudes on Trident Test," *Aviation Week and Space Technology*, January 25, 1982, pp. 20–22; "Trident Missile Launch Viewed by USSR Ship," *Aviation Week and Space Technology*, December 10, 1984, p. 23.

52. Charles Mohr, "Army Test Missile Is Said to Destroy a Dummy Warhead," *New York Times*, June 12, 1984, pp. 1, 9.

53. "News Digest," *Aviation Week and Space Technology*, June 13, 1983, p. 29.

54. Robert Fish, "Soviet Spy Ship Keeps Eye on Israelis," *London Times*, June 17, 1983, p. 1.

55. David Rees, "Soviet Sea Power: The Covert Support Fleet," *Conflict Studies* 84 (June 1977).

56. Submarine Defence Commission, *Countering the Submarine Threat: Submarine Violations and Swedish Security Policy* (Stockholm: Ministry of Defense, 1983), p. 74.

57. "The Undersea Intruder," *Newsweek*, October 18, 1982, p. 53.

58. Peter Osnos, "Sweden Charges Six Soviet Subs Violated Waters," *Washington Post*, April 27, 1983, p. A1; R. W. Apple, "Sweden Warns Moscow Over Subs and Temporarily Recalls Its Envoy," *New York Times*, April 27, 1983, pp. A1, A12; Submarine Defence Commission, *Countering the Submarine Threat*, p. 10.

59. James C. Bussert, "Signal Troops Central to Soviet Afghanistan Invasion," *Defense Electronics*, June 1983, p. 102; John K. Cooley, "Soviets in Libya: A New Mediterranean Power," *Washington Post*, March 10, 1981, p. 15.

60. Drew Middleton, "U.S. Officers Report a Buildup by Cuba," *New York Times*, March 28, 1983, p. A3; William J. Broad, "Evading the Soviet Ear at Glen Cove," *Science* 217 (September 1982): 910–11; Department of Defense, *Soviet Military Power—1984* (Washington, D.C.: U.S. Government Printing Office, 1984), p. 126; Ralph Kinney Bennett and Jay Mallin, "Rising Flow of Soviet Arms to Cuba Poses Three Threats," *Washington Times*, July 13, 1982, p. 6.

61. "China Warns of Soviet Elint Activities from Cam Ranh Bay," *Defense Electronics*, June 1984, p. 25; *Pacific Area Update* (P.4048, 1P1-4), (Hickam AFB, Hawaii: Pacific Command, February 17, 1984), p. 12.

62. Ian Ward, "New Soviet Spying Complex in Vietnam: Russians Set Up an Electronic Watch over Asia," *Australian*, July 8, 1981, p. 5.

63. M. F. Beg, "Afghan Rebel Offensive Threat to Russians," *Daily Telegraph*, November 2, 1979, p. 4; James C. Bussert, "Signal Troops Central to Soviet Afghanistan Invasion"; "Tuning In: Soviets Set Up Spy Station," *Time*, March 8, 1982, p. 32.

64. Beg, "Afghan Rebel Offensive Threats to Russians."

65. Desmond Ball, *Soviet Ears in the Ether*, forthcoming.

66. John Barron, *KGB Today: The Hidden Hand* (New York: Reader's Digest Press, 1983), p. 227.

67. "The KGB's Spies in America," *Newsweek*, November 23, 1981, pp. 50–61; James Bamford, *The Puzzle Palace: A Report of NSA, America's Most Secret Agency* (Boston: Houghton-Mifflin, 1982), pp. 177–78; Lawrence Meyer, "Tuning in on Washington: The Soviets Are Listening," *Washington Post Magazine*, February 20, 1983, pp. 10ff.

68. "Security Unit Seeks Electronic Building Shield," *New York Times*, April 1, 1984, p. 29; U.S. Congress, House Appropriations Committee, *Military Construction Appropriations for 1985, Part 5* (Washington, D.C.: U.S. Government Printing Office, 1984), p. 689.

69. "Hill with Topflight Electronic View," *New York Times*, January 28, 1985, p. A12.

70. Broad, "Evading the Soviet Ear at Glen Cove"; Gregory C. Sieminski, *The Search For a Balance between Scientific Freedom and National Security: A Case Study of Cryptology* (unpublished M.S. thesis, Defense Intelligence College, 1983), pp. 6-7.

71. "The KGB's Spies in America."

72. Broad, "Evading the Soviet Ear at Glen Cove."

73. David Kahn, "The Bugging of America," *Penthouse*, October 1984, pp. 69ff.

74. Freemantle, p. 57; Barron, *KGB Today*, pp. 92, 93, 126; John Sawatsky, *Men in the Shadows: The RCMP Security Service* (New York: Doubleday, 1980), p. 161; John Sawatsky, *For Services Rendered: Leslie James Bennett and the RCMP Security Service* (New York: Doubleday, 1982), pp. 201, 236-37; Andrew Kruger, "How the Russian Bear in Canberra Watches Us Watching Him," *Sydney Morning Herald*, March 28, 1981, p. 42.

75. Perry, "Soviet ELINT Satellites Cover the Globe."

76. Ibid.

77. Geoffrey E. Perry, "Russian Ocean Surveillance Satellites," *Royal Air Forces Quarterly* 18 (Spring 1978): 60-67.

78. *SIPRI Yearbook 1976—World Armaments and Disarmament* (Cambridge, Mass.: MIT Press, 1976), p. 111.

79. Ibid; David Wood, "A-Powered Soviet Satellite May Plunge to Earth Soon," *Los Angeles Times*, January 6, 1983, pp. 1, 18; "Soviets Seen Operating Two Types of Ocean Surveillance Satellite," *Aerospace Daily*, June 2, 1976, pp. 169-70.

80. Leo Heaps, *Operation Morning Light: Terror in Our Skies, The True Story of Cosmos 954* (New York: Paddington Press, 1978); John Noble Wilford, "Soviet Denies Peril from Satellite; U.S. Differs and Sets Up an Alert," *New York Times*, January 7, 1982, pp. A1, A8.

81. Ibid.

82. U.S. Congress, Senate Committee on Commerce, Science and Technology, *NASA Authorization for Fiscal Year 1984* (Washington, D.C.: U.S. Government Printing Office, 1983), pp. 4, 7; Richard D. Lyons, "Soviet Launches a Spy Satellite to Track U.S. Ship," *New York Times*, May 2, 1980, p. 37; "Washington Report," *Defense Electronics*, June 1984, p. 19.

83. Richard Halloran, "Soviet Satellites Reported over Area," *New York Times*, May 4, 1982, pp. 4, 7.

84. Nicholas L. Johnson, "Soviet Satellites Eye Grenada and the Persian Gulf," *Defense Systems Review*, January 1984, p. 42; Jack Anderson, "GAO Audits Soviet Spy Satellites," *Washington Post*, February 11, 1985, p. C12.

85. U.S. Congress, House Appropriations Committee, *Department of Defense Appropriations for 1985, Part 2* (Washington, D.C.: U.S. Government Printing Office, 1985), p. 195.

86. Johnson, *The Soviet Year in Space 1983*, p. 31.
87. "Soviet Intelligence Satellite Fails, Reenters over Europe," *Aviation Week and Space Technology*, February 4, 1985, p. 21; Nicholas Johnson, *The Soviet Year in Space 1984* (Colorado Springs, Co.: Teledyne Brown Engineering, 1985), pp. 31, 33.
88. Dismukes and McConnell, *Soviet Naval Diplomacy*, p. 57.
89. Ibid.; Department of Defense, *Soviet Military Power—1984*, p. 126.
90. Polmar, *Soviet Naval Development*, p. 104.
91. "2 Soviet Bombers Spy on New U.S. Carrier Off Va.," *Baltimore Sun*, June 27, 1982, p. 9.
92. Department of Defense, *Soviet Military Power—1984*, p. 126.
93. "Tracking the Russian Bear," *Sea Technology*, January 1983, p. 9.
94. Polmar, *Soviet Naval Developments*, p. 105.
95. Ibid.
96. Dismukes and McConnell, *Soviet Naval Diplomacy*, p. 52.
97. Ibid.
98. Ibid.
99. Ibid.
100. U.S. Congress, Senate Committee on Appropriations, *Department of Defense Appropriations Fiscal Year 1971, Part 3* (Washington, D.C.: U.S. Government Printing Office, 1970), p. 38; Dismukes and McConnell, *Soviet Naval Diplomacy*, p. 54; James Mistretta, *Soviet Naval Indian Ocean Operations* (Washington, D.C.: Defense Intelligence Agency, 1979), p. 4.
101. Dismukes and McConnell, *Soviet Naval Diplomacy*, p. 54.
102. Ibid.
103. Paul Stares, "Space and U.S. National Security," *Journal of Strategic Studies* 6, no. 4 (1983): 31–48.
104. Desmond Ball, "The Soviet Target Base," in Demond Ball and Jeffrey Richelson, eds., *Strategic Nuclear Targeting* (Ithaca, N.Y.: Cornell University Press, forthcoming); U.S. Congress, Senate Committee on Aeronautics and Space Sciences, *Soviet Space Programs 1971-1975, Part I* (Washington, D.C.: U.S. Government Printing Office, 1976), p. 64; U.S. Congress, Senate Committee on Commerce, Science and Technology, *Soviet Space Program 1976-1980 Part I* (Washington, D.C.: U.S. Government Printing Office, 1982), p. 122.
105. U.S. Congress, Senate Committee on Commerce, Science and Technology, *Soviet Space Programs 1976-1980 Part I*, p. 124.
106. Philip J. Klass, "U.S. Scrutinizing New Soviet Radar," *Aviation Week and Space Technology*, August 22, 1983, pp. 19–20; Michael Getler, "Soviets Veto Bid for SALT Talks," *Washington Post*, September 4, 1983, p. A14.
107. Department of Defense, *Soviet Military Power—1984*, pp. 32–33.

108. U.S. Congress, Senate Committee on Commerce, Science and Technology, *Soviet Space Programs 1976–1980 Part I*, p. 124.
109. Ibid.
110. Ibid., p. 105.
111. Ibid., p. 125.
112. Ibid., p. 133.
113. "Soviet Spy Ships Monitor U.S. Nuclear Tests," report June 1, 1962, Executive Files ND 21–1, JFK Library, pp. 1–3.
114. Charles Shishkevish, *Soviet Seismographic Stations and Seismic Instruments, Part I* (Santa Monica, Calif.: RAND Corporation, 1974), p. 1.
115. Ibid., pp. 7, 34.
116. William J. Broad, "Some Atomic Tests Being Kept Secret by Administration," *New York Times*, January 29, 1984, pp. 1, 12.

6 OPEN SOURCES

Soviet intelligence activities are usually associated in the public's mind with clandestine human and technical collection operations. Yet, although the Soviet Union and the United States spend the major portion of their intelligence budgets on such clandestine operations, the vast majority of the information employed in intelligence analysis is obtained from open sources. This is particularly true with respect to the Soviet Union, which benefits from the more open nature of Western society. Open sources include the newspapers, magazines, and trade and technical journals as well as government and contractor reports available to anyone for the asking or for purchase. Open sources also include public gatherings, hearings, or meetings open to the public as well as unclassified discussions.

Soviet attention to the value of open source information is evident from a variety of writings. In an article in the Soviet newspaper *Soviet Russia* for December 19, 1967 an article was published that said:

On 20 March 1935, the affair of the writer Berthold Jacob, kidnapped from Switzerland by agents of the Hitlerite Secret Service, resounded throughout the world.

Jacob at that time was writing much on the German Army, in a state of rearmament. He was able to reveal all the organizational details of the fascist army in a small book. The book gave short biographic information on 168 Hitlerite generals, the disposition of many divisions was revealed and so on.

When the kidnapped Jacob was brought for interrogation to Walter Nikolay, the Chief of the fascist secret service, he proved that he had borrowed all his information for this book from the open German press, from journals, and papers. So, for example, the basis of the assertion that General Haase commands the 17th Division billeted at Nuremberg was taken from an obituary notice in a Nuremberg paper which said that the Commander of the 17th Division, recently transferred to Nuremberg was present at the funeral. In an Ulm paper he turned attention to the description of the marriage ceremony of a Major Stemmerman at which Colonel Virov, Commander of the 36th Regiment of the 25th Division was present. Evidently, in order to give the wedding a more solemn character, the local journalists had mentioned that the Commander of this Division himself, General Shaller, was at the wedding. For what sort of wedding is it without a General! And so, patiently, Jacob had collected information on 168 Generals and on what they are doing.[1]

Similarly, in his authoritative *Soviet Military Strategy*, Marshal V.D. Sokolovskiy wrote:

The information service uses all legal sources, such as, for example, the press and periodicals, radio and television broadcasts and motion picture films concerning the country being studied, etc.

The painstaking and systematic study of all legal information, its methodical processing, and its comparison with data from illegal sources can supply intelligence with very important and detailed information concerning all questions of preparation for war in peacetime. This branch of intelligence activity is just as important as the others.[2]

According to one account, the FBI estimates that the Soviet Union gets 90 percent of its intelligence information from open sources.[3] Thus, one KGB agent in Washington begins his day by reading the *Washington Post, New York Times, Baltimore Sun*, and the *Wall Street Journal*, looking for defense-related articles—including those concerning START, defense spending, MX, and developments concerning rapid deployment forces. Additionally, he finds information in the *Wall Street Journal* as to which defense contractors have been awarded contracts and by whom.[4]

He then turns to specialized publications such as *Aviation Week and Space Technology* as well as to other trade publications that contain information on electronics and avionics. In addition, the agent also attends open congressional committee hearings on defense questions. By both the congressional questions and official answers he can gain a sense of trends in thinking on particular issues.[5] The same pattern applies in other areas of Soviet interest, such as foreign policy, energy, and international economic policy.

The remainder of this chapter examines the rationales for open source collection, the origins of open source information, and three types of intelligence that can be obtained from open sources: political, military, and economic. Open source acquisition of scientific and technical intelligence is dealt with in Chapter 9.

RATIONALES FOR OPEN SOURCE COLLECTION

One can distinguish three rationales for Soviet open source collection activities. In some cases, the activity is used as a "come on," that is, as a means of recruiting foreign nationals. Thus, it is well known that a KGB officer will often begin his recruiting pitch by asking for unclassified documents, paying the source if he can to establish a financial relationship. Once such a relationship is established, they will move on to seeking the delivery of classified information, using the financial relationship as a lever.

Second, open source collection can provide directions for clandestine collection. Information indicating the existence of plans, programs, organizations, or weapons systems will provide new targets for clandestine collection activities. Thus, it is possible that first Soviet knowledge of the Army's Intelligence Support Activity, the Chalet signals intelligence satellite, and the Stealth bomber came from open source disclosures.

Third, and directly related to the discussion in the remainder of the chapter, open sources provide information concerning political, military, scientific and technical, and economic matters. The press, academia, the media, think tanks, and business organizations constitute a massive intelligence/information network with thousands of collectors and agents and analysts. Since a significant overlap exists in interests, it is to be expected that Soviet intelligence would make use of their efforts.

AVAILABILITY AND ORIGINS OF OPEN SOURCE INFORMATION

The availability of open source information varies significantly from nation to nation—even within the U.S.-European bloc of nations that are the major targets of the KGB and GRU. This variation in availability is a function of each nation's secrecy laws and the ability of parliaments or legislatures to inquire into certain executive branch activities, particularly national security activities.

The United States is by far the most "lenient" of the Western countries, lacking an Official Secrets Act (which would be unconstitutional) but having a relatively powerful Freedom of Information Act. Nations such as Britain, Canada, France, and Sweden are much more inclined to view defense matters as classified. Those countries have little or no mechanisms by which members of the public can acquire even unclassified national security information that government agencies would rather not make public.

In Britain public officials will make no significant comments on intelligence operations beyond the amount of the yearly "vote" (budget) for "secret services" unless forced to do so by a public scandal. Thus, in one of his memoirs, Harold Wilson included a less-than-one-page chapter on the secret services—noting only the budget voted in Parliament and that further comment would be inappropriate.[6]

Further, since its passage in 1911 the present-day Official Secrets Act has been employed against both former government employees and journalists. In his memoirs concerning his service in the Secret Intelligence Service during World War I, Compton MacKenzie revealed that the head of the British Secret Service was known by the code letter "C"—a revelation that landed him in the Old Bailey dock, charged with violation of the act.

In the late 1950s two undergraduates who worked in a British signals intelligence station in West Germany were jailed for describing such activities in a university magazine.[7] And in 1977 a former corporal who also worked in the British signals intelligence organization was arrested for talking to news magazine reporters. The reporters were also arrested and tried.[8] More recently, a government clerk was sentenced to a jail term for leaking a memo (concerning cruise missile deployments) to the press.

In Norway in 1981, two researchers were tried on the charge of publishing classified information in a study they did for the International Peace Research Institute, Oslo. The study, *Intelligence Installations in Norway*, detailed the existence and operations of signals intelligence and satellite tracking stations, the number of personnel, and their equipment.[9] The report also speculated on the specific functions of the stations. All the information employed was obtained from unclassified documents and legal activities—phone books, trade union lists, observation of antennae from public roads, and the study of books on electronics and radio. However, the very act of combining the unclassified information was considered a breach of the Norwegian secrecy laws.[10]

In any case, information of significance to Soviet intelligence appears throughout the Western press. This information can be categorized in two ways. One distinction is between authorized and unauthorized disclosures. Authorized disclosures are those that involve material considered unclassified or declassified by the "proper authorities"; the vast majority of open source information falls in this category. Declassification often results from an administration seeking to support its programs or version of events. Thus, much material that would otherwise be classified was officially declassified as a result of the 1983 KAL 007 disaster. Likewise, much of the information and drawings in the *Soviet Military Power* pamphlets that have been published by the U.S. government would ordinarily be considered classified.[11]

Unauthorized disclosures are disclosures to the public of material considered by the government, although not necessarily by others, to be properly classified. Such disclosures stem from a variety of motives—a desire to kill or support a particular program or the desire to inform the public of an activity believed to be dangerous, immoral, or illegal. Thus, the initial leak concerning the U.S. Holystone submarine reconnaissance program appears to have stemmed from an official concerned over what he considered its provocative nature, and the leak that revealed the existence of the Chalet signals intelligence satellite appears to have been motivated by a desire to sell SALT II.[12]

Classified information may also be disclosed inadvertently, either due to slips of the tongue by government officials or slips of the scissor by the censors of congressional testimony. In the first category is President Nixon's stating that the United States *knew* that North Korean radar screens showed the EC–121 aircraft that was shot down to be outside North Korean airspace, thus revealing a U.S. capability to read enemy radar screens. Likewise, during the SALT I hearings a U.S. official unwittingly revealed that U.S. reconnaissance satellites had a slant angle capability that allowed the United States to determine what was taking place under the nets the Soviet Union used to cover submarine construction. The Soviets promptly closed the front end of the nets.[13]

Censors have failed to delete classified information in congressional hearings dealing with intelligence collection systems and capabilities and weapons systems. The description of a planned satellite called Clipper Bow as a radar satellite as well as the specification of a 0.075 nautical mile Circle of Equal Probability (CEP) for MX warheads appeared in publically available congressional hearings due to such errors.[14] Most recently, two satellite photographs of Soviet fighters slipped through a Pentagon censor and appeared in similar hearings.[15]

Whatever the origin, information concerning political, military, economic, and scientific and technical matters appear in a variety of publications. Most visible are the newspapers—the *New York Times, Washington Post, Baltimore Sun, Los Angeles Times, Wall Street Journal, London Times*—and national magazines such as *Time, Newsweek,* and *The Economist.*

Less visible to the general public are the trade journals such as *Aviation Week and Space Technology, Defense Electronics, Air Force Magazine,* and *Defense Systems Review.* The journals focus in greater and with greater technical precision on specialized topics that would not receive coverage in the mass media.

A third, even less visible, category is the academic/technical journals. One subset of this category includes the academic foreign policy and strategic studies journals. In addition, there are technical journals that deal with a variety of scientific matters, often matters with direct military applications. Technical academic journals such as *Physical Review* concentrate on theoretical issues; journals such as the *Proceedings of the IEEE* and *Applied Optics* focus on more applied issues. In some cases, reading of such journals can provide an additional payoff beyond their direct value. For example, one indication to Soviet intelligence that the United States had embarked on a project to develop an atom bomb was the sudden and complete disappearance of articles from *Physical Review* by the best-known nuclear physicists.[16]

Congressional and executive branch documents represent another set of publications of interest to the KGB and GRU. Government (whether U.S., British, or French) white papers on defense, security, and diplomatic issues are of interest, as are the U.S. congressional hearings mentioned above. In addition, there are congressional—

Office of Technology Assessment (OTA), Congressional Budget Office, General Accounting Office (GAO)—assessments of military plans and programs, such as GAO's studies on Trident and strategic C^3 and OTA's study of MX missile-basing options.[17] Furthermore, there is a vast amount of material published by all government agencies—including the Department of Defense—for basically internal purposes but which can be obtained by subscription or purchase. This material includes phone books, directives, instructions, organization charts, and mission statements.

Contractors conduct thousands of studies each year for government agencies on both technical and policy issues. Unclassified reports are obtainable via the National Technical Information Service for a fee, and until recently, when their purchase rights were cut off, the Soviets would purchase all such reports.

In addition to reports and products, contractors also produce brochures extolling their products, which often include strategic and other systems, such as the MX, B-1, and SR-71. Exhibits or conferences bring numerous contractors together and provide a means of gathering information with little effort.

Newsletters of various kinds also provide information of value in that they concern defense, foreign policy, energy, trade, and other matters of importance. The newsletters are often geared toward would-be contractors, who want to know how much money the government has to spend, what it wants to spend it on, and who has been awarded what contract.

OPEN SOURCE POLITICAL INTELLIGENCE

As noted earlier, Soviet intelligence desires information on domestic politics as well as on foreign policy. The impact of domestic affairs on foreign policy is both direct and indirect. The state of the economy or the level of social conflict, for example, can determine or influence the ability of the United States, NATO, or China to undertake certain foreign policy or military initiatives. The course of domestic politics determines who has control of the foreign and military policy apparatus and how much leeway.

It is particularly in the area of domestic politics that open source information is of the greatest relative value to the Soviet Union, in terms of quantity, quality, and efficiency. Coverage of domestic politics occupies a substantial portion of the press and media throughout the West. The major newspapers, news magazines, and national television networks devote tremendous resources to covering domestic politics, especially in an election year. Resources include manpower ("star" journalists and technicians), money, print, and airtime.

More significantly, the domestic media and their representatives have an access that is generally unobtainable by Soviet intelligence personnel, certainly Soviet embassy employees. This access involves not only coverage of day-to-day events on the domestic political/campaign front but an access to inside information concerning positions, strategies, and future plans. Columnists such as George Will, Rowland Evans and Robert Novak, and David Broder, to name a few, by virtue of friendship or position or both can obtain a view of the inner workings of a campaign or political conflict that would be virtually impossible for Soviet intelligence officers to match, regardless of the funds they had available.

Coverage of domestic social movements, whether in the United States or elsewhere, is another area where open sources can be of primary importance. Often, such movements, whether or not they involve foreign policy issues, function on a nationwide basis; Soviet coverage might be restricted, depending on the country, to the areas where they are officially represented. Thus, open sources provide a breadth of coverage that would otherwise be unavailable.

This is not to say that Soviet clandestine activity in such areas would be pointless, particularly if the agent went on to a position in the federal government, especially the national security establishment. Such a penetration would be of major importance. However, in terms of the information already available on domestic politics from open sources, an extensive effort to gather additional information would likely be of very marginal benefit.

Open source information is also of significant value in the area of foreign policy. Reporting on U.N. relations with NATO and other countries, U.S. policy toward the Middle East or Central America all receive significant attention in the mass media as well as specialist journals such as *Foreign Affairs* and *Foreign Policy*. Additionally, U.S. congressional committees produce reports and hearings running into thousands of pages per year dealing with such topics.

As was the case with the domestic political side, elite columnists, journalists, and reporters have access to highly placed sources—sometimes the President or Secretary of State—who provide them with information concerning directions in policy or specific decisions.

In these columns, the journalist often spells out in detail the thinking of administration officials on key issues. Of course, in nondemocratic nations, particularly those with heavy government control of the media, both domestic and foreign policy information will be harder to obtain and thus require clandestine penetration.

OPEN SOURCE MILITARY INTELLIGENCE

One can distinguish eight basic, sometimes overlapping. military areas about which the Soviet Union would like to obtain information: organizational structures, systems in place, systems under development, system vulnerabilities, development and deployment schedules, contracts, plans and programs, and foreign bases. "Systems" refers to weapons, C^3, and intelligence systems. Whether dealing with the United States, France, China, or Iran, the intelligence organs would prefer total and complete information about military matters.

Information on such matters comes from a vast number of sources, particularly in the United States. A Strategic Air Command pamphlet on operations security listed twenty-two different examples of open source information on military affairs:

1. *Congressional Record*
2. National Technical Information Service documents
3. Defense Documentation Center unclassified documents
4. *Aviation Week and Space Technology*
5. *Jane's Fighting Aircraft*
6. *Flight Operations*
7. *Military Affairs*
8. *Military and Space Daily Newsletter*
9. *Military Electronics/Countermeasures*
10. *The Infra-red Handbook*
11. *Aerospace Daily*
12. *Air Force Times*
13. *Combat Crew*
14. *Airman*
15. *Defense Management Journal*
16. *Commerce Business Daily*

17. Armed Forces Communications and Electronics Association
18. *Electronic News*
19. *Electronic Warfare Markets, USA*
20. *Defense Electronics*
21. Notices to Mariners/Airmen
22. Various Base and Community Newspapers[18]

Such a list represents only a minute fraction of the total number of available publications dealing in whole or in part with military affairs. Nor does it represent all the different types of publications that contain relevant information.

Major newspapers and magazines are of value on an intermittent basis since they report on only a small fraction of the information available. They do from time to time provide significant and sometimes classified information concerning plans and capabilities, as illustrated by the almost yearly publication of extracts from the Secret U.S. *Defense Guidance* document that states basic U.S. defense policy. Local newspapers often cover in detail events at the local base; thus, Omaha's newspapers would be of value for their coverage concerning the Strategic Air Command, and newspapers in the vicinity of Patrick AFB, Florida would provide information on the Central Command and its activities.

Outside of their main news sections, newspapers provide defense-related information in their business and employment sections. The business section of both major and local newspapers often contains detailed analysis of the economic impact of a weapons program, discussing the contractors and subcontractors and their roles as well as the system itself. For a system such as MX it is possible to identify the major contractor as well as the subcontractor for each component of the missile.[19] In addition, the Sunday edition of any major newspaper or newspaper located in an area with major aerospace, communications, or naval firms will often be full of engineering, physicists positions relating to defense projects. The Sunday, December 4, 1983 edition of the *New York Times*, for example, contained two large advertisements indicating openings in the area of sonar and ocean surveillance, including

- Manager, Towed Array Development;
- Manager, Vertical/Bottom Arrays;
- Manager, Marine Navigation Systems; and
- Surveillance Systems Engineers.[20]

A November 18, 1983 TRW advertisement in the *Los Angeles Times* listed over ten different defense-related job categories and approximately ten different functions within each category.[21]

It is, however, the trade, technical, academic, and official publications that provide the most systematic coverage of military matters. Thus, information on the organization of many military and intelligence establishments can be found in the *Department of Defense Telephone Directory*, which can be purchased at the Pentagon's Government Book Store or through the Government Printing Office. Although not all organizations are included, either due to being classified organizations or being located outside the Washington area, in the latter case, phone books for a particular organization can usually be obtained legally.

Although the organizational information in the *Department of Defense Telephone Directory* may stop at the division or branch level, it provides a unique and generally quite detailed source of information. The organizational structure of such units as the Naval Electronics Systems Command—an organization heavily involved in the development of space, antisubmarine warfare, and intelligence systems—the Defense Intelligence Agency, and the Defense Nuclear Agency are given in great detail. In addition, the directory identifies heads of divisions, sections, and so on—information that can be exploited in recruitment and disinformation attempts.

Likewise, other nations such as Canada and Australia have publicly available government phone directories that provide organizational and personnel information on military and intelligence organizations. The prospect of a publicly available *British Defence Directory* has alarmed some British officials. Presently sold for £150 a year to a select audience, it covers the Ministry of Defence, Army, Navy, Air Force, and NATO command. According to one account, the proposal, by the publisher, to sell the directory in open market has led to

security officials in the Ministry of Defence becoming alarmed at the prospect of the KGB being able to purchase dial-up directories of everyone working in the Whitehall headquarters or other British military establishments, simply by presenting their American Express Card. . . . 'foot-dragging . . . security people' . . . are concerned that handing all their internal directories to the computers of an outside agency would make the ministry vulnerable to easy electronic espionage.[22]

Ironically, in the case of the United Kingdom, a reporter was able to identify signals intelligence stations in the United Kingdom via the use of ordinary telephone directories for cities and regions.[23]

Information on systems—both those in place and those under development—comes from a combination of official and unofficial sources. Each year four congressional committees—the Appropriations and Armed Services committees of each branch of Congress—hold hearings on the Defense Department budget for the forthcoming fiscal year. These hearings consist of a combination of open and closed hearings and produce several thousand pages of publicly available (sanitized) hearings. Thus, the 1983 hearings by the House Appropriations Committee produced a nine-volume set on the FY 1984 defense budget, each volume running between 600 and 1,000 pages.

Part 4—on Research, Development, Test, and Evaluation—is 795 pages and deals with, among other subjects, remotely piloted vehicles, the Pershing II missile, Ballistic Missile Defense, lasers, strategic communications, cruise missiles, and strategic defense. It is not uncommon for the discussion and testimony of particular subjects and categories to run 100 or more pages. For example, Part 7 of FY 1984 hearings devotes 123 pages to Air Force procurement programs (excluding MX and B-1B, which are dealt with elsewhere); 129 pages to command, control, and communications programs; and almost 100 pages to the military role in space.

The section on C^3 programs contains testimony on antisatellite systems, the TACAMO aircraft, present and projected military satellite communications, the NAVSTAR Global Positioning System Satellites, the Ground Wave Emergency Network, and the Defense Data Network—with the discussion focusing on present and projected capabilities, vulnerabilities, and development schedules. The space segment discusses ASATs, early warning space-based surveillance of space, and laser experiments.

In addition to the hearings, material is available in the form of Congressional Justification Books dealing with specific areas of activity for the Department of Defense as well as the individual services. This material deals in even greater detail with specific systems or programs—for example, the Defense Support Program, early warning, or nuclear monitoring.

Supplementing and complementing the hearings are trade journals such as *Aviation Week and Space Technology, Military Electronics/Countermeasures*, and *Defense Electronics.* In focusing on specific systems or programs, these journals often "fill in" the deleted portions of testimony. Since these journals tend to be advocates of greater military strength, they often are the beneficiaries of leaks concerning particular systems—usually focusing on either the problems of a present system or the virtues of a planned system or both.

Technical journals may also deal on occasion with specific systems. For example, the 1965 issue of the *Proceedings of the IEEE* devoted an entire issue to the Vela nuclear detection satellite system—its internal logic as well as the operations of its sensing system.[24]

Reports on weapons and military technology can be obtained from the National Technical Information Service (NTIS), a government organization, in Springfield, Virginia. NTIS serves as a clearinghouse for the sale of unclassified government technical documents. Thus, the report entitled *Simultaneous Line of Sight Terrain Effects on Remoted Weapon Systems*, a report prepared by the Combined Army Combat Developments Activity, could be purchased in 1974 on microfiche for $2.25. According to its abstract,

> the report contains an analysis of the impact of terrain on the dual simultaneous line of sight (LOS) requirements of a remote target designation weapon system when both parties are operating at surface or near surface terrain environments. . . . Study results include comparisons of autonomous single sites with remoted systems for quantities such as rare LOS probabilities, duration of moving target intervisibility, and distributions of multiple target intervisibility.[25]

Likewise, the Los Alamos Scientific Laboratory (LASL) in New Mexico prepared a report in 1973 entitled *Electron-Beam-Controlled Lines: Discussion from the Engineering Viewpoint* that could also be purchased in 1974 for $2.25. According to its abstract,

> the LASL CO_2 laser program was organized to design, fabricate and evaluate high energy, short pulse CO_2 lasers for use in fusion studies. A general discussion of electron-beam-controlled lasers is included along with details of component designs. This includes a discussion of the high voltage pulsers, electron guns, pumping chamber vessels, timing and operational experience with the 1–LJ CO_2 system components.[26]

Soviet concern over U.S., West European, and other foreign military systems begins from the moment a contract in awarded for development and steadily increases as the system progresses toward full deployment. Information obtained concerning the contractor, the number and identity of personnel involved, and the money allocated allows assessment of the importance and significance of the system as well as of recruitment possibilities. Recent experience shows that the payoffs of recruiting contractor personnel can be quite significant. One means of tracking such developments has already been noted—the business and employment sections of newspapers. Another, in the United States, is the *Commerce Business Daily*, which lists all unclassified government requests for proposals and contracts awarded.

Information on policies, plans, programs, and procedures varies significantly as to sources and availability. Information on general policies is often available via public testimony, speeches, academic journal articles, and news reports. Information on plans and programs is often much harder to come by, particularly if it concerns nuclear war plans or "black" (classified) programs. Thus, under the Reagan administration there is almost no official discussion of nuclear targeting issues. Virtually the only open source material available consists of newspaper articles, journal articles, and unclassified contractor reports.

The procedures and policies governing all the aspects of the operations of the U.S. Department of Defense and the military services are contained in a series of regulations, directives, and instructions. These documents cover administrative practices, weapons, procurement, and intelligence operations. Many are classified; others are freely available.

Information on domestic and foreign bases is available through a variety of sources. In addition to intermittent newspaper stories, there are the *Autovon Directory*, the Real Property inventories, and the individual base telephone books. The *Autovon Directory* is a phone book listing the phone numbers on the Automatic Voice Network (hence Autovon) for U.S. installations in the United States and abroad, identified by the organization responsible for the installation or activity. The Real Property inventories (one for each service) specifies the function, size, and location owned by each of the services—to the extent that such information is unclassified. The telephone books for U.S. and overseas commands and bases—for example, the Pacific Command (PACOM) in Hawaii or Fort Bragg in North Carolina—can be employed to identify personnel, organizations present at the base, and organizational structures.

OPEN SOURCE ECONOMIC INTELLIGENCE

Probably the most detailed and systematic open source information available is that concerning economic matters—the economy; foreign trade; energy; and specific industries such as oil, steel, and computers. Such information is useful in assessing the dimensions of instability in a country, its mobilization capacity, its stake in its relations with another nation, its peacetime and wartime vulnerabilities. The latter data are useful both for peacetime economic warfare and development of nuclear targeting plans.

Economic information available to the U.S. public, and therefore to the Soviet Union, includes a voluminous amount of official documents—the hearings of the Joint Economic Committee and other congressional committees, reports by the Departments of Commerce and Energy, and company reports to the Securities and Exchange Commission. The last-mentioned reports allow an interested party to determine how the U.S. energy, steel, or chemical industries are structured and how they are investing.

Outside the government there is an even more voluminous quantity of material available. Virtually every major bank publishes a weekly or monthly newsletter on the U.S. economy. These newsletters focus on special industries as well as trends in the economy. Additionally, specialized newsletters such as Platt's *Oilgram* provide detailed coverage of the oil industry, and investment firms such as Merrill Lynch provide detailed analysis on companies such as Exxon.

Further, economic analysis firms such as DRI, Chase, and Wharton publish monthly newsletters on the U.S. economy and selected industries. More importantly, they provide customers with computer data bases with which one can estimate the impact on the U.S. economy of particular economic/physical events. Attempts by the Soviet embassy to subscribe to such services have, in at least one case, been rebuffed, but the material could be obtained via a dummy or friendly company.

PROBLEMS OF OPEN SOURCE COLLECTION

Open source collection does present Soviet intelligence with some problems. One problem, at least with respect to the United States, is the sheer volume of data—a problem that could threaten to make a "vacuum cleaner" approach counterproductive. Once collected, such data must be analyzed and integrated with the data from clandestine sources in a timely and coherent fashion in order to be useful.

The quantity of data is partially a product of overlapping information due to competition in all fields of publishing on defense, foreign affairs, and economic issues. Also, within this vast quantity of data will be numerous errors, particularly with respect to officially classified matters. The inability to count on perfect accuracy thus poses an additional burden on Soviet analysts.

In addition to honest errors there is the possibility of disinformation, either by using an unwitting reporter or with the reporter's cooperation. There is no known instance of a U.S. reporter publishing, at the government's request, information he or she knew to be false, but at least one British reporter has acknowledged publishing assertions he knew to be false concerning the scheduled date of a nuclear test.

NOTES TO CHAPTER 6

1. U.S. Congress, House Permanent Select Committee on Intelligence, *Soviet Active Measures* (Washington, D.C.: U.S. Government Printing Office, 1982), pp. 213–14.

2. V.D. Sokolovskiy, *Soviet Military Strategy*, 3rd ed. (New York: Crane, Russak, 1975), p. 320.

3. "The KGB's Spies in America," *Newsweek*, November 23, 1981, pp. 50ff.

4. Tad Szulc, "The KGB in Washington," *Washington Post Magazine*, March 2, 1980, pp. 1ff.

5. Ibid.

6. Harold Wilson, *A Personal Record: The Labour Government 1964–1967* (Boston, Mass.: Little, Brown. 1971).

7. Duncan Campbell, "Spy in the Sky," *New Statesman*, September 9, 1983, pp. 8–9.

8. Crispin Aubrey, *Who's Watching You?* (London: Penguin, 1981), p. 11.

9. Owen Wilkes and Nils Petter Gleditsch, *Intelligence Installations in Norway: Their Number, Location, Function and Legality* (Oslo: International Peace Research Institute, 1979).

10. *The Oslo Rabbit Trial* (Oslo: Solidarity Campaign for Gleditsch and Wilkes, 1981), pp. 16–17.

11. Department of Defense, *Soviet Military Power—1984* (Washington, D.C.: U.S. Government Printing Office, 1984).

12. Richard Burt, "U.S. Plans New Way ro Check Soviet Missile Tests," *New York Times*, June 29, 1979, p. A3; Seymour Hersh, "Submarines of U.S. Stage Spy Missions Inside Soviet Waters," *New York Times*, May 25, 1975, pp. 1, 42.

13. See Jeffrey Richelson, "The Keyhole Satellite Program," *Journal of Strategy of Strategic Studies* 1, no. 2 (June 1984): 121–53.

14. U.S. Congress, House Committee on Armed Services, *Hearings on Military Posture and HR 5068, Book 1, Part 3* (Washington, D.C.: U.S. Government Printing Office, 1977), p. 751; U.S. Congress, Senate Committee on Appropriations, *Department of Defense Appropriations FY 1982, Part 5* (Washington, D.C.: U.S. Government Printing Office, 1981), p. 445.

15. U.S. Congress, House Committee on Armed Services, *Department of Defense Authorization of Appropriations for Fiscal Year 1984, Part 3* (Washington, D.C.: U.S. Government Printing Office, 1983), p. 1105.

16. David Holloway, "Entering the Nuclear Arms Race: The Soviet Decision To Build the Atomic Bomb, 1939–1945," *International Security Studies Program Working Paper No. 9.*

17. Office of Technology Assessment, *MX Missile Basing* (Washington, D.C.: U.S. Government Printing Office, 1981).

18. Strategic Air Command, *Operations Security Officer's Guide*, SACP 55–31 (Offutt AFB, Nebraska: Headquarters, Strategic Air Command, June 11, 1982), pp. 5-1 — 5-2.

19. David Gold, Christopher Paine, and Gail Shields, *Misguided Expenditure: An Analysis of the Proposed MX Missile Systems* (New York: Council on Economic Priorities, 1981), pp. 173 to conclusion.

20. Gould Electronics advertisement, "Entrepreneurial Technical Leaders: For Expansion Beyond Core Business into New and Existing Areas," *New York Times*, December 4, 1983, p. F35.

21. TRW advertisement, "Defense Is Our First Name," *Los Angeles Times*, November 13, 1983, p. 33.

22. Duncan Campbell, "Publisher Tries To 'Privatise' Defense List," *New Statesman*, September 16, 1983, p. 4.

23. Aubrey, "Who's Watching You?" p. 107.

24. Sidney Singer, "The VELA Satellite Program for Detection of High Altitude Nuclear Detonations," *Proceedings of the IEEE* 53, no. 12 (1965): 1935–48.

25. U.S. Air Force, Office of Special Investigations, *Special Report: Soviet Overt Intelligence Collections in the United States* (Washington, D.C.: AFOSI, 1975), p. 16.

26. Ibid.

7 ACTIVE MEASURES

Active measures represent a significant aspect of Soviet intelligence/ national security activity. The term "active measures" encompasses a variety of tactics designed to influence foreign events in favor of the Soviet Union. Included among these tactics are forgeries, propaganda, agents of influence, paramilitary operations, and assassinations.

In contrast to the U.S. term "covert action," the term "active measures" includes both overt and covert activities. Thus, such activities are directed by a variety of Soviet institutions—the KGB's Service A, the International Department and International Information Department of the Central Committee Secretariat, and the Foreign Ministry. The discussion in this chapter will focus mainly on the covert activities of the KGB and the International Department.

In seeking to enhance the Soviet position, combinations of active measures may be employed toward the same objective, the specific combination being a function of the situation and country. Whatever the active measures employed, they may be part of an attempt to attain a variety of objectives. A former KGB active measures officer has stated that the KGB's active measures goals in Japan included:

- the prevention of further political and military cooperation between Japan and the United States;
- the provocation of distrust between Japan and the United States;

- the inhibition of closer relations between Japan and China, especially in the political and economic fields;

- the prevention of the formation of anti-Soviet triangle of Washington, Peking, and Tokyo;

- the creation of a new pro-Soviet lobby among Japanese politicians;

- the persuasion of the Japanese government to broaden economic ties with the Soviet Union;

- the organization of the movement for signing a Japanese-Soviet friendship treaty;

- the penetration of the main opposition parties, especially the Japanese Socialist party, and the influencing of their political platforms to prevent dominance by the Liberal-Democratic party;

- the discouragement of opposition parties from creating a coalition government; and

- the discouraging of the Japanese government from disputing Soviet control of the Kuril Islands.[1]

The above list demonstrates that only part of the objectives in Soviet active measures are concerned with blocking U.S. or Chinese strategy. Others are concerned with enhancing Soviet positions in diplomatic or economic relations.

FORGERIES

There are two basic types of forgeries: alterations and fabrications. Altered documents (or tapes) are documents (tapes) in which portions of the document are true but other portions are falsified. The original documents may be obtained by theft or from an inside agent. Such documents are the more difficult to demonstrate as forgeries since none of the nomenclature, classifications, or procedural/routing markings need be fabricated. Further, the existence and general subject nature of the document cannot be denied.

Completely fabricated documents are those wholly created by Service A and might bear no resemblance to their actual counterpart document, if such a document even exists. In some cases the fabricators may employ an actual blank form.

The target audiences of forgeries include both governments and large groups—indeed, entire populations, races, or religions. When targeted at a government audience the objective is often to undermine their relations with the United States, China, West Germany, or some other government considered hostile to the Soviet Union. In some cases it is intended to cause a breach with respect to a particular subject—for example, bases, trade—and in others a general deterioration of relations is the goal.

Forgeries targeted at groups or populations may be intended to damage the reputations of either individuals—politicians, movement leaders, hostile journalists—or nations, especially the United States and China. The forgery may be part of a larger campaign intended to produce a specific result by a specific time—for example, cancellation of the Pershing II deployments—or simply continue agitation against those the Soviets consider hostile. Forgeries may also be disseminated to support Soviet claims—such as those regarding the mission of KAL 007—or to distract attention from a Soviet embarrassment—such as the beaching of a Soviet submarine on the Swedish coast.

To be successful a forgery need not remain unexposed, even for a moderate amount of time. Even if the United States can convince a foreign leader or government that a particular document is a forgery, the forgery may serve to remind the government of similar U.S. activities in the past or plant a seed of doubt concerning the U.S. explanation. When dealing with groups or populations, any explanation may be impossible, either because the media carrying the report of the forged document will not carry the disclaimer or because the audience is unwilling to be convinced, especially on "technical" grounds.

The success of such forgeries may often depend on their suggesting activities in which the United States is known or has been widely alleged to have been involved in the past. Thus, some U.S. military and intelligence personnel, when contacted about specific items, will be unable to confirm their authenticity but will note that the United States engages in the type of activities described.[2]

There are nine typical elements in the Soviet modus operandi for forgery operations: (1) use of security classification, (2) use of official letterheads, (3) surfaced as copy, not original, (4) key document not in sharp focus or full size, (5) accompanying cover letter, (6) use of logical plots, (7) documents given gratis, (8) designed for media replay and (9) aimed at foreign government or leaders.[3] Of course, for a variety of reasons, not all elements will occur in each operation.

The use of security classification is employed because such documents attract more attention. In particular, SECRET-NOFORN documents attract attention since they contain "information" the U.S. designates as not available to foreign nationals—even allies. When possible, official letterhead or government forms are employed to lend an aura of truth to the operation. It is known that the Soviet and Soviet Bloc intelligence services collect U.S., NATO, and other nations' forms, letters, and official signatures. U.S. agencies the letterheads of which have been employed in forgery operations have included the United States Information Service (USIS), Peace Corps, Defense Department, FBI, and CIA.[4]

Surfacing the document as a copy not an original and in blurred focus or not in full size complicates forensic analysis—that is, detection of the forgeries by analysis of the paper, signatures, and typewriter. A cover letter usually accompanies the document explaining the senders' "disgust" and why the recipient is receiving it. It is often signed with a signature of a nonexistent individual or with "A Concerned Citizen," "A Fellow Arab," or "A Friend."[5]

Rather than fanciful scenarios about specific plots or coups, Soviet forgeries tend to contain a more generalized matter designed to exacerbate negative feelings about the American presence or American intentions in the target country. Vague charges about spying by the Peace Corps, anti-host government intrigue by the U.S. government, or anti-host country attitudes by key U.S. officials are easy to believe, difficult to disprove and in the latter two cases sometimes true.[6]

Documents are given gratis via mail—in contrast to the amateur or conman, who invariably seeks to sell the document in person. There is no personal link between the person offering the documents and the recipient, and no opportunity to ask questions.[7]

In the 1950s the Soviets used to publish forgeries in their own controlled press as opposed to their present practice of surfacing the document outside the Bloc. Although they had automatic access to the publication, the effect was limited since the Soviet Bloc press is not widely read in the West or Third World and is considered an obviously biased source.[8] Finally, often times the document will be sent to a foreign government or political personage who may raise a "Question in Parliament" or initiate a government inquiry. This technique is equally effective as media splashes in making a political point. Also, if an inquiry or parliamentary discussion results, the operation is carried forward by reports on the discussion or the parliamentary report.[9]

The identified Soviet forgeries since 1945 are too numerous to review. Several of these that serve to illustrate the different targets and objectives of Soviet forgeries include FM 30-31B, U.S. Nuclear War Plans, two Defense Intelligence Agency (DIA) intelligence collection requirements, PRM-46, the Chou-En-Lai letter, the U.S.-Swedish agreement, U.S. documents concerning Egypt, and a tape of an alleged Reagan-Thatcher conversation.

FM 30-31B, published in the *Covert Action Information Bulletin*, purports to be Supplement B to Army Field Manual 30-31 and its "SECRET NOFORN classified supplement FM 30-31A, providing guidance on doctrine tactics, and techniques for intelligence support to U.S. Army stability operations in the internal defense environments," is titled *Stability Operations Intelligence-Special Fields*.[10] It has been characterized by the CIA as a very sophisticated fabrication containing a minimum number of errors in style, format, and phraseology and constructed with use of appropriate typewriters, paper, and terminology.[11]

The manual purports to contain operational guidance to U.S. military security services regarding measures for influencing the internal affairs of friendly countries where U.S. armed forces are stationed and which are confronted by internal security threats from leftist and Communist forces. The "message" to be conveyed is that the United States interferes in the domestic affairs of governments the internal stability of which is considered important to U.S. national security. Additionally, the document seeks to suggest that in dire cases the United States envisions the use of extreme leftist organizations to convince allies of the need for harsher internal security measures.[12]

Mention of the field manual was first made in late 1975 in an obscure left-wing Turkish paper, but a copy did not surface until 1976, when a fascimile was left at the Philippino embassy in Bangkok, reappearing two years later when a Cuban intelligence officer in Madrid began offering copies of the document to Spanish publishers. It was reprinted in September 1978 in two Spanish periodicals and was subsequently reported in the European press, especially in Italy. According to the CIA, one of the main objectives was to "document" a Red Brigades-CIA link.[13]

As opposed to FM 30-31B, the several documents purporting to be authentic U.S. nuclear war plans and related documents include a combination of forged, altered, and authentic documents. These documents include the Top Secret *CINCEUR Operation Plan NR 100-6* and the *Nuclear Weapons Yield Requirements Handbook*. The original documents were apparently delivered to the Soviets by Army Sgt. Robert Lee Johnson in the early 1960s.[14]

NR 100-6 speaks of preemptive U.S. attack in the event of unequivocal strategic warning of a Soviet attack, and the handbook includes targets located in the Western European/NATO countries. The surfaced version of the latter document apparently consisted of the original target list from another document but with the addition of Western European targets. First surfaced in the latter 1960s, the intent was to exploit European concern about U.S. employment policies and their implications for Europe.[15]

The reemergence of these documents since summer 1980 suggests that they are part of a Soviet effort to encourage West European opposition to the modernization of NATO nuclear forces by raising concerns about U.S. employment policies.[16] The use of these documents represent the integrated approach of active measures—as Soviet attempts to stimulate opposition to Pershing II and ground-launched cruise missile (GLCM) deployment include propaganda and other active measures plus conventional diplomacy.

Soviet forgeries have also been designed to promote fears of U.S. intelligence collection against countries friendly to the United States, whether against the country's intelligence services or its political groups. Thus, a recent Soviet forgery resulted in the *Toronto Star* article entitled "U.S. Secretly Probed Canada's Intelligence Service: Report."[17] The article reported that a three-page Special Intelligence Collection Requirement (SICR) dictated by Army Operational Security requirements called for intelligence collection on the intelligence services of thirty-four friendly countries. Collection was to be directed at information concerning Targeting, Collection Operations, Special Operations, Characterization and Order of Battle, and Relations with FISS (Foreign Intelligence and Security Services).[18]

While the United States certainly collects and analyzes information on foreign intelligence services, including those on friendly nations, the SICR is an easily spottable forgery. First, SICRs are issued using a standard form, whereas the alleged SICR was typed on blank paper. Second, and most important, such collection is the responsibility of the CIA alone; reports by other U.S. agencies on foreign intelligence and security services are derived from CIA reports.

Another forgery of a DIA SICR was more competent. Surfaced in 1978, the document appeared on a genuine DIA DD Form 1365 which was completed and given the title "Anti-U.S. Activities and Their Sponsors in Western Europe." The document purported to be instructions for U.S. spying on forty-three Greek political parties and organizations. Despite its greater competence, the forgery was unconvincing to the newspaper recipient, and it did not publish it. Errors in the document included the absence of paragraph markings, incorrect expiration dates and downgrading instructions, and reference to superseded forms [19]

A forgery intended to cause damage both overseas (in Africa) and in the United States was a document dated March 17, 1978 purporting to be a presidential review memorandum—PRM/NSC-46—on "Black Africa and the U.S. Black Movement" and the associated report by the National Security Council (NSC) groups for Africa. The alleged report noted that "the nationalist liberation movement in black Africa can act as a catalyst with far reaching effects on the American black community" and that "a recurrence of the events of 1967–68 would do grievous harm to U.S. prestige."[20]

The recommendations of this "report" stated:

1. Specific steps should be taken with the help of appropriate government agencies to inhibit coordinated activity of the black movement.
2. Special clandestine operations should be launched by the CIA to generate mistrust and hostility in American and world opinion against joint activity to the two forces, and to cause division among black African radical national groups and their leaders.
3. The FBI should mount surveillance operations against black African representatives and collect sensitive information on those, especially at the U.N., who oppose U.S. policy toward South Africa; the information should include facts on their links with the leaders of the black movement in the U.S.[21]

Although surfaced in a manner unusual for Soviet forgeries—hand delivered by an unknown individual to a radio station in the Washington, D.C. area followed by delivery to a member of the U.S. delegation to the United Nations by a journalist four days later (September 16, 1980)—other signs indicate it is a Soviet forgery. The authentic

PRM/NSC-46 was dated May 4, 1979 and dealt with Central America. At least one of the individuals responsible for surfacing the document has been identified as a former Communist Party of the USA (CPUSA) member and is now affiliated with the World Peace Council.[22]

One forgery directed not at the United States but at the People's Republic of China (PRC) surfaced in January 1976 in a respected Japanese newspaper. Purportedly Chou-En-Lai's political testament, the document was placed via a Soviet agent in the newspaper's hierarchy.[23] The document alleges that the Chinese cultural revolution was a mistake, that China's economy should stress the expansion of heavy industry, and that there should be greater cooperation among the "democratic" and socialist forces to ensure world peace. The intent was to encourage political rivalries in China and support those elements favoring closer ties with the Soviet Union.[24]

One example of "diversionary" forgeries were ones surfaced in response to the grounding of a Soviet Whiskey-class submarine on the Swedish coast near a top secret naval base on which it had been spying.

Between November 8 and 11, 1981 at least eleven falsely attributed Western Union mailgrams circulated in the Washington area. The mailgrams were sent to U.S. and foreign journalists, including one TASS and one Polish correspondent. The mailgrams alleged a secret agreement between neutral Sweden and the United States to permit a satellite-monitoring facility on the Karlskrona Naval Base, Sweden. The mailgrams alleged the facility was required to allow photoreconnaissance of Poland—apparently a reference to the need for low-orbiting satellites to make frequent contacts with ground stations.[25] All alleged senders, including Undersecretary of Defense Fred Ikle, denied having sent the mailgrams. The purpose, in addition to distracting attention from Soviet violations of Swedish territorial waters, involved creating tension in U.S.-Swedish relations and raising questions about Swedish neutrality.[26]

Forgeries have also been employed in attempts to damage U.S.-Egyptian relations, with the audience or target being President Anwar el-Sadat. Thus, in mid-March 1977 prints from a film negative of a forged letter from U.S. Ambassador to Egypt Herman F. Eilts to his Saudi Arabian counterpart turned up at the Sudanese embassy in Beirut, Lebanon. The letter purported to outline a joint U.S.-

Egyptian plot to gain influence in the Sudan, its purpose apparently being to embarrass and isolate Sadat in the Arab world.[27]

The following month a photocopy of the purported notes taken by a U.S. aide to Secretary of State Vance for a confidential report to President Carter was delivered anonymously to the Egyptian embassy in Rome. The bogus notes attributed to Vance critical remarks about Sadat, King Hussein, President Assad, and the Saudi Arabian and Kuwaiti leaderships. The result was an Egyptian government inquiry.[28] In June photocopies of a forged operations memorandum (O.M.) bearing the forged signature of Ambassador Eilts was mailed to ten Egyptian newspapers. The "O.M." attacked Sadat for lack of leadership, foresight, and political acuity and indicated that the opinion was shared by the CIA chief of station.[29] Other letters directed at Sadat followed in July and August.

The Falklands war of 1982 led to several forgeries. The KGB may have faked a tape of a telephone conversation between President Reagan and British Prime Minister Margaret Thatcher that allegedly dealt with the Falklands war and cruise missiles. Reagan's part seemed to be constructed from a November 1982 speech on nuclear armaments. The drift of the tape was to blame Thatcher for the sinking of the *Sheffield* and Reagan for the failure of negotiations on intermediate nuclear forces. A late June 1982 bogus Pentagon news release—obviously bogus due to errors in grammar, coloring, and numbering—was said to grossly overstate the nature and extent of U.S. support for Britain with a view to damaging U.S.-Argentinian relations.[30]

Several forgeries surfaced in 1982 and 1983 in Europe and Africa. On February 7, 1983, *Tiempo*, a Madrid weekly newspaper, published extracts from a forged 1978 NSC memorandum on Poland from Zbigniew Brezinski to President Carter. The memorandum identified Poland as "the weakest link in the chain of Soviet domination of Eastern Europe" and proposed a destabilization policy involving "politicians, diplomats, labor unions, the mass media and covert activity."[31] In Italy forged State Department cables suggested that the United States was orchestrating a campaign to blame the Bulgarians and the Soviet Union for the attempted assassination of the Pope, and in Austria a forged letter signed by the U.S. ambassador to Austria seemed to disclose "a clumsy attempt to push Austria toward military ties with the West."[32]

Forgeries surfaced in Africa suggested U.S. plans to supply South Africa with new warplanes as well as plans to assassinate two Nigerian politicians and stage a coup in Ghana. One story alleged Reagan administration collusion in allowing U.S. companies to offer to supply new warplanes and trained helicopter pilots to South Africa in defiance of a U.N. arms embargo. A photocopied letter appeared in print in the November 1982 French-language weekly *Jeune Afrique* and later in the *Times* of Zambia, alleging that the Northrop aviation company was offering to sell FSF fighters to South Africa. The letter was addressed to Lt. Gen. A.M. Muller of the South African Air Force and invited him to visit Los Angeles at Northrop's expense to test fly new planes. In March 1983 Ghanaian officials called a press conference to accuse the U.S. embassy in Accra of plotting a coup. The officials cited an alleged report by the West German embassy to Bonn claiming that U.S. Ambassador Thomas W.M. Smith had instructed CIA operatives to overthrow the Ghanaian government.[33]

On April 13, 1983 two major opposition party newspapers in Ibadan, Nigeria—the *Nigerian Tribune* and the *Daily Sketch*—charged that U.S. Ambassador Thomas Pickering had ordered the assassination of two prominent Unity party of Nigeria figures. The papers published a forged document purporting to be an internal U.S. embassy memorandum which stated that "Chief Abiola has outlived his usefulness to our service. . . . [H]is flirtation with the opposition led by Obafemi Awolowo exemplifies the need to go ahead with operations Heartburn and Headache to solve the problem of these two personalities. . . . The Department must be well briefed on these wet affairs." "Wet affairs" is Soviet, but not Western, terminology for assassination.[34]

PROPAGANDA

It is in the area of propaganda that the interaction between overt and covert methods and the agencies responsible for these methods—the KGB's Service A, the International Department, and the International Information Department—is the greatest. Soviet propaganda activities involve Soviet news agencies, foreign Communist parties, and Soviet front organizations as well as black propaganda activities such as the operation of clandestine radio stations.

The Soviet organizational structure for active measures, especially propaganda, is illustrated in Figure 7-1. As indicated, the International Information Department is responsible for managing the most overt portion of the Soviet propaganda apparatus, which includes two newspapers (*Pravda* and *Izvestiya*), two news services (TASS, Novosti (APN)), Radio Moscow, and the Soviet embassy information departments.[35]

Of the two news agencies, TASS is the "official" agency and Novosti (APN) is the "unofficial" agency. TASS maintains bureaus and correspondents in about 100 countries; Novosti claims information exchanges with more than 100 international and national news agencies, more than 100 radio and television stations, more than 7,000 newspapers and magazines, and 120 publishing houses.[36]

Both agencies operate under official control and are used to take advantage of international events. Within hours of the assassination of Iranian Ayatollah Motahhari in May 1979, a TASS dispatch read on Radio Moscow's Persian-language service implied that the CIA was responsible for the terrorist organization that took credit for the Ayatollah's death.[37]

Similarly, *Pravda* and *Izvestiya* are used as conduits for propaganda and disinformation—through their staffs as well as through the material printed. According to the CIA, an occasional writer on international affairs for *Izvestiya*, sometimes identified as a government official, has been a source of official disinformation to West German journalists and politicians for the past twenty years.[38]

The activities that are supervised by the International Department are spread over the spectrum of overt and covert activities, including foreign Communist party activity, international Communist fronts, friendship societies, and clandestine radios.

Soviet propaganda makes use of Communist parties in power as well as those in Western and non-Communist nations. Thus, in 1979, the Belgian section of the World Peace Council (WPC), which is controlled by the Belgian Communist party, was instructed to organize front activity on the disarmament issue, with three distinct rallies to be organized immediately. The Belgian Communist party planned three meetings in October 1979, prepared the publication of a brochure on the theme "No missiles in Belgium," and held a mass demonstration for disarmament in December.[39] In the same year a CPSU Central Committee delegation to a West European Communist

Figure 7-1. Soviet Organizational Structure for Propaganda.

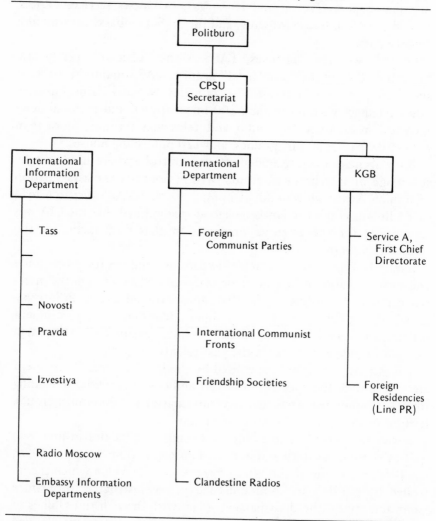

Source: Central Intelligence Agency, "Soviet Covert Action and Propaganda," in U.S. Congress, House Permanent Select Committee on Intelligence, *Soviet Covert Action* (The *Forgery Offensive*) (Washington, D.C.: Government Printing Office, 1980), p. 61.

party provided information on Soviet disarmament and defense issues with instructions that it should be used immediately in the Party's newspaper—the purpose being to ensure that the Party's press appeared to be as well informed as the non-Communist media.[40]

Soviet use of front organizations is an aspect of Soviet propaganda operations that has gained significant attention. These organizations claim non-Communist goals and therefore are, under certain circumstances, of more use than groupings with clear Communist affiliations. Such fronts accept virtually in toto Soviet foreign and defense policies, whether concerning disarmament or the invasion of Afghanistan.[41]

Front groups allow non-Soviet Bloc representatives to expound the Soviet position at a variety of international and regional conferences while being labeled independent or neutral. Four of these groups have qualified for official status with the United Nations. Such status permits their presence at worldwide U.N.-sponsored meetings.[42]

The priorities of such front groups are support of the Soviet positions on START, deployment of cruise and Pershing II missiles, and the neutron bomb. Major importance is also given to creating dissidence among the armed forces of the NATO countries. Hence, a March 1979 meeting in Malmo, Sweden was attended by "anti-militarist" delegates from France, West Germany, Belgium, the Netherlands, Sweden, Norway, Denmark, Italy, Austria, Spain, Finland, and U.S. forces in Germany. The keynote address was delivered by a WPC member calling for anti-militarist participation in a People's Assembly for European Security under WPC sponsorship and for continued organizational work among anti-militarist groups.[43]

The WPC is the best known of the front groups and is one of the four awarded official U.N. status. The WPC was founded in 1949 as the World Committee of Partisans for Peace and adopted its present title in 1950, the same year it was expelled from its French base for what the French government called "fifth column activities." It first moved to Prague and then to Vienna in 1954, where it remained until 1957. In 1957 it was banned by the Austrian interior minister for "activities directed against the Austrian state" but continued to operate there until 1968 under the cover of the International Institute for Peace. In that year it moved to Helsinki, its present location.[44]

The WPC was created to support Soviet national defense and international military objectives and foreign policy through worldwide campaigns. In addition, it was to coordinate the activities of other fronts. It presently has affiliates in approximately 130 countries. Directives from the CPSU to the WPC are routed through the Soviet Committee for the Defense of Peace, a propaganda and liaison organization. An employee of the International Department, Oley Kharkhardin, is Vice-Chairman of the committee. The committee directs the activities of the WPC headquarters and arranges for Soviet and East European financing of WPC activities.[45]

The WPC stages major events approximately every three years. The majority of participants at these peace assembles are Soviet and East European Communist party members, representatives of foreign Communist parties, and representatives of other Soviet-backed international fronts. According to the U.S. State Department, the discussions are "usually confined to inequities of Western socioeconomic systems and attacks on the military and foreign policies of the United States and other "imperialist, fascist nations." Resolutions advocating policies favored by the Soviet Union and other Communist nations are passed by acclamation, and any attempts by non-Communist delegates to discuss or criticize Soviet actions such as the invasion of Afghanistan are rejected as anti-Soviet propaganda or interference in Soviet internal affairs.[46]

The yearly budget of the WPC runs to about $49,380,000—which includes $600,000 in salaries for its forty-five-person staff; $150,000 for administration; $230,000 for travel; $110,000 for publications; $31,400,000 for public meetings; and $6,000,000 for in-house meetings.[47]

The other three U.N.-certified organizations are the World Federation of Trade Unions (WFTU), World Federation of Democratic Youth (WFDY), and the International Union of Students (IUS). The WFTU was originally formed by the British Trades Union Congress, American Congress of Industrial Organizations, and the Soviet All-Union Central Council of Trade Unions, but by 1949 all non-Communist Western trade unions had left over the policies of the federation.[48] The purposes of the federation were to consolidate trade unions throughout the world under Soviet control, to conduct or support strikes in non-Communist countries, and to serve as a major Soviet propaganda outlet.[49]

As with the WPC, the WFTU was expelled from Paris and Austria in succession. In 1951 the French government charged the WFTU with conducting "subversive activities" and expelled its headquarters staff from Paris. In 1956 it was expelled from Austria for "endangering Austrian neutrality."[50] Presently headquarted in Prague, it is second to the WPC in size (with a staff of thirty) and budget (approximately $8,575,000).[51] The WFTU has shown some slight independence from the Soviet line. Although it supported the Soviet invasion of Hungary in 1956, it was silent on the invasion of Czechoslovakia and events in Poland in 1981.[52]

The WFDY is headquarted in Budapest and has a membership of 150 million spread over 110 countries. Like the WFTU, it was formed in 1945. Its purposes are to support Soviet policy, oppose the activities of non-Communist youth organizations, promote Soviet disarmament in developing countries, and gain local acceptance for Soviet policy in the Third World. It has the same size staff as the WFTU (thirty), but it has a smaller budget—$1,575,000.[53] The IUS is also headquartered in Prague with 118 member organizations that have 10 million members. It was formed to complement the WFDY, conducting similar activities among students and often cosponsoring events such as world youth festivals. With a staff of twenty-five, it spends approximately $900,000 a year.[54]

Additional fronts include:

International Institute for Peace (IIP), Vienna. Member organizations in nine countries of West and East Europe. Formed in 1958 to provide a legal cover mechanism for the WPC secretariat to circumvent the WPC's expulsion from Austria. Now an independent entity.

Afro-Asian People's Organization (AAPSO), Cairo. AAPSO committees exist in most African and Asian countries. Formed in 1957 as an offshoot from the WPC to provide Third World channels for propaganda, political action, and support (including arms and paramilitary training) to national liberation movements and various political entities in opposition to their own governments.

Women's International Democratic Federation (WIDF), East Berlin. Formed in 1955 to support propaganda campaigns with special emphasis on women's and children's affairs.

International Organization of Journalists (IOJ), Prague. Membership over 150,000 in 112 countries. Formed in 1952 to "further revolutionary proletarian journalism," to act as arbiter and propagandist for the Soviet Union, and to participate in the breakdown and overthrow of capitalism and to discredit international news agencies.

International Association of Democratic Lawyers (IADL), Brussels. Membership approximately 25,000 in fifty-seven countries. Formed in 1946 to support Soviet propaganda and to issue "legal" statements and appeals on Soviet foreign policy priorities and to condemn non-Communist causes.

Christian Peace Conference (CPC), Prague. Membership in forty-eight countries but no totals available. Formed in 1958 to appeal to religious leaders and communities in support of Soviet propaganda and campaigns.

International Federation of Resistance Fighters (FIR), Vienna. Claims five million members in twenty-two countries (all but Israel are from Europe). Formed in 1951 to support Soviet initiatives on disarmament.

World Federation of Scientific Workers (WFSW), Paris. Claims 400,000 members, affiliated groups in thirty-one countries, corresponding members in twenty-six countries, mostly Communist. Formed in 1946 to organize scientific activities on behalf of the Soviet Union.

International Radio and TV Organization (OIRT), Prague. Formed in 1946 in Brussels by twenty-eight radio organizations in Europe and Africa. Most non-Communist countries have left OIRT. However, it still operates from Prague as a "non-governmental" organization aimed at influencing Third World countries.[55]

Table 7–1 lists the budgets of the above-named fronts, broken down by category.

Another mechanism used by the Soviet Union are Soviet binational organizations. Called Soviet Friendship and Cultural Societies, they exist in approximately 80 nations. Their charter is "to spread a thorough and reliable knowledge of the culture, history, social structures and national law, the language and economy of the Soviet Union and its significance for world peace."[56]

Thus, the National Council of American-Soviet Friendship (NCASF) was established in 1943 by the U.S. Communist party. The NCASF has been urged by the Soviet Union to concentrate its activities on arms control, disarmament, and the peace movement. Thus, "local chapters were instructed by national headquarters in April 1981 to join peace coalitions in their areas and to ensure that such matters as a freeze on nuclear weapons and Soviet attitudes toward peaceful co-existence are brought to the attention of the American people."[57]

The most covert of the International Department's propaganda activities are the clandestine radio operations. Such radios are located in the Soviet Union or in Bloc countries but are represented as being in the target countries. Two clandestine radios broadcast to Turkey—"Our Radio" and "Voice of the Turkish Communist Party"—from Magdeburg, East Germany. The broadcasts to Turkey have generally followed the Soviet line on the policies of NATO member Turkey and seek to discredit the United States, NATO, and Western policies. The broadcasts have urged the ouster of a Justice party government and an end to the U.S. presence in Turkey.

Operating from the Baku area of the Soviet Union is the "National Voice of Iran" (NVOI). Apparently started in 1959, the NVOI has given the Soviets the capability to pursue a two-track policy toward both the Shah and the present government. Between the Shah's departure and the return of Khomeini, NVOI expanded its broadcast time and added a second daily program.[58]

In the aftermath of the hostage seizure of November 1979 it sought to incite Iranian mobs to further violence. Subsequently, it has attempted to link the CIA with a terrorist organization responsible for a number of assassinations of prominent Iranian political and religious leaders.[59] Since February 1983 it has grown increasingly critical of the Khomeini regime. It has condemned Tehran's suppression of the Communist Tudeh party, urged the release of Tudeh leaders, and warned that "groundless charges of espionage" against them will damage Iranian-Soviet relations.[60]

The Soviets also operate a clandestine radio station, Radio Ba Yi, aimed at the People's Republic of China. Radio Ba Yi (August First Radio) purports to broadcast from China and speak for dissident members of the Chinese armed forces. The radio attempts to sound patriotic, strongly Communist, anti-Western, and sympathetic to

Table 7-1. Soviet Front Organizations, Budget by Category.

Front	Staff	Salaries	Administration
World Peace Council _____	45	$600,000	$150,000
International Institute for Peace _____	20	100,000	50,000
World Federation of Trade Unions _____	30	450,000	100,000
International Union of Students _____	25	400,000	75,000
World Federation of Democratic Youth_____	30	450,000	100,000
Women's International Democratic Federation __	15	50,000	10,000
International Association of Democratic Lawyers __	10	50,000	10,000
World Federation of Scientific Workers _____	10	50,000	10,000
International Organization of Journalists _____	15	75,000	15,000
International Federation of Resistance Fighters _____	10	30,000	5,000
Christian Peace Council _____	10	75,000	15,000
Afro-Asian People's Solidarity Organization __	27	500,000	200,000
International Radio and TV Organization _____	5	15,000	10,000
Total _____	253	$2,845,000	$745,000

Source: Central Intelligence Agency, "Soviet Covert Action and Propaganda," in U.S. Congress, House Permanent Select Committee on Intelligence, *Soviet Covert Action (The Forgery Offensive)* (Washington, D.C.: Government Printing Office, 1980), p. 60.

Army gripes. Thus, it charged that Peking insulted the armed forces by giving the military last priority in the four modernizations—after industry, agriculture, and science.[61]

It has accused Deng-Hsiao-Ping of creating a personality cult and letting "degenerate" Western values into China. Its main target, though, is U.S.-China relations. When Ronald Reagan visited China in April 1984 it likened the visit to "the weasel going to pay his

Table 7-1. continued

Travel	Publications	Public Meetings	In-House Meetings	Total
$230,000	$11,000,000	$31,400,000	$6,000,000	$49,380,000
10,000	100,000	—	—	10,160,000
225,000	2,000,000	2,800,000	3,000,000	11,350,000
100,000	30,000	200,000	100,000	905,000
75,000	100,000	500,000	350,000	1,575,000
50,000	30,000	150,000	100,000	390,000
10,000	10,000	10,000	10,000	100,000
10,000	10,000	10,000	10,000	100,000
25,000	100,000	200,000	100,000	515,000
10,000	20,000	50,000	10,000	125,000
10,000	20,000	40,000	50,000	210,000
100,000	10,000	300,000	150,000	1,260,000
10,000	5,000	5,000	5,000	50,000
$865,000	$13,345,000	$35,365,000	$9,885,000	$63,050,000

respects to the hen"—an old Chinese proverb for treachery. It has played up the size of continuing U.S. military sales to Taiwan and accused Defense Secretary Caspar Weinberger of describing Chinese as impolite and odious yellow-skinned dogs.[62]

The yearly expense of propaganda activities runs to about $3 billion, broken down as shown in Table 7-2. Of course, part of this $3 billion—especially as it relates to TASS, *Pravda*, and *Izvestiya*—involves domestic propaganda, while only part of Service A's $150 million budget is applied to purely propaganda activities.

Table 7-2. Soviet Propaganda Budget, 1979.

Organization/Activity	Millions ($)
CPSU International Department	100
CPSU International Information Department	50
TASS	550
Novosti (APN)	500
Pravda	250
Izvestiya	200
New Times and other periodicals	200
Radio Moscow foreign service	700
Press sections in Soviet Embassies	50
Clandestine radios	100
International Communist Fronts	63
Subsidies to foreign Communist parties	50
KGB's Service A	50
Covert Action Operations by KGB's foreign residencies	100
Support to National Liberation Fronts	200
Special campaigns in 1979, including anti-Nato TNF modernization campaign	200
Total	3,363

Source: "Soviet Covert Action and Propaganda," in U.S. Congress, House Permanent Committee on Intelligence, *Soviet Covert Action (The Forgery Offensive)* (Washington, D.C.: Government Printing Office, 1980), p. 60.

Propaganda assets can be mobilized in a very dramatic and visible way in the case of emergencies or situations of particular importance. Thus, during 1977 the Soviet Union initiated an intensive worldwide campaign against U.S. production of the enhanced radiation warhead, and in 1979 the Soviet-directed WPC began planning for massive demonstrations against NATO's response to Soviet SS-20 deployment.

Communist front groups mobilized in support of anti-enhanced radiation warhead campaign activities included peace councils in various East European states, which held protest meetings and passed resolutions. In Istanbul a peace committee demonstrated in front of a U.S. consulate general; in Accra a group, described as "completely out of local character," delivered a protest letter to the U.S. embassy. In Stuttgart, Frankfurt, and Dusseldorf front groups delivered notes to U.S. consulates general, and a front group in Lima, Peru sent a protest to the United Nations.[63]

In the spring of 1981 the Soviet Union advised the WPC to focus its attention on current and planned activities relating to the modernization campaign. It was suggested that the WPC concentrate its efforts on broadening the publication of anti-NATO themes in the Western media and organize an international meeting of media representatives "to discuss the role of the mass media in publicizing the dangers inherent in the arms buildup." In August 1981 national affiliates of the WPC were instructed to accelerate the "peace offensive" to attempt to involve more unions, churches, and civic organizations.[64]

Front groups were also employed to stage conferences in support of the Soviet position at the U.N. Special Session on Disarmament, held in New York from May 23 to June 28, 1977. Thus, the WPC, through a subsidiary front (the International Liaison Forum of Peace Forces), organized a symposium in Vienna on "Nuclear Energy and the Arms Race" in collaboration with the U.N.'s International Atomic Energy Agency. During the Second Special Session on disarmament in 1982, front groups such as the U.S. Peace Council and the National Council of American-Soviet Friendship were among the sponsors of a June 12 rally and attempted to tone down the official rally call so that it was predominantly critical of the United States.[65]

AGENTS OF INFLUENCE

The term "agent of influence" has been employed in an elastic and sometimes misleading sense. Some individuals may be labeled agents of influence for no reason other than expressing or supporting policies that some consider too favorable to the Soviet Union. Others may by no means be agents in the conventional sense—people hired to carry out work assigned them by a case officer—and may not consider themselves to be agents of any kind. They may not be aware that the Soviet diplomat they are in touch with is a KGB officer and may be "agents" only in the eyes of their Soviet friends. Finally, there are those who are recruited and possibly paid to perform influence operations.

Thus, the term "agent of influence" can cover a broad spectrum of social relationships, from casual luncheon partners to close personal friends. The "agents" may be politicians, government servants, industrialists, bankers, journalists, or university professors. In many of these cases, the KGB has been assigned the essentially diplomatic function of maintaining contact simply because the Soviet Foreign Ministry has not been judged up to the task.[66]

According to Harry Rositzke, true agents of influence who have come to light include a British businessman helpful in evading export restrictions, one of the German negotiators on a truck-plant deal with the Soviet Union, a New Zealand cabinet minister, an Italian television director, and the wife of a Western European prime minister.[67]

A prominent agent of influence was Pierre-Charles Pathé, a French journalist who acted as a KGB agent for twenty years until he was arrested in 1980 at seventy years of age. Pathé apparently first came to Soviet attention in 1959 when he wrote an extremely favorable article about the Soviet Union.[68] In 1960 he was introduced to a Soviet employee of a U.N. organization who recruited him to act as a source of information and as an asset who could put Soviet propaganda material in the Western press.[69]

In 1961 Pathé began to publish a confidential journal entitled *Center for Scientific, Economic and Political Information*, for which he received Soviet encouragement and financial assistance. Additionally, Pathé wrote for several other French publications under the pseudonym Charles Morland. Rather than being provided with completed articles, Pathé was given general instructions and thematic guidelines on which to base his writings.[70]

In 1976 Pathé began a new biweekly newsletter, *Synthesis*, which was partly funded by the Soviets. The newsletter's main topics concerned French, European, and international political, economic, scientific, and military issues. At its height the newsletter reached 70 percent of the French Chamber of Deputies (299 deputies) and 47 percent of the French Senate (139 Senators) as well as forty-one journalists, fourteen ambassadors, and only seven private individuals.[71]

The main objective of the articles appearing in *Synthesis* was to exacerbate or create a split between and among the United States and Europe. In one article Pathé asserted that many French politicians were of the view that NATO no longer served any purpose. In another he raised doubts about U.S. willingness to defend Europe.

With regard to economic issues, *Synthesis* articles claimed that U.S. restrictions on landing rights for the Concorde were part of an attempt by the United States to maintain a quasi-monopoly of the airlines industry. They also portrayed the United States as more opposed to free trade than any other member of the General Agree ment on Tariffs and Trade and as doing everything possible to maintain an ineffective Common Market.[72]

PARAMILITARY, TERRORIST, AND SABOTAGE OPERATIONS

Along with assassinations, involvement in paramilitary, terrorist, and sabotage operations represents one end of the spectrum of active measures. Within the paramilitary category, one can distinguish between direct involvement in such activities and support and training for national liberation and other groups that engage in such activities.

The most recent known KGB paramilitary operation took place on December 27, 1979. After the Politburo was convinced by the KGB that Afghani President Hafizullah Amin had to be eliminated, his assassination was approved. However, attempts by a KGB illegal failed and a more open operation was approved.[73]

On December 26, 1979 Soviet paratroopers began arriving at Kabul airport. The following day an armored column moved out of the airport and toward the palace. It consisted of a few hundred Soviet commandos, including a specially trained assault group of KGB officers. When the force reached the palace, the special troops attacked from three sides with Colonel Bayernov of the KGB leading the assault.[74]

National liberation movements can be characterized as those that attempt to seize power in a specific country. They may or may not engage in terrorist acts (defined below). The Soviets have clearly stated their support for such movements, often materially. For example, in October 1979 when the Patriotic Front (Rhodesia) had temporarily withdrawn from the negotiations over a Rhodesian settlement, the Soviet Union informed the Zimbabwe African People's Union (ZAPU) that it was prepared to provide whatever amount of military aid was necessary to achieve a military victory in Rhodesia, if the Patriotic Front decided to withdraw from the negotiations permanently.[75]

In early November officers from the Main Political Directorate of the Soviet Armed Forces arrived in Lusaka to conduct a training course in covert political action for senior Zimbabwe People's Revolutionary Army officers. The course was to include briefings on the recruitment of agents of influence able to subvert balloting, the recruitment of agitators, and other tactics.[76]

A more dramatic effort had the government of Mexico as its target. The KGB effort began in 1963 and continued until 1971 with the objective of establishing a Moscow-directed guerilla group that would lead a popular movement against the government, employing violent tactics.[77] The plan developed from the efforts of the Soviet embassy in Mexico City to recruit university students through either of two organizations: the Mexican Communist party or the Institute of Mexican-Russian Cultural Exchange. One student, selected as the key individual in the plan, was sent to Moscow in 1963. After four years of training, the Movement of Revolutionary Action (MAR) was established among Mexican students in Moscow.[78]

Those recruited into the MAR were sent to North Korea for training during the summer of 1970. By September the trainees, of whom there were more than forty, were back in Mexico. Their initial tasks were to recruit new members as well as set up training bases and safe houses. They were also to engage in "expropriations" of bank funds; procurements of weapons from the police and Army; coordination of bombings and terrorist attacks; and the sabotaging of power lines, railways, and factories. All these actions were intended to arouse the populace, create an atmosphere of emergency, and provoke an extreme reaction by the government.[79]

Before the campaign really got underway the accidental discovery of a MAR safe house led to the arrest of several MAR members. Subsequent arrests and interrogations led to complete exposure of the operation and the exact role of the KGB.[80]

It is Soviet support for the Palestine Liberation Organization (PLO) that has attracted the most notice and raised the question of possible Soviet support to terrorist groups. There is no doubt that the Soviet Union has trained between 2,000 and 3,000 Palestinians.[81] These have been trained at several sites in the Soviet Union in addition to sites in Eastern Europe. Sites in the Soviet Union include Simferpol in the Crimea (for ground troops), a site near Moscow (for pilots), and a GRU site at Doupov.[82]

The PLO has in turn supported groups that would clearly fall into the terrorist category—where terrorism is defined as the "threat or use of violence [against innocent individuals] for political symbolic effect aimed at achieving a psychological impact on target groups wider than its immediate victim."[83]

The question of whether there is direct Soviet involvement with such groups has been a source of controversy. Many of the charges of direct Soviet involvement seem to come from General Jan Sejna, a former Czechoslovakian military officer who defected to the United States in 1968. At that time he apparently informed the CIA and other Western intelligence services that the Soviets had trained terrorist groups like the Baader-Meinhof Gang and the Red Brigades. However, according to U.S. intelligence officials, there is little evidence to back up his assertion of direct Soviet involvement.[84]

Rather, in the judgment of intelligence personnel—in line with Khrushchev's support for wars of national liberation—the Soviet Union established training and support centers in the Soviet Union and in other East Bloc countries for Libyans, Iraqis, North Koreans, Angolans, PLO members, and others for the purpose of aiding those groups with training in guerilla techniques and weapons. Some of those centers were in turn employed by the Libyans, PLO, and others to train groups like the Baader-Meinhof Gang, the Red Brigades, and the Japanese Red Army.[85]

Thus, while some intelligence officials say that Soviet complicity is "clear," others believe that the centers created for support of national liberation movements have turned into Frankenstein monsters that could not be controlled. The later groups point to evidence that the Soviet leadership has talked about the uncontrollability of the groups and have referred to their members as "adventurists."[86]

The judgment of Brian Jenkins, a RAND Corporation expert on terrorism, is that the Soviet Union provides direct and indirect support, including arms and training, to many groups that have employed terrorist tactics. He finds no convincing evidence, however, that the Soviets are orchestrating terrorism worldwide.[87] Likewise, speaking of terrorist groups, the Undersecretary of State for Management has stated that "there are interrelationships among them. They change from time to time in different ways. They doubtless exchange information. But to be able to say that all of those are then somehow directly linked back to the Soviet Union I think is probably overstating it."[88]

In the event of war, the Soviet Union would employ special purposes forces controlled by the GRU to carry out a variety of sabotage operations. These forces, known as SPETSNAZ, conduct peacetime reconnaissance programs to meet wartime intelligence requirements. In wartime, SPETSNAZ troops would operate behind enemy lines for extended periods of time.[89] These troops would be tasked with:

- hunting down and assassinating the enemy's political and military leaders;
- seeking out the enemy's nuclear facilities and either designating them as targets for Soviet aircraft and missiles or destroying them by independent action;
- naturalizing command systems by acting against command centers, staffs, and lines of communication;
- destroying important targets such as airfields, naval bases, and air defense installations in enemy territory; and
- disrupting the enemy's power system, the highest priority targets being power stations, oil and gas storage centers, pipelines, electricity power lines, and transformer stations.[90]

The peacetime strength of the SPETSNAZ forces is estimated at 27,000 to 30,000.[91]

ASSASSINATIONS

One form of active measures that the Soviet Union has resorted to frequently in the past is assassination. The targets of past assassinations fall into two basic categories: activist emigrés and renegades or defectors from Soviet official circles, mainly the intelligence services.

The most notorious Soviet assassination operation was that directed against Leon Trotsky. Trotsky had lived in exile in Turkey, France, and Norway since his expulsion from the Soviet Union in 1929. In January 1937 he found political asylum in Mexico. During his entire exile, the Soviet intelligence service kept close track of his activities—movements, associations, writings, lectures, and organizational efforts.[92]

After one attempt on his life in Mexico in January 1938, Trotsky had heavy security provided by his own guards as well as the Mexican police. The task of killing him was assigned to Leonid Eitingon, a senior KGB official. The first attempt by Eitingon employed the services of a Mexican Communist painter named Sigueiros in a straight-forward terrorist attack.[93]

On May 23, 1940 Sigueiros, disguised as a Mexican Army major, raided Trotsky's villa with a goon squad of twenty men. Equipped with submachine guns, incendiaries, and a dynamite bomb, they cut the telephone lines, subdued the Mexican police guards and an American sentry, unleashed their machine guns on the bedroom, and left the dynamite bomb—which did not explode. Trotsky escaped with a slight wound in his right leg.[94]

The next attempt was to be an inside job. It revolved around Ramon Mercador, son of a Spanish Communist woman who had worked with Eitingon in the guerilla operations set up by the People's Commissariat for Internal Affairs (NKVD) in the Spanish civil war. Mercador was provided with a false passport under the name of Jacson and placed under the direction of the NKVD legal resident in New York. Accepted in New York's left-wing circles, Mercador became a friend of a devoted follower of Trotsky, through whom he gained entrée to Trotsky's household.[95]

On his last visit on August 20, 1940 he entered Trotsky's study for the ostensible purpose of having him critique an article he had written. However, he was equipped with a revolver, a dagger, and a short ice ax in his raincoat pocket and proceeded to crush Trotsky's skull with the ice ax as he began to read the article. Trotsky died the next day.[96]

The following year Walter Krivitsky was found shot to death in a Washington hotel room—a case of murder or suicide. Krivitsky had been a GRU resident in Holland who sought asylum in France. A hit team was dispatched to Paris to murder Krivitsky, his wife, and son but Krivitsky and his family eluded them. He had warned that should he ever turn up a "suicide" it would really be a case of murder.[97]

During the 1950s the Soviet assassination targets were emigrés. One of the first targets was the operations chief of the People's Labor League (NTS), a group of ethnic Russians devoted to the destruction of the Soviet regime by building secret cells within the Soviet Union itself. The NTS "was particularly troublesome because of its efforts to contact and recruit Soviet soldiers stationed in East Germany and Soviet officials stationed abroad."[98]

The operations chief was fortunate in that his intended assassin defected rather than carry out his mission. Less fortunate were Stefan Bandera and Lev Rebet. The first victim was Rebet, a Ukrainian nationalist emigré. On October 10, 1957 Rebet was assassinated by a spray of prussic acid from a seven-inch-long noiseless "pistol." The inhaled gas had the same effect as sniffing glue—the severe contraction of blood vessels so that Rebet's heart simply stopped. Death was attributed to a heart attack.[99]

In April 1959 the assassin of Rebet, Bogdan Stashinsky was called to Moscow and assigned the task of assassinating Stefan Bandera, also a Ukrainian nationalist emigré and director of the Organization of Ukrainian Nationalist Revolutionaries. In October 1959 Stashinsky killed Bandera by the same method as Rebet. This time, however, a careful autopsy detected traces of prussic acid in the stomach, indicating murder.[100]

More importantly, Stashinsky grew remorseful and turned himself in to West German authorities. His trial, beginning in October 1962, became a worldwide sensation and a propaganda disaster for the Soviet Union. In 1964 the Soviet Union signed a protocol with the Bulgarian security service, turning over to them the responsibility for "wet affairs."

However, it appears that the KGB took on itself the direct responsibility of one assassination attempt—that of Hafizullah Amin. After deciding that Amin needed to be eliminated, a KGB illegal, one of Amin's personal cooks, was assigned the job. He attempted to poison Amin's food, but Amin kept switching his food and drink. The job had to be carried out by the KGB-GRU commandos who stormed the palace on December 27, 1979.[101]

NOTES TO CHAPTER 7

1. Hikaru Kerns, "Red Faces in Tokyo," *Far Eastern Economic Review*, March 24, 1983, p. 18.
2. U.S. Congress, House Permanent Select Committee on Intelligence, *Soviet Covert Action* (The Forgery Offensive) (Washington, D.C.: U.S. Government Printing Office, 1980), p. 19.
3. Central Intelligence Agency, "Soviet Covert Action and Propaganda," in Ibid., pp. 173–75.
4. Ibid.
5. Ibid.
6. Ibid.
7. Ibid.

8. Ibid.
9. Ibid.
10. "The Mysterious Supplement B; Sticking It to the Host Country," *Covert Action Information Bulletin* 3 (January 1979): 9.
11. Central Intelligence Agency, "Soviet Covert Action and Propaganda," p. 66.
12. Ibid.
13. Ibid.
14. U.S. Congress, House Permanent Select Committee on Intelligence, *Soviet Active Measures* (Washington, D.C.: U.S. Government Printing Office, 1982), pp. 74–75.
15. Ibid.
16. Ibid.
17. *Toronto Star*, September 28, 1972.
18. "Special Intelligence Collection Requirement," copy in possession of the author.
19. Central Intelligence Agency, "Soviet Covert Action and Propaganda," in U.S. Congress, House Permanent Select Committee on Intelligence, *Soviet Covert Action*, p. 122.
20. Forged document entitled "National Security Council Interdepartmental Group for Africa, Study in Response to Presidential Review Memorandum NSC-46 Black Africa and the U.S. Black Movement."
21. Ibid.
22. U.S. Congress, House Permanent Select Committee on Intelligence, *Soviet Active Measures*, p. 111.
23. Ibid., p. 87.
24. Ibid.
25. Ibid., p. 105.
26. Ibid.
27. Central Intelligence Agency, "Soviet Covert Action and Propaganda," in U.S. Congress, House Permanent Select Committee on Intelligence, *Soviet Covert Action*, p. 145.
28. Ibid.
29. Ibid., p. 154.
30. "Reagan Tape May Be Soviet Fake, U.S. Says," *Washington Post*, July 30, 1983, p. A17; U.S. Congress, House Permanent Select Committee on Intelligence, *Soviet Active Measures*, p. 133.
31. U.S. Department of State, Special Report No. 110, *Soviet Active Measures* (Washington, D.C.: DOS 1983), p. 3.
32. Stephen Engelberg, "If It's Too Bad to Be True, It Could Be 'Disinformation,'" *New York Times*, November 18, 1984, p. E3.
33. Glenn Frankel, "Officials See Soviets between the Lines of Phony Stories about U.S. in Africa," *Washington Post*, December 3, 1983, p. A22.

34. U.S. Department of State, Special Report No. 110, *Soviet Active Measures*, p. 4.
35. Central Intelligence Agency, "Soviet Covert Action and Propaganda," in U.S. Congress, House Permanent Select Committee on Intelligence, *Soviet Covert Action*, p. 61.
36. Ibid., p. 76.
37. Ibid., p. 77.
38. Ibid.
39. Ibid., p. 81.
40. Ibid., p. 82.
41. Ibid., pp. 79–81.
42. Ibid.
43. Ibid., p. 81.
44. Department of State, "World Peace Council: Instrument of Soviet Foreign Policy," *Foreign Affairs Note* (Washington, D.C.: DOS April 1982).
45. Central Intelligence Agency, "Soviet Covert Action and Propaganda," in U.S. Congress, House Permanent Select Committee on Intelligence, *Soviet Covert Action*, p. 80; Director of Central Intelligence, "Soviet Active Measures," in House Permanent Select Committee on Intelligence, *Soviet Active Measures*, p. 39.
46. Department of State, "The World Peace Council's Peace Assembles," *Foreign Affairs Note*, May 1983.
47. Central Intelligence Agency, "Soviet Covert Action and Propaganda," in U.S. Congress, House Permanent Select Committee on Intelligence, *Soviet Covert Action*, p. 79.
48. Department of State, "World Federation of Trade Unions: Soviet Foreign Policy Tool," *Foreign Affairs Note*, August 1983.
49. Central Intelligence Agency, "Soviet Covert Action and Propaganda," in U.S. Congress, House Permanent Select Committee on Intelligence, *Soviet Covert Action*, p. 80 n. 29.
50. Department of State, "World Federation of Trade Unions: Soviet Foreign Policy Tool."
51. Central Intelligence Agency, "Soviet Covert Action and Propaganda," in U.S. Congress, House Permanent Select Committee on Intelligence, *Soviet Covert Action*, pp. 79, 80 n. 29.
52. Department of State, "World Federation of Trade Unions: Soviet Foreign Policy Tool."
53. Central Intelligence Agency, "Soviet Covert Action and Propaganda," in U.S. Congress, House Permanent Select Committee on Intelligence, *Soviet Covert Action*, pp. 79, 80 n. 29.
54. Ibid.
55. Ibid.
56. Ibid.

57. Ibid.; "FBI Intelligence Divison on Soviet Active Measures Relating to the U.S. Peace Movement," *Congressional Record*, March 24, 1983, pp. H 1793–1797.
58. Central Intelligence Agency, "Soviet Covert Action and Propaganda," in U.S. Congress, House Permanent Select Committee on Intelligence, *Soviet Covert Action*, p. 78.
59. Ibid.
60. Department of State, Special Report No. 110, *Soviet Active Measures*, p. 6.
61. Christopher Wren, "Peking Finds the Airwaves Filled with Unkind Remarks," *New York Times*, May 7, 1984, p. A4.
62. Ibid.
63. Central Intelligence Agency, "Soviet Covert Action and Propaganda," in U.S. Congress, House Permanent Select Committee on Intelligence, *Soviet Covert Action*, pp. 75–76.
64. U.S. Arms Control and Disarmament Agency, *Soviet Propaganda Campaign Against NATO* (Washington, D.C.: ACDA, 1983), p. A4.
65. "FBI Intelligence Division on Soviet Active Measures Relating to the U.S. Peace Movement."
66. Harry Rositzke, *The KGB: The Eyes of Russia* (Garden City, New York: Doubleday, 1981), p. 193.
67. Ibid.
68. Richard H. Shultz and Roy Godson, *Dezinformatsia: Active Measures in Soviet Strategy* (New York: Pergamon-Brassey's, 1984), pp. 133–34.
69. Rositzke, *The KGB*, p. 193.
70. Shultz and Godson, *Dezinformatsia*, p. 134.
71. Ibid.
72. Ibid., pp. 139, 142.
73. "Coups and Killings in Kabul," *Time*, November 22, 1982, pp. 33–34.
74. Ibid.
75. Central Intelligence Agency, "Soviet Covert Action and Propaganda," in U.S. Congress, House Permanent Select Committee on Intelligence, *Soviet Covert Action*, p. 85.
76. Ibid.
77. Rositzke, *The KGB*, p. 226.
78. Ibid., p. 227.
79. Ibid.
80. Ibid.
81. John Vinocur, "The KGB on the Offensive and the West Begins Striking Back," *New York Times*, July 24, 1983, p. 1.
82. Henry Kamm, "Israelis and Germans Doubt Bulgarian Link in Attack on Pope," *New York Times*, December 18, 1983, p. 10.

83. U.S. Congress, Senate Committee on the Judiciary, *Terrorism: Origins, Direction and Support* (Washington, D.C.: U.S. Government Printing Office, 1981), p. 8.

84. Leslie Gelb, "Soviet Terror Ties Called Outdated," *New York Times*, October 18, 1981, p. 9.

85. Ibid.

86. Ibid.

87. Brian Jenkins, *International Terrorism: Choosing the Right Target* (Santa Monica, Calif.: RAND Corporation, 1981).

88. U.S. Congress, Senate Committee on Foreign Relations, *International Terrorism* (Washington, D.C.: U.S. Government Printing Office, 1981), p. 52.

89. Department of Defense, *Soviet Military Power—1984* (Washington, D.C.: U.S. Government Printing Office, 1984), pp. 69–70.

90. Viktor Suvorov, "Spetsnaz: The Soviet Union's Special Forces," *Military Review*, March 1984, pp. 30–46.

91. Ibid.

92. Rositzke, *The KGB*, p. 106.

93. Ibid.

94. Ibid.

95. Ibid.

96. Ibid.

97. Ibid., p. 112.

98. Ibid., p. 104.

99. Ibid., p. 109.

100. Ibid.

101. "Coups and Killings in Kabul."

8 ACQUISITION OF ADVANCED TECHNOLOGY

Soviet attempts to acquire and benefit from advanced Western technology date back to at least the 1930s and Stalin's industrialization program, the program being motivated, in part, by Stalin's interpretation of Russian history and the damaging consequences of "falling behind." Then, as now, the technology sought included civilian technology, dual-use technology, and military technology.

There has been a significant increase in recent years in the emphasis on the acquisition of Western advanced technology. The major advances in the computer laser, and microelectronic fields, among others, have led to significant improvements in the methods and efficiency of producing consumer and industrial goods. Since the advances cannot be realized through a more intensive use of labor or rubles, even if that option was considered acceptable, the Soviets must seek to acquire existing technology from the West.

The acquisition is of utmost importance not because of its impact on civilian and heavy industrial goods production but because its military significance is enormous, producing a quantum leap in capabilities. Thus, in the area of strategic nuclear weaponry, technological advances have enhanced, in a major fashion, capabilities—in terms of accuracy, retargeting, attack assessment and command, control, and communications—all of which, for better or worse, have permitted strategists to think in terms of selective targeting options, counterforce targeting, and prolonged nuclear war. The accuracy foreseen for a variety of weapons systems has even led to suggestions that non-nuclear warheads could take the place of nuclear warheads in some circumstances.[1]

At the same time, advances in military-related technology may, in the future, threaten the invulnerability of submarines—through enhanced sonar/acoustic technology or the ability to image in clear ocean water via laser technology.[2] Likewise, the viability of ballistic missile defenses may hinge on a combination of advanced laser technology and computer capabilities.

There are five ways in which militarily relevant technology might be acquired, according to Peter Sharfman:

- legal transfers made possible by the open nature of Western society;

- legal transfers occurring through purchase of technologies of a general license;

- legal transfers through purchase of technologies under a validated license;

- illegal transfer through purchase; and

- illegal transfer through industrial espionage or the actual theft of classified materials.[3]

The last two ways may be required because the United States and its European allies and Japan place restrictions on the technology that can legally be exported to the Soviet Union and Soviet Bloc states. Operating via both national institutions (e.g., the Department of Commerce) and international institutions (e.g., the Paris-based Coordinating Committee for Multilateral Export Controls—COCOM), an attempt is made to distinguish between items of technology that can be exported to the Soviet Union without damaging Western security and those that cannot.

ACQUISITION APPARATUS

Given the high stakes involved, it is not surprising that the Soviet Union has a major and well-planned national-level program for the acquisition of advanced technology—a program involving legal and illegal methods and involving both overt organizations such as the Ministry of Foreign Trade and covert organizations such as the KGB.

Soviet foreign trade organizations, although quasi-independent entities, are partially subordinated to the Ministry of Foreign Trade, and their activities are coordinated by the ministry. The foreign trade organizations have responsibilities with regard to legal and illegal acquisitions and purchases.[4]

The State Committee for Science and Technology (GKNT) is the primary actor in arranging government-to-government science and technology agreements to facilitate access to and acquisition of established and new technologies, including those just emerging from Western universities, laboratories, and high technology firms.[5] Within the GKNT the Technical Center acts as a clearinghouse for technology acquisition and exploitation activities. The center is responsible for collecting the requirements and reports submitted to the Military-Industrial Commission (VPK) by the defense industry ministries and for the intelligence information and material acquired by the collection agencies.[6]

The requirements collected by the center are compiled into a book entitled *Coordinated Requests for Technological Information* and known informally as the "Red Book." The Red Book constitutes a "shopping list" for Soviet intelligence officers, detailing specific items to be acquired, such as microelectronic equipment, radar, and super minicomputers. According to a West German Interior Ministry report, the items are divided into twenty-six chapters such as "Theoretical Physics," "Lasers," and "Atomic Technology" and one chapter that specifies "non-secretive, seemingly harmless items that the Soviet Union appears highly interested in."[7]

On the covert side, as noted in Chapter 2, both the KGB and the GRU have major responsibilities for the acquisition of classified or embargoed technology. Part of these responsibilities are fulfilled by the placement of intelligence officers in overt organizations. Thus, the GRU has made substantial use of the GKNT, and the First Deputy Chairman of the Soviet Chamber of Commerce, Yevgeniy P. Pitovranov, is a KGB general who was the KGB resident in Peking in the early 1960s.[8]

As noted in Chapter 4, the KGB acquisition role abroad manifests itself in the form of an embassy line—Line X for the collection of scientific and technical intelligence, the highest priority for the specially trained Line X officers being the classified and embargoed technologies. A secondary priority is the open acquisition of unclassified documents and purchase of unrestricted machinery.[9]

LEGAL ACQUISITIONS

For a variety of reasons, the Soviet Union would prefer to acquire most advanced Western technology that it desires by legal methods. The difficulty and overall cost involved is certainly less. More importantly, legal acquisition allows for the possibility of repair or replacement, as well as ensuring a continued supply via long-term contracts. The only possible circumstances where covert acquisition would be advantageous are those where an advantage is obtained due to Western underestimation of Soviet capabilities in a particular area.

There are a variety of methods by which the Soviet Union can acquire technology legally. The simplest is the acquisition of unclassified journals or documents detailing scientific advances, industrial processes, and construction plans. Included may be some of the same journals discussed in Chapter 6—for example, *Aviation Week and Space Technology and Applied Optics*—as well as the documents available through the National Technical Information Service.

Another technique involves the purchase of an entire plant—the machinery, the assembly line, and so on. Once it has been set up in the Soviet Union it can be copied piece by piece. Other methods include use of Soviet- and East European-owned companies locally chartered in the United States; scientific technical agreements and exchanges (including student exchanges); participation in joint ventures and joint product development; attendance at scientific and technical conferences, trade shows, and exhibits; and the collection of unclassified documents.

Soviet- and East European-owned firms locally chartered in the United States number approximately 20. Near the end of the 1970s there were more than 300 similar firms in Western Europe. Particularly heavy concentrations of such firms appear in the United Kingdom, Sweden, Canada, and West Germany.[10] Such firms can be employed for both legal and illegal acquisitions.

Soviet-U.S. scientific exchanges began in 1958. In May 1972 the United States and Soviet Union signed an "Agreement on Cooperation in the Field of Science and Technology," which establishes the U.S.-U.S.S.R. Joint Commission on Science and Technology to conduct a broad range of scientific and technical efforts. Approximately

463 Soviet scientists were sponsored by various exchange programs and came to the United States in 1973. Of those, 60 were involved in agricultural studies, 34 in environmental protection studies, 116 in space studies, and 63 in health studies.[11]

Additionally, the Graduate Student/Young Faculty Exchange Program, administered by the International Research and Exchange Board (IREX), sponsors most of the Soviets involved in scientific and technical work that come to the United States for a full academic year. Among the Soviet participants there has been a growing trend toward concentration on technical subjects. In the years 1958–1968, 30 percent of those involved came to study in the social sciences and humanities. Between 1968 and 1973, 96 percent have been involved in the study of natural/physical science subjects.[12] In 1976–1977 a Russian scholar named S. A. Gubin studied the technology of fuel air explosives under an American professor who was also a consultant for the U.S. Navy. Gubin returned to the Soviet Union to perform similar studies.[13] In 1980 and 1981 more than a third of the program proposals were deemed unacceptable because of the possible technology loss that it was felt could occur.[14]

In addition to exchanges, acquisition can occur via the scientific and technical agreements between U.S. firms and Soviet ministries. The agreements are of a general nature: Rather than calling for the delivery of specific products or services, they call for cooperative development in certain fields. In 1972–73 U.S. firms that entered into cooperative agreements with Soviet organizations included Bechtel, Boeing, Control Data, Dresser Industries, General Dynamics, General Electric, Hewlett-Packard, ITT, Litton Industries, Monsanto, Occidental Petroleum, Singer, SRI, Tenneco, and Texas Eastern Transmission.[15]

The agreement with Boeing called for cooperation in the development of civil aviation and air transport; the agreement with General Dynamics involved shipbuilding, aircraft construction, and the manufacturing of telecommunications equipment and computers. An agreement with General Electric specified cooperation in the fields of power engineering, electronic engineering, and atomic power plants. Agreements with ITT and Singer called for cooperation in the areas of communications technology, electronic components, computers, electronic instruments, and textile equipment.[16]

Soviet commercial delegations to the United States have included representatives from a number of ministries with military functions, including the Ministry of Machine Building (which designs and manufactures ammunition, explosives, fuses, projectiles, and solid propellants); Ministry of Aviation Industry (military aircraft, aerodynamic missiles, and defensive ballistic missiles); Ministry of Shipbuilding (naval vessels, underwater weapons, and fire control systems); Ministry of Radio Industry (communication, navigational, and guidance equipment); and the Ministry of Electronic Industry (electronic components for military systems).[17] Many of these representatives attempt to visit small and medium-sized firms that are involved in developing new technologies.[18]

In some cases, the Soviets will use what is known as the "whipsaw" technique. A Soviet ministry will indicate to one or more companies that are competing for a contract that its competitors are prepared to provide certain information in their proposal. Unless the whipsawed company provides the same or additional information they will be eliminated from the competition.[19] Whatever the specific method of legal acquisition, such acquisitions generally have their greatest impact on the Soviets' broad industrial base and thus affect military technology on a relatively long-term basis. Thus, the Soviet Kama Truck Plant was built over a seven-year period with more than $1.5 billion worth of U.S. and West European automotive production equipment and technology.[20]

A large number of military-specification trucks (but no tanks) produced at the Kama plant in 1981 are now being used by Soviet forces in Afghanistan and by Soviet military units in Eastern Europe opposite NATO forces. Likewise, large Soviet purchases of printed circuit board technology and numerically controlled machine tools from the West have been employed in the military manufacturing sector.[21]

ILLEGAL ACQUISITIONS

Illegal acquisition can also be accomplished by a variety of means. Acquisition of classified government documents concerning scientific and technical matters can be attained in the same way other classified documents can be acquired—via theft or recruiting an agent, by whatever means, to provide those documents. With regard to unclassified documents concerning "sensitive" technologies employed by private corporations, agents can be recruited to commit industrial espionage. In a variant on false-flag procedures, a Soviet agent can pose as a representative of a competing firm, thus avoiding entirely the national issue.

Another means is smuggling illegally acquired documents or equipment from the United States to a safe location and then on to the Soviet Union. In some cases, equipment has been seized at U.S. airports shortly before it would have been shipped out of the United States—for example, a multispectral scanner that would enhance overhead reconnaissance capabilities.[22] In other cases, Soviet intelligence officers or trade officials have been expelled for seeking to make illegal purchases. In 1982 Canada expelled a Soviet assistant trade commissioner in Ottawa for offering a large sum of money to a Canadian businessman for information on fiber optics technology—a technology involving flexible glass strands that can transmit large numbers of simultaneous voice or data items by light. Likewise, a recently expelled Soviet diplomat based in the United States was seeking to buy information concerning military laser technology.[23]

The most sophisticated means of acquiring technology formally prohibited is via either third-country diversions or end-user diversions. Certain critical technologies are licensed for sale under the provision that no other companies or nations are granted access to the technology without U.S. approval. The Export Administration Act of 1979 requires exporting companies to insist on contracts with buyers of defense-sensitive products that prohibit reexport to the Soviet Bloc. Soviet attempts to evade those provisions involve both the setting up of bogus companies and enlisting the help of third parties. According to the CIA there are 300 companies engaged in diversionary schemes. Bogus companies have been set up in Holland, Austria, Switzerland, Canada, Finland, and France with names such as Analog Digital Techniques, Continental Technologies Corporation, and Continental Industries.[24]

One operation involved setting up a bogus company in Canada via false-flag recruitment. In 1972 a Canadian attorney named Peter Virag incorporated a firm called De Vimy Test Labs Ltd. for the apparent purpose of manufacturing and testing integrated circuits. Over the next four years De Vimy bought sophisticated computer and electronic equipment from U.S. manufacturers for its "plant" near Montreal. Virtually all of the equipment was of strategic military value, and the sales were permitted because Canada was the perceived final destination.[25] In fact, Virag's company existed only on paper. The computer equipment destined for its plant was shipped to Amsterdam and then to the Soviet Union, where it is presumably manufacturing and testing high-quality semiconductor chips of potential use in Soviet missiles and weapons. A twist was added by Virag's disclosure that, although formally the president of the company, he was actually in the employ of Jacob Kelmer, who presented himself as an Israeli major and told Virag that the material was destined for Israel. It was Kelmer, who had been recruited by someone in London, who arranged the shipments to Eastern Europe.[26]

In another instance, front companies were established in reaction to a failure to anticipate demand for an advanced technology item. Planning engineers had underestimated the demand for photoelectric repeaters. Soviet trade officials in countries of the West identified the best source as the David Mann Company in the United States. Contact was made with Western middlemen to act as their brokers who in turn established front companies in Yugoslavia, Switzerland, and Germany and began to buy embargoed photorepeaters from the U.S. company. Some of the middlemen even set up special facilities, which the Americans were allowed to inspect.[27]

In some cases, a legitimate third-party user either conspires to divert technology or simply looks the other way. Thus, in late 1982 the United States threatened to impose trade sanctions against Austria if it did not stop the transfer of militarily sensitive technology to the Soviet Union. As of that time there were over 100 Austrian companies with access to U.S. data banks and microprocessor technology as well as several with access to information concerning metals technologies, including the production of advanced alloys used in weapons manufacturing.[28]

Finally, end-user diversion can involve Soviet or East Bloc countries using technology sold to them under the provision that it would only be used in civilian industry, not for military purposes. The prime example of such a diversion was the use of ball bearing grinders by the Soviets to produce pinhead-size ball bearings for use in the SS-18 guidance system—ball bearings crucial to produce a guidance system capable of ensuring a high degree of accuracy.

TARGETS

The fields of technology and the institutions that are the target of Soviet technology acquisition activities are numerous and varied. Table 8-1 lists twenty-two categories of targeted technology, some of which overlap, according to the CIA and Defense Department.

Table 8-1. Target Technologies.

CIA	DOD
Computers	Automated production and control
Materials	technology
Semiconductors	Computer technology
Communications, navigation,	Directed energy
and control	Sensor technology
Vehicular/transportation	Guidance and navigation
Laser and optics	Microelectronics/semiconductors
Nuclear physics	Optics/optoelectronics
Microbiology	Power generation and propulsion
	Production and manufacturing
	Structural materials
	Genetic engineering/BW/CW
	Telecommunications technology
	Transportation technologies

Sources: Central Intelligence Agency, *Soviet Acquisition of Western Technology* (Washington, D.C.: CIA 1982), p. 4; "Key Western Technology is Target of Soviet Military," *Aviation Week and Space Technology*, December 10, 1984, pp. 67–68.

Specific items of interest in the Automated Production and Control category include artificial intelligence, CAD/CAM (computer-aided design/computer-aided manufacture), robotics, robotics sensors, automated test and production, numerical control, and computerized numerical control. Aspects of computer technology of interest include architecture, data, image-processing design and retrieval, memories, networking, software, and pattern recognition. Information concerning particle beam technology, high-energy lasers, and microwave technology falls under the directed energy category; sensor technology includes radar, array processors, infrared technology, and signal processing.[29]

The communications, guidance, and navigation field has as its components antennae, inertial components, system integration, and radio wave propagation. The microelectronics/semiconductors field involves production technology, research and development, components, and materials. Subcategories of the optics/electronics field include fiber optics technology, lenses/mirrors technology, electro-optic devices, and infrared devices. Targeted power generation and propulsion technologies include power sources technology, research and development, and propulsion technology.[30]

Lathes, furnaces, presses, and heavy industry machinery are among the targeted items in the production and manufacturing category. Advanced composites technology, carbon-carbon technology, metallurgy, superconductors, and cryogenics are examples of the type of materials of interest to the Soviet Union. Genetic engineering information in the form of information on gene splicing, recombinant DNA/RNA, and production technology is also of considerable interest.[31]

Three additional categories of interest are nuclear physics, telecommunications technology, and transportation technology. Specific items of interest in the field of nuclear physics include cryogenics, fusion, magnetohydrodynamics, reactors, structural designs, and superconductors. Telecommunications technologies of interest include Extremely Low Frequency technology, hostile radiation environment communication, networking/switching, IFF (Identification Friend or Foe), and electronic warfare R&D. The transportation information and technologies of interest include aircraft design, spacecraft design, sea vessel design, and aerodynamics/fluid dynamics.[32]

As a result of the wide range of targeted technologies, a wide range of companies in the United States and abroad have been targeted by the KGB and GRU in addition to particular military agencies. In the United States defense-electronics area alone, seventeen companies are known to have been targets of foreign agents who either stole or were caught trying to steal defense-related technologies between 1973 and 1981: Advanced Computer Technologies, Advanced Micro Devices Inc., Boeing, Computer Technology Corporation, Geo Space Corporation, Hewlett-Packard, Intel, Kasper Instruments, Lockheed, McDonnell, Micro-Tel, Mostek, National Semiconductor, Texas Instruments, TRW, Watkins-Johnson, and Zilog.[33] Some of these companies are located in Silicon Valley, a primary target of Soviet scientific and technical intelligence collection operations conducted out of the Soviet consulate in San Francisco.[34] At one given time in Silicon Valley there may be over 40 top secret and 400 secret high technology projects underway.[35]

Among the Soviet targets in Sweden are two in Goteborg. L. M. Ericsson is a giant electronics firm that took over Datasaab, a company that illegally sold the Soviet Union a radar system in the 1970s. The second target is Saab Scania, which manufactures Sweden's combat aircraft and has a marine electronics division in Goteborg. Among the naval equipment the Soviets seek to acquire is Saab Scania's automatic piloting system for ships.[36]

ACQUISITIONS AND ATTEMPTED ACQUISITIONS

The KGB, GRU, and other organizations engaged in technology acquisition have achieved many notable successes. They have been able to purchase or acquire complete computer system designs, concepts, hardware, and software—including a wide variety of Western general purpose computers and minicomputers for military applications.[37]

Among the computer systems the Soviet Union has attempted to acquire is the VAX 11/782, produced by the Digital Equipment Corporation. The VAX 11/782, according to defense experts, could be critical to the production of integrated circuits for the military circuits and chips that can be used to improve the targeting and guidance systems for future aircraft, missiles (offensive and defensive), and warheads. A small number of chips should be able to process information at a substantially greater rate than present systems and make future systems smaller, more efficient, and easier to service.[38]

Containers destined for the Soviet Union and containing components of the VAX 11/782 system were seized in Hamburg and Sweden in November 1983. The computer components had originally been shipped from the United States to South African front companies. It appears that a VAX 11/782 and eight containers of U.S. strategic goods were also diverted to the Soviet Union early in 1983.[39]

In the microelectronics field the Soviets have acquired complete industrial processes and semiconductor manufacturing equipment capable of meeting a large number of Soviet military requirements. Manufacturing acquisitions include automated and precision manufacturing equipment for electronic, optical, and future laser weapons technology.[40] From November 1975 to February 1977 Spawr Optical Research Inc. supplied the Soviet Union with dozens of sophisticated laser mirrors in at least six separate illegal shipments. Spawr, who had done work for TRW, Rocketdyne, Los Alamos National Laboratory, Red Stone Arsenal, Lawrence Livermore Laboratories, and other similar organizations, produced a breakthrough in the manufacturing of laser mirrors. Using his techniques he was able to produce absolutely smooth mirrors. Previously, laser mirrors were insufficiently smooth, leading to a diffusion of the light beam reflected off their surface and decreasing effectiveness. Spawr's innovation made it possible to achieve pinpoint accuracy when the light beam was bounced off and the mirrors were rotated to face the target.[41]

Additional manufacturing acquisitions included information on manufacturing technology related to weapons, ammunition, and aircraft parts—including turbine blades, electronic components, and machine tools for cutting large gears for ship propulsion systems.[42]

Soviet acquisitions in the microelectronics areas include hundreds of pieces of equipment related to wafer preparation, including expitaxial growth furnaces, crystail pullers, rinsers/dryers, slicers, and lapping and polishing units. They have also acquired technology concerning computer-aided design, pattern generators, compilers, digital plotters, electron-beam generators, and ion-milling equipment.[43]

In the guidance and navigation area they have obtained marine and other navigation receivers, advanced inertial guidance components (including miniature and laser gyros), missile guidance, subsystems, precision machinery for ball bearing production for missiles, missile test range instrumentation systems, and documentation and technology relating to missile test telemetry collection.[44]

Structural materials acquired by both purchase and other means include titanium alloys, welding equipment, and furnaces for producing titanium plates large enough to be applicable to submarine construction. Acquisitions in the propulsion technology area include some related to missile technology and ground propulsion (diesels, turbines, and rotaries) and advanced jet engine fabrication technology and design information.[45]

Sensor technology acquired includes both acoustical and electro-optical technology. Acoustical sensor technology acquired includes underwater navigation and direction-finding equipment. When a Soviet ocean buoy was examined by U.S. experts, it was discovered that the printed board circuits inside the buoy (which was designed to help track U.S. submarines), were pin-for-pin compatible with those of Texas Instruments.[46] Electro-optical sensor technology acquired includes satellite technology, laser range finders, underwater low-light television cameras, and the systems for their remote operation.[47]

Finally, the Soviet Union has acquired technology involving antenna designs for missile systems and air defense radars. Thus, Datasaab Contracting AB sold sophisticated U.S.-made radar tracking systems to the Soviet Union in the late 1970s. In the early 1970s the Soviets began seeking Western assistance in developing an advanced radar tracking system for airports in Moscow, Kiev, and Mineralnye Vody near the Afghanistan border. Soviet representatives approached Sperry Rand about selling them the proposed Terminal and En-Route Control Automated Systems (TERCAS). The Commerce Department approved a sale on the condition that the system was to be used only for tracking civilian aircraft for safety purposes, but the Soviets wanted also to buy a system that would track "non-cooperative" airplanes and missiles that would not be equipped with a beacon for communicating with the radar systems.[48]

BENEFITS

According to the 1982 CIA study *Soviet Acquisition of Western Technology*, the Soviet strategic weapons program has benefited substantially from the acquisition of Western technology. The similarities between the U.S. Minuteman silo and the Soviet SS-13 silo very likely, according to the study, resulted from the acquisition of U.S. documents and resulted in a faster deployment of the SS-13, the first Soviet solid propellant ICBM. Additionally, acquisition of 3-D carbon-carbon weaving technology has been useful in developing heat shields for reentry vehicles and portions of the rocket motors for large missiles.[49]

Likewise, the Soviet Union's ballistic missile systems have, in the last ten years, demonstrated qualitative improvements that probably would not have been achieved without acquisition of U.S. ballistic missile guidance and control technology. The most important single improvement—in the area of accuracy—may, given the poor accuracy of a decade ago, have been the result of the exploitation and development of good quality guidance system components such as gyroscopes and accelerometers, the quality of which depends largely on the quality of the small, precision, high-speed ball bearings used.[50]

Throughout the 1950s and 1960s the Soviet precision bearing capability trailed substantially behind that of the West. Legal purchases in the 1970s allowed the Soviet Union to acquire U.S. precision grinding machines that permitted the production of the small, high-precision bearings. Similar machines, although with lower production rate capabilities, were available from several other countries. A small number of such machines would have been adequate to produce all the quality ball bearings required by Soviet missile designers. According to the CIA study, these machines "provided the Soviets with the capability of manufacture precision bearings in large volume sooner than would have been likely through indigenous development."[51]

Aircraft technology acquisitions have had two purposes: to aid in the development of countermeasures against Western systems and to aid the development of their own systems, with primary emphasis on the latter. Much Soviet information in this area has been acquired from U.S. planes lost over Vietnam.[52] In a more recent case, a U.S. advanced drone aircraft that was recovered by the crew of a Soviet intelligence ship was held for two days before being dismantled and dumped into the ocean. The Northrop BMQ-74C, used to train gunners, represented state-of-the art technology in pilotless aircraft.[53]

Aircraft technology acquisitions have been applied to both the military and aircraft development programs. Thus, aircraft from certain Soviet military design bureaus are to a significant extent copies of Western aircraft. Soviet acquisition of documents on the C-5A transport plane during its early development stages contributed to Soviet development of a new strategic military cargo plane. Additionally, Soviet development of the IL-76 and IL-86 transports may have been aided by Soviet acquisition of information concerning the Boeing 747.[54]

An internal Soviet report on the various ways in which the Soviet aeronautics industry has benefited from technology acquisition was apparently leaked by the French intelligence service to Le Monde. The document states that 156 technical "samples" and 3896 technical documents were collected in 1979. It further states that 87 samples and 346 documents "have been used in a practical way in research projects and in the development of new weapons systems and new military materials, as well as in the improvement of weapons systems in current use."[55]

In the naval area Soviet acquisitions have had two benefits: It has permitted acquisition of equipment that the Soviet Union was not capable of producing, and it has permitted the diversion of resources to higher priority naval programs. In the latter case, the equipment is producible in the Soviet Union but with a greater expenditure of resources than required if they were simply to be purchased. Soviet acquisitions have focused on aircraft carriers, deep sea diving capabilities, sensor systems for antisubmarine warfare (ASW) and navigation and ship maintenance facilities. In additon, two large floating drydocks were purchased from the West, allegedly for civilian use, and were diverted to military use. One was diverted to the Pacific Naval Fleet, the other to the Northern Fleet. They are the only drydocks capable of servicing the new Kiev class V/STOL aircraft carriers. Among the first ships repaired at the drydocks included Soviet SSBNs, the Kiev aircraft carriers, and Soviet destroyers.[56]

The Soviet Union has also contracted for or purchased foreign-built oceanographic survey ships equipped with advanced technology. These ships are used in the development of Soviet weapons and antisubmarine weapons systems against the West.[57]

In the tactical area Soviet acquisitions appear to focus mainly on tank, antitank, and air-defense-related technology. As with aircraft technology acquisitions, there appear to be two objectives: to improve Soviet capabilities and to develop countermeasures to U.S. and other Western systems. Thus, the Soviet SA-7 heat-seeking shoulder-fired antiaircraft missiles contain many features of the U.S. Redeye missile, and the AA-2 Atol family of air-to-air missiles has been alleged to be copied from the U.S. AIM-9 Sidewinder missile.[58]

In addition to the conclusions related to specific weapons or other systems given above, the 1982 CIA study also concluded that Soviet technology acquisitions programs have allowed the Soviet Union to:

- save hundreds of millions of dollars in R&D costs and years in R&D development lead time;

- modernize critical sectors of their military industry and reduce engineering risks by following or copying proven Western designs, limiting their rise in military production costs;

- achieve greater weapons performance than if they had to rely solely on their own technology; and

- incorporate countermeasures to Western weapons early in the development of their own weapons programs.[59]

It is clear that acquisitions of advanced Western technology can and have produced significant benefits to the Soviet Union, both in the military and nonmilitary spheres. Two issues, to be discussed in Chapter 13, are the extent to which advanced Soviet technologies are based on the acquisition of advanced Western technologies and the threat such acquisitions represent.

NOTES TO CHAPTER 8

1. John Deutch, H. Rowan, and A. Wohlstetter, *Defense Implications of Technologies of Precision and Discrimination* (Los Angeles: Pan Heuristics, 1975).

2. Walter Sullivan, "Can Submarines Stay Hidden?," *New York Times*, December 11, 1984, pp. C1, C9.

3. Testimony of Peter Sharfman, in U.S. Congress, House Armed Services Committee, *Technology Transfer* (Washington, D.C.: U.S. Government Printing Office, 1984), p. 7.

4. Central Intelligence Agency, *Soviet Acquisition of Western Technology* (Washington, D.C.: CIA, 1982), p. 2.

5. Ibid.

6. Edgar Uslamer, "Moscow's Technology Parasites," *Air Force Magazine*, December 1984, pp. 52ff.

7. "Soviets Seeking to Pirate West's Technology," *Washington Times*, January 25, 1985, p. 5A.

8. Uslamer, "Moscow's Technology Parasites."

9. Testimony of John Stein, CIA Deputy Director for Operations, in U.S. Congress, House Permanent Select Committee on Intelligence, *Soviet Active Measures* (Washington, D.C.: U.S. Government Printing Office, 1982), p. 23.

10. Central Intelligence Agency, *Soviet Acquisition of Western Technology*, p. 5.

11. Air Force Office of Special Investigations, *Soviet Overt Intelligence Collections in the United States* (Washington, D.C.: AFOSI, 1975), p. 7.

12. Ibid.

13. "Keeping High-Tech Secrets," *Newsweek*, January 25, 1982, pp. 34–36.

14. Central Intelligence Agency, *Soviet Acquisition of Western Technology*, p. 5.

15. Air Force Office of Special Investigations, *Soviet Overt Intelligence Collections*, p. 11.

16. Ibid., p. 20.

17. Ibid., p. 8.

18. Central Intelligence Agency, *Soviet Acquisition of Western Technology*, p. 5.
19. Air Force Office of Special Investigations, *Soviet Overt Intelligence Collections*, pp. 11–12.
20. Central Intelligence Agency, *Soviet Acquisition of Western Technology*, p. 3.
21. Ibid., p. 3.
22. Mark Potts, "Device Sold to Soviets Seized after Repair Bid," *Washington Post*, August 25, 1982, p. D7.
23. "The Soviet Spy Sought 'Star Wars' Secrets," *Newsweek*, May 2, 1983, p. 21.
24. Central Intelligence Agency, *Soviet Acquisition of Western Technology*, p. 5.
25. R. Jeffrey Smith, "Eastern Bloc Evades Technology Embargo," *Science* 211 (January 1981): 364–68.
26. Ibid.
27. Linda Melvern, David Hebditch, and Nick Anning, *Techno-Bandits: How the Soviets Are Stealing America's High Tech Future* (Boston: Houghton Mifflin, 1984).
28. "U.S. Says Austria Lets Soviet Have Sensitive Goods," *New York Times*, December 14, 1982, p. A12.
29. Central Intelligence Agency, *Soviet Acquisition of Western Technology*, p. 4; "Key Western Technology is Target of Soviet Military," *Aviation Week and Space Technology*, December 10, 1984, pp. 67–68.
30. Ibid.
31. Ibid.
32. "Targets of Arms Espionage," *Los Angeles Times*, October 23, 1983, pp. 1, 6–8.
33. Harry V. Martin and Robert Carroll, "Electronics Companies Combat Increased Soviet Spying," *Defense Electronics*, July 1981, pp. 34ff.
34. C. Simpson, "Soviet Espionage in the Silicon Valley," *Current Analysis* 2, no. 10 (December 1980).
35. Ibid.
36. Jack Anderson, "Swedes, Soviets in Secret War for High-Tech," *Washington Post*, April 16, 1984, p. C13.
37. Central Intelligence Agency, *Soviet Acquisition of Western Technology*, p. 7.
38. "Moscow's Computer Capers," *Newsweek*, January 2, 1984, p. 19.
39. Paul Mann, "Smuggling Advances Soviet Technology," *Aviation Week and Space Technology*, April 9, 1984, pp. 24–25.
40. Central Intelligence Agency, *Soviet Acquisition of Western Technology*, p. 7.
41. Ehud Yonay, "Mirrors for Moscow," *New West*, September 1981, pp. 87ff.

42. Central Intelligence Agency, *Soviet Acquisition of Western Technology*, p. 7.
43. Ibid.
44. Ibid.
45. Ibid.
46. "Some of Our Chips Are Missing," *Time*, March 14, 1983, p. 32.
47. Central Intelligence Agency, *Soviet Acquisition of Western Technology*, p. 7.
48. Ronald Kessler, "Swedish Firm Fined on Sale of Radar to Soviets," *Washington Post*, April 28, 1984, pp. A1, A2.
49. Central Intelligence Agency, *Soviet Acquisition of Western Technology*, p. 6.
50. Ibid., pp. 6-7.
51. Ibid., p. 7.
52. Ibid.
53. "U.S. Says Soviet Kept Drone," *New York Times*, June 3, 1984, p. 6.
54. Central Intelligence Agency, *Soviet Acquisition of Western Technology*, p. 8.
55. David Dickson, "Soviet High-Tech Spying Detailed in France," *Science*, April 19, 1985, p. 306.
56. Ibid.; Central Intelligence Agency, *Soviet Acquisition of Western Technology*, p. 8.
57. Ibid.
58. Ibid., p. 7; Uslamer, "Moscow's Technology Parasites."
59. Central Intelligence Agency, *Soviet Acquisition of Western Technology*, p. 10.

9 COUNTERINTELLIGENCE

Much of the activity of the KGB falls under the heading of counter-espionage—that is, preventing and detecting the espionage activities of hostile intelligence services in the Soviet Union. A related but distinct activity is counterintelligence, which seeks to limit the effectiveness and, if possible, completely neutralize hostile intelligence services. Rather than simply focusing on their activities in and against the Soviet Union, Soviet counterintelligence operations seek to penetrate to the heart of hostile intelligence services and disrupt their activities throughout the world. These activities are the responsibility of Directorate K of the First Chief (Foreign) Directorate of the KGB.

Neutralization can be attained or made more likely by a variety of means. The most basic means is the collection and analysis of information concerning foreign intelligence and security services and their personnel. Such information aids understanding of how those services operate and how they can be discredited and helps in penetrating them. Penetration involves recruiting an individual who is already in the service or can be expected to attain such a position. Another means of neutralization is the acquisition of classified information concerning technical collection systems (e.g., satellites) which can then be used to limit or eliminate the effectiveness of those systems. Disinformation provided by double agents or false defectors is yet another means of neutralizing the operations of the covert action and human intelligence operations of a hostile service; cover, concealment, and deception are means of neutralizing the effectiveness of technical collection systems, sometimes aided by the acquisition of classified information concerning those systems.

ANALYSIS

Little is known about the counterintelligence analysis operations of Directorate K other than that it voraciously collects information relevant to the operations of foreign, particularly hostile, intelligence services and their personnel. Much of the information concerning the organization and structure of U.S. and other Western intelligence agencies can be found in official telephone and other directories as well as in the press. This is particularly true in the case of the United States, where detailed organizational and personnel information is available concerning almost all agencies other than the CIA, the National Security Agency (NSA), and the National Reconnaissance Office. In the case of the CIA, the organizational structure of all but the Directorate of Operations is unclassified. Likewise, information on intelligence officials can be gathered from newspapers, directories, and congressional hearings.

It is probably safe to assume that Directorate K's analysts prepare lengthy reports on the intelligence communities of foreign nations of interest to the KGB—just as the CIA's Counterintelligence Staff prepares such studies concerning the intelligence communities of the Soviet Union, Cuba, China, and even Israel. These reports probably discuss the structure and functions, history, methods of operation, relationships to supervisory agencies, and key personnel of the intelligence community's components.

Information on personnel is probably provided in other reports as well, allowing KGB and GRU officers to know who they are operating against. And, of course, information on individuals with problems or weaknesses susceptible to exploitation is always helpful in seeking to penetrate a foreign intelligence or security service.

Additionally, Directorate K probably produces studies on Western intelligence activity in specific countries. Such studies would provide a KGB operative with vital information concerning the opposition in those countries.

PENETRATIONS

The Soviet Union has had considerable success in penetrating several Western intelligence communities—most notably the British and West German—at high levels. At lower levels the United States, particularly the security-conscious NSA, has also shown itself susceptible to penetration.

Soviet penetrations of the British intelligence community have reached into the Secret Intelligence Service (SIS), the Security Service, and the Government Communications Headquarters (GCHQ). The two best-known and serious penetrations into the SIS were those by Kim Philby and George Blake—the former recruited prior to his entrance into the secret world, the latter after his entrance.

Born in 1912, Philby began his university education in 1929 at Cambridge. Between then and 1933, when he graduated, he met Guy Burgess and Donald MacLean and apparently became a Marxist. Shortly after graduation he went to Vienna, where he married a Communist party member. When he returned to London in May 1934 he buried the image of a young left-wing activist and began constructing a political disguise, indicating that he had already been recruited by the Soviets.[1] This disguise involved taking trips to Spain in the summers of 1934 and 1935—trips apparently financed by the Soviets—as well as joining the Anglo–German Fellowship and editing its magazine. In May 1937 he became the Spanish correspondent for the *Times of London* and demonstrated clear sympathies with Francisco Franco's Fascists. All this, especially his position with the *Times*, apparently made him a candidate for recruitment to SIS.[2]

In the 1939–40 period he was recruited into the sabotage section of SIS (Section D) and then transferred along with that section to the newly formed sabotage and resistance agency, Special Operations Executive. He was subsequently recruited back into SIS, winding up in the Iberian subsection of Section V, the counterintelligence section of SIS. During the war he passed on a variety of material to his Soviet contacts.[3]

By 1944 he became head of the newly created Section IX, the counterintelligence section targeted against the KGB. Philby soon put his position to use to possibly save his neck. In 1946 Konstantin Volkov, the new Soviet consul in Instanbul, contacted an SIS officer and offered what he said was valuable counterintelligence information in exchange for £27,500. The material offered included

- the addresses and descriptions of NKVD (People's Commissariat for State Security) buildings in Moscow;
- details of their burglar alarm systems;
- key imprints and guard schedules;
- numbers of all NKVD cars;
- a list of Soviet agents in Turkey and their means of communication; and
- the names of three Russian agents operating in government departments in London, one of whom was in counterintelligence.

The offer was passed along to Philby to review, and he promptly alerted his controller, resulting in the removal of Volkov.[4]

Philby subsequently served as SIS station chief in Istanbul and then Washington—a position from which he was able to supply the Soviets with a variety of items. He was able to ensure that a joint U.S.-British operation directed at overthrowing the Communist government of Albania would not succeed. The first guerilla groups were dropped into Albania in 1950, and for the next two years small groups departed regularly from training camps in Malta, Cyprus, and Germany, either to be dropped by parachute into the Albanian mountains or to be infiltrated across the Greek-Albanian border. Each time, the police were waiting.[5]

In January 1951 the Minister of the Interior reported a large unsuccessful infiltration attempt in the north resulting in twenty-nine killed and fourteen captured. The final operation took place a few weeks before Easter in 1952. Similar attempts by the Organization of Ukrainian Nationalists to infiltrate resistance teams failed because the Ukrainian police were always aware of their presence.[6]

Born in Rotterdam in 1922, George Blake's original name was George Behar. In 1940 he was arrested by the Gestapo, but escaped in 1942 and made his way to Spain, where he was interned. Eventually, he reached Gibraltar, joined the Royal Navy, and changed his name to Blake.[7]

His fluency in three languages resulted in his being commissioned into the Royal Navy Volunteer Reserve (RNVR) and attached to the Naval Intelligence Division (NID) of the Admiralty. From NID he was subsequently transferred to the Dutch section of Special Operations Executive (SOE). He later moved from SOE to SIS and became a senior agent, being sent to Korea in 1950 as a key agent with the rank of vice-consul. He was captured by the North Koreans in 1950 and interned for three years, a period during which he was apparently converted to Communism.[8]

Blake was repatriated in 1953 and was sent to Germany in April of 1955—an assignment he obtained at the request of his KGB controller. Several months after arriving he became privy to the existence of Operation Gold, the Berlin Tunnel operation involving the tapping of the telephones of the Soviet *Kommandatura* in Germany. Thus, the Soviet Union apparently knew of the operation from its very beginning, although it was not until April 21, 1956 that the KGB and East German police burst into the tunnel.[9]

While in Germany Blake was assigned to the job of organizing a network of agents and informers to obtain information from the Soviet Bloc—most especially concerning Soviet intelligence operations. Blake was particularly concerned with whether any Germans employed by the British were simultaneously employed by the KGB or other Soviet agency. He tried to convince his British superiors that he should be given control over all German informers and agents and was placed in command of an extensive network of British agents in East Germany and Czechoslovakia, which led to the KGB being informed regularly of their activities and whereabouts.[10]

Among the agents given away by Blake was Johann Baumgart, an official of the East German railways, who produced twenty-five detailed reports about railway transportation. Baumgart received a fifteen-year sentence for espionage. Altogether, Blake informed the KGB of forty British and West German agents while he was in Berlin.[11] Additionally, he inadvertently discovered that a GRU officer serving in Vienna, Lt. Colonel Peter Popov, had defected in place to the CIA.[12]

Blake left Berlin in April 1959. Probably in conjunction with advice from the KGB, he decided to apply for a Middle East posting, which resulted in his arrival in Beirut in September 1960 as a student of the Middle East College for Arabic Studies, a well-known "cover" for SIS officers. While in London waiting for his departure he obtained and passed to the Soviets a number of Foreign Office documents concerning Berlin.[13] Blake's role as a Soviet penetration agent was finally blown by a Polish defector in 1961.

Two further SIS officers who spied for the USSR were John Cairncross and Charles Howard Ellis. Cairncross joined the Government Code and Cypher School (GCCS) in 1942 and proceeded to supply ULTRA material to the Soviets, allowing them to destroy hundreds of German aircraft on the ground. In 1944 he joined SIS, being assigned first to counterintelligence operations against Germany and then to Yugoslav affairs. He turned over a variety of material about both subjects to the NKVD.[14] Ellis joined SIS in 1924 and by 1944 became Controller for Southeast Asia and the Far East. Shortly thereafter he received another promotion—Controller of North and South American operations. During these later years he also served as a Soviet agent. In 1953 he left the British SIS to join the Australian Secret Intelligence Service (ASIS) but subsequently rejoined SIS to help in the weeding out of SIS files.[15]

Within the Security Service (commonly known as MI5) only one certain penetration has been established: the wartime penetration of Anthony Blunt, who left the service after the war and subsequently became the Queen's art historian.[16] However, at times suspicion has revolved around several high-ranking Security Service officers, including two director-generals. One of the two, Sir Michael Hanley, was conclusively cleared. The other, the late Sir Roger Henry Hollis, Director-General from 1957 to 1963, has been the subject of controversy in recent years and has been accused of having been recruited by the GRU in the 1930s and having been a Soviet agent throughout his intelligence career.[17]

The most recently discovered penetration was that of GCHQ by Geoffrey Arthur Prime. Prime joined a branch of GCHQ, the Joint Technical Language Service (JTLS), on September 30, 1968. JTLS consisted of translators, mostly of voice communications that had been intercepted by transmitters planted in embassies and foreign residencies in London and via the interception of phone calls.[18]

Prime had previously made contact with the KGB in January 1968 while he was stationed in Berlin. He was given training in hidden messages, microdots, and radio transmitting and given a supply of one-time pads. While at JTLS he probably passed on what JTLS was able to extract from open telephone channels into and out of the Soviet embassy and residencies as well as information as to whether any of the scrambler phones had been penetrated and the extent to which the British had succeeded in eavesdropping on communications within Soviet buildings in London.[19]

For a variety of reasons, Prime became a sleeper for several years but was reactivated by 1975, at which time he moved from JTLS to GCHQ proper. In 1976 he was transferred to the most sensitive division: the J or Special Sigint Division of GCHQ's Directorate of Sigint Operations and Requirements. J Division is directed at the Soviet Union. On November 1 he became a section head and regularly attended meetings where discussions concerning GCHQ's most sensitive operations were discussed. However, in 1977 Prime left due to his inability to handle the pressure under which he was working.[20]

The West German intelligence community has also been penetrated at high levels by the KGB. The West German intelligence community consists of the Federal Intelligence Service (BND for *Bundesnachrictendienst*), the Federal Office for the Protection of the Constitution (BfV), and the Military Security Service (MAD). The BND is responsible for all foreign intelligence activities; the BfV and MAD are responsible for counterintelligence and countersubversion activities.[21]

There have been at least two Soviet penetrations of the BND. The most significant involved Heinz Felfe, who was born in 1918 and served as a member of the Nazi's SS Security Service (SD). As the result of being a SS officer he was imprisoned by the Allies and sent to Canada. He was released in 1946, probably because he had offered his services to British intelligence and they had accepted.[22]

Upon his return to Germany he became an SIS informer at the University of Bonn. In his informant role Felfe joined a variety of Marxist and left-wing student groups. He was classified by the British as "uninvolved" in Nazi activities and was accepted into the BND. His entrance was arranged by an already functioning KGB agent in the BND, Hans Clemens.[23] With Felfe's entrance into the BND, the KGB managed to achieve their objective of penetrating Department IIIF, Counterespionage, of which Felfe became chief. IIIF operated against all East Bloc services. As senior intelligence officer of a department, Felfe had access to the reports of the BND and MAD. Additionally, he regularly was informed of those individuals who were suspected of being Soviet agents and were being investigated and subjected to surveillance.[24]

Felfe's photographic activities in aid of the KGB included practically every document that went through his hands. Included were personnel reports on the BND staff, minutes of classified meetings, and reports on clandestine field operations. Felfe was arrested in

November 1962 based on information provided by an East German intelligence officer who defected in 1961. At their trial, Felfe and Clemens admitted to delivering 15,000 photographs of secret West German intelligence documents. Felfe also made two further admissions: that he betrayed ninety-four agents and that the head of the counterespionage division of MAD had been blackmailed into supplying the Soviets with secret information for a period of seven years.[25]

One case involving possible penetration or defection or both is that of Otto John, the first President of the BfV. John joined the BfV with an impeccable anti-Nazi reputation. Born in 1909, he joined the resistance in 1939. From 1942 he was in regular contact with both the SIS and the U.S. Office of Strategic Services in Madrid and Lisbon. In January 1944 he informed them of the plan to assassinate Adolf Hitler on July twentieth of that year. After the attempt failed, he flew to Madrid, made contact with British intelligence, and joined its black propaganda unit.[26]

At the end of the war he became a lawyer, and in 1950 he was offered the job of President of the BfV. On July 30, 1954 he announced over East German radio that he had defected and shortly afterward held a news conference—open to both Eastern and Western reporters—to explain the reason for his defection. On December 12, 1955 John reappeared in West Germany, claiming that his defection was the result of having been drugged and kidnapped. In August 1956 he was charged with treason and subsequently spent several years in prison.[27]

Soviet penetrations of U.S. and Canadian intelligence and security services have not reached the same levels as in the British and West German cases. U.S. agencies that have been penetrated to varying extents include the National Security Agency, Federal Bureau of Investigation, and the Central Intelligence Agency.

In 1958 Sgt. Jack F. Dunlap was assigned to NSA as a chauffeur for Major General Garrison B. Cloverdale, an assistant director and the agency's chief of staff. In 1960 he was recruited by the KGB, his motivation being purely monetary. Exactly what he passed on is unknown, as he committed suicide in 1963. However, between 1960 and 1963 U.S. authorities were unaware of those activities, and Dunlap would have had access, through Cloverdale, to a large number of highly classified documents.[28]

On the same day that Dunlap's body was discovered, Victor Norris Hamilton turned up in Moscow. Hamilton had joined NSA's Production Organization in June 1957 and, due to his outstanding knowledge of Arabic, had been assigned to its Near East Sector, which was concerned with the United Arab Republic, Syria, Iraq, Lebanon, Jordan, Saudi Arabia, Yemen, Libya, Morocco, Tunisia, Turkey, Iran, Greece, and Ethiopia. By February 1959 he began to show psychological problems and was declared mentally ill. NSA retained him despite this finding because of his Arabic-language expertise.[29] Whether Hamilton was in contact with the Soviets prior to his defection and passed them classified material is not known.

In 1984 the first certain KGB penetration of the FBI was uncovered. In August, Richard Miller, a twenty-year veteran, assigned to the counterintelligence squad of the FBI's Los Angeles Field Office, offered to sell classified FBI documents to the KGB for $65,000. Allegedly he previously had passed one classified document—a twenty-four-page manual entitled "Reporting Guidance: Foreign Intelligence Information"—which would give the KGB a "detailed picture of FBI and U.S. intelligence activities, techniques and requirements."[30]

Although Miller's case is the first confirmed case of penetration, two cases where penetrations may have occurred are detailed in *The Bureau*, a book by a former FBI assistant director, William Sullivan. At one point during Sullivan's tenure, the FBI was running a series of successful operations against the KGB and Soviet officials. Suddenly, all of the defections to the United States ceased and the programs no longer worked. Additionally, the Washington Field Office (WFO) was found to be missing three Top Secret documents connected with naval operations.[31]

According to a Soviet defector, the documents had been sold by an FBI agent to the Soviet embassy. One particular WFO agent came under suspicion due to unusually large gambling debts and because of information provided by Soviet defectors. It was determined that he was contacted by Soviet agents from a certain phone booth at certain hours. Nothing further was developed, and the agent requested and received early retirement.[32]

Less certain is whether there was also a penetration of the FBI's New York Field Office. According to Sullivan, the Soviets abruptly broke contact with an FBI man being "dangled." They apparently learned who he was and that he was operating against them—information Sullivan asserts could only have come from an agent inside the field office. A plan to transfer, over a period of time, all those with counterespionage functions from the New York Field Office was vetoed by Director J. Edgar Hoover, who feared that this was too conspicuous and would fan negative publicity.[33]

The case of David Henry Barnett is not quite a case of penetration. That is, the KGB did not recruit him while he was employed by the CIA. Barnett was employed by the CIA in the 1950s and 1960s as a contract employee and staff officer. He had responsibility for a variety of intelligence operations including several concerned with collecting information concerning the Soviet Union. Barnett quit the agency in 1970 for financial reasons.[34]

Heavily in debt, Barnett approached the KGB in 1976 with an offer to sell them classified information that he had obtained as a CIA employee. Over the next several years he received over $90,000 in exchange for telling the KGB about CIA operations and the identities of Soviet officials who had been targeted by the CIA for possible recruitment. He also agreed to seek reemployment in the intelligence field at the urging of the KGB and applied for positions on the staffs of the Intelligence Oversight Board and the congressional intelligence committees.[35]

The only known penetration of the Royal Canadian Mounted Police (RCMP) Security Service occurred in the 1950s when an employee known as "Long Knife" offered to sell a Soviet agent information. For $5,000 he provided the agent with a pocket-sized notebook containing the names of everybody in the Security Service.[36]

The impact of these penetrations has been significant: The effectiveness of numerous Western agents has been curtailed or negated. Beyond that, the impact has been profound in either "increasing vigilance" *or* consuming a significant amount of resources in a possibly useless effort to find nonexistent moles. Additionally, the fear of moles may have diverted Western agencies from considering errors in procedures and operations security as the true cause of operational failures.

In Canada sixteen years had passed—from 1954 to 1970—in which the RCMP Security Service had been constantly outwitted by the KGB. Dangles had been dropped, meetings that had been intended to lead to arrests did not materialize, as the target suddenly ceased showing up, and so on—almost as if the KGB had an inside agent. During most of that time, the responsibility for the Russian Desk of the Counterespionage Branch was that of Leslie James Bennett. Bennett had emigrated to Canada after having served with Britain's

GCHQ. During his GCHQ tenure he served in Istanbul as well as GCHQ liaison to the Australian Defense Signals Division. After his Australian posting he was moved to Hong Kong. Because of his involvement for such a long period of time he became a suspect—a suspicion furthered by his crossing of paths with Kim Philby during his posting in Istanbul. Although no case was proved against Bennett, he felt compelled to resign.[37]

The most prolonged and acrimonious mole hunt involved the CIA and the long-time chief of the CIA's Counterintelligence Staff, James Jesus Angleton. Accepting the claim of defector Anatoli Golytsin (see below) of a high-level CIA mole, Angleton conducted a twelve-year hunt which did not even exclude those who supported his position. Thus, during his time several Soviet Bloc Division chiefs and other CIA executives came under suspicion. Angleton tried to isolate the entire Soviet Bloc Division and informed the chief of French counterespionage that the CIA chief of station in France was a KGB agent—the latter act resulting in his dismissal by CIA Director William Colby.[38]

RHYOLITE AND THE KH-11

In an era where technical collection is the most important means by which the superpowers collect information about each other, it follows that seeking to deceive and neutralize the other nation's intelligence activities involves activities directed toward neutralizing, at least to some extent, the effectiveness of technical collection systems. The means of doing this is via the acquisition of information about those systems—about their functions, operation capabilities and characteristics, and vulnerabilities. Acquisition of information beyond that which is available in open sources can result from the penetration of intelligence agencies or contractors.

Two systems about which the Soviet Union has acquired classified information are RHYOLITE and the Keyhole (KH)-11. Beginning in 1975 information concerning RHYOLITE was sold to the Soviet Union by Christopher Boyce, a $145-per-week code clerk at TRW Inc., the satellite's manufacturer.[39]

RHYOLITE was described in Boyce's TRW briefing as a "multipurpose covert electronic surveillance system." Specifically, the RHYOLITE system consisted of a series of satellites placed in geosynchronous orbit to monitor Soviet missile test telemetry as well as intercept communications. The first RHYOLITE satellite was launched in 1970 with four subsequent launches in 1973, 1977, and 1978. RHYOLITE satellites were stationed over the Horn of Africa, primarily to intercept telemetry signals transmitted by liquid-fueled ICBMs launched from Tyuratam toward Kamchatka as well as over Singapore to monitor telemetry from the SS-16 and SS-20 missiles launched from Plesetsk in north Russia.[40]

RHYOLITE's communications intercept capabilities extend across the VHF, UHF microwave frequency bands. With respect to microwave frequencies, Robert Lindsey has written that the RHYOLITE satellites "could monitor Communist microwave radio and long-distance telephone traffic over much of the European land mass, eavesdropping on a Soviet Commissar in Moscow talking to his mistress in Yalta or on a general talking to his lieutenants across the great continent."[41]

In addition to passing on information concerning RHYOLITE, Boyce and his partner, Andrew Daulton Lee, also passed on information concerning the Advanced Rhyolite or ARGUS satellite. ARGUS satellites would have had a greater intercept capacity than RHYOLITE satellites due to an antenna that would be twice the diameter. The ARGUS project was never funded, however, due to congressional resistance.[42]

The KH-11 satellite is the latest and most advanced U.S. photographic reconnaissance spacecraft. First launched on December 19, 1976, it flies in a north-south, sun-synchronous polar orbit that covers each area twice a day. According to one account, the "KH-11 optical system uses an array of light sensitive silicon diodes and the array's charge is read off by an amplifier and converted from analog to digital signals for transmission."[43]

These digital radio pulses are then transmitted to Satellite Data System spacecraft and then to a Washington-area ground station at Ft. Belvoir, Virginia. This permits real-time transmission rather than the delays necessitated either by film recovery or initial transmission to overseas ground stations. The most important difference between the KH-11 and previous photographic reconnaissance satellites after readout speed is its lifetime. With one exception, all of the KH-11s launched since 1976 (a total of five) have had lifetimes of two years or more.[44]

In 1977 the KH–11 *Technical Manual* was removed from the CIA Operations Center by a $15,000-a-year "Watch Officer," William Kampiles. Kampiles subsequently left the CIA in frustration at being unable to become a covert operator. On or about March 2, 1978 he sold the manual for $3,000 to a KGB agent in Greece.[45]

COVER, CONCEALMENT, AND DECEPTION IN REGARD TO TECHNICAL COLLECTION SYSTEMS

Reducing the effectiveness of technical collection systems does not require possession of classified information—for example, manuals—concerning those systems. As noted in Chapter 5, the Soviet Union maintains an extensive network for spacetracking and detection. Thus, they are aware of the orbital periods and ground tracks of U.S. reconnaissance satellites. Given this information, the Soviet authorities can seek to reduce the effectiveness of U.S. reconnaissance efforts by covering up (with tarpaulin or other means) weapons systems or facilities they do not wish to be viewed; by concealing planes or other movable weapons systems by moving them into hangars or other facilities; or by actually deceiving the United States about the existence or capabilities of various facilities (e.g., C^3 bunkers) or weapons systems. Deception measures may extend to the creation of false or "shadow" targets to divert warheads from real targets.[46]

Soviet cover, concealment, and deception operations are conducted by the Chief Directorate for Strategic Deception of the General Staff. According to Suvorov,

A huge U.S. computer, which has been installed at the Central Command Post of the Chief Directorate of Strategic Deception, maintains a constant record of all intelligence-gathering satellites and orbiting space stations and of their trajectories. Extremely precise short- and long-term forecasts are prepared of the times at which the satellites will pass over various areas of the Soviet Union and all the other territories and sea areas in which the Armed Services of the Soviet Union are active. Each Chief Directorate unit serving with a military district, a group of armies, or a fleet makes use of data provided by this same U.S. computer to carry out similar work for its own force and area. Each army, division, and regiment receives constantly updated schedules showing the precise times at which enemy reconnaissance satellites will overfly their area, with details of the type of satellite concerned (photo-reconnaissance, signals intelligence, all-purpose, etc.) and the track it will follow. Neither the soldiers nor most of the officers know the precise reason for daily orders, like "From 12.20 to 12.55 all radio transmissions are to cease and all radars are to be switched off," but they must obey them. At the same time, each division has several radio transmitters and radars which work only during this period and which are there solely to provide signals for the enemy's satellites.[47]

DISINFORMATION AND DECEPTION

Counterintelligence objectives can be achieved by deception as well as penetration—by sending opposition intelligence services down false trails and turning their suspicions on themselves. One deception operation, discussed in Chapter 1, was the Trust operation.

A similar operation was employed in the aftermath of World War II. During that war the Germans virtually destroyed the Polish Home Army during the Warsaw uprising of October 1944. The survivors maintained a sporadic communication with the government in exile in London until 1947, when they were apparently wiped out in a determined Soviet drive that eliminated the remaining cells of resistance, including an organization known as WIN (Freedom and Independence).[48]

A few years later a Pole escaped to the West and made contact with General Wladyslav Anders. WIN, Anders was told, still existed and with funds and equipment from the West might become a significant force. Anders informed the British SIS and soon both the SIS and the CIA were trying to build up WIN. As part of this effort the CIA's covert action arm of that time, the Office of Policy Coordination (OPC), dropped significant amounts of supplies and money to WIN. OPC was thus quite chagrined when at the end of December 1952 a Polish broadcast detailed OPC's support efforts for WIN and revealed that the present WIN was a Soviet and Polish invention.[49]

The defections of several KGB officers in 1962 sparked controversy over whether a Soviet counterintelligence operation was involved in either or both of the defections. The controversy stemmed from the defection in 1962 of Anatoli Golitsin and has been resurrected in recent years by the alleged suicide of highly placed CIA official and the realization that a Soviet U.N. employee supposedly working for the United States had been under Soviet control all along. The severity of the controversy was in part due to the persistence in pursuing the mole by James Jesus Angleton, chief of the CIA's Counterintelligence Staff.

Golitsin defected to the CIA from Helsinki, Finland. He identified himself as a major in the First Chief Directorate of the KGB, working primarily against targets in the NATO alliance. He was brought to Washington and was given the pseudonym John Stone. The information Stone provided in his debriefing caused a sensation. According to Stone, the KGB had already planted an agent within the highest echelons of U.S. intelligence. This penetration agent would be assisted by "outside" men—other Soviet-controlled agents masking themselves as defectors or double agents—who would supply pieces of disinformation designed to bolster an "inside" man's credibility. The inside agents, in turn, would be in a position to help confirm the authenticity of the outside agent.[50]

During his debriefing sessions with Angleton in 1962, Stone had called particular attention to a trip made by V. M. Kovshuk to the United States in 1957 under diplomatic cover, using the alias Komarov. Stone identified Kovshuk as the then-reigning head of the all-important American embassy section of the KGB and stressed that only an extremely important mission would account for his leaving his post in Moscow to come to the United States. He suggested that Kovshuk's mission might have involved contacting or activating a high-level Soviet penetration agent within the CIA who had been recruited years before in Moscow.[51]

Stone further cautioned that the KGB, realizing that he knew about Kovshuk's mission, would almost certainly attempt to discredit or deflect the CIA from the information he was providing. He warned Angleton that Soviet disinformation agents could be expected to make contact with the CIA for this purpose. Six months later Yuri Nosenko defected to the CIA. Nosenko's information ran counter to that of Stone in many instances and tended to downplay the possibility of a Soviet penetration of the CIA. Thus, the explanation Nosenko gave concerning Soviet detection of a CIA agent in the GRU, Lieutenant Colonel Peter Semyonovich Popov, stressed Soviet security measures.[52]

There were several problems with Nosenko's story and bona fides that made him and his explanations suspect. His initial claim of being a Lieutenant Colonel was, according to Nosenko himself, false—a confession made only after intense interrogation. In numerous other instances interrogators got him to admit that his initial claims were false. As a result, doubts about Nosenko began to grow. Indeed, the extent of doubt about Nosenko led to his being incarcerated by the CIA for a period of three years, until Director Richard Helms set him free.[53]

Complicating matters further, Nosenko's story was confirmed by an FBI source codenamed FEDORA. FEDORA was a Soviet intelligence agent working under diplomatic cover at the United Nations. In March 1962 he had contacted the FBI with information about Soviet espionage operations, claiming to be a disaffected First Chief Directorate officer and offering to supply the FBI with secret information of Soviet missile capability and nuclear development plans.

FEDORA's veracity eventually came to be doubted by the FBI — a doubt fostered by Nosenko's admission to having lied about being a Lieutenant Colonel, a lie backed up by FEDORA. FEDORA also falsely claimed that Daniel Ellsberg delivered a copy of the Pentagon Papers to the Soviet embassy. In 1981 when FEDORA retired he returned to the Soviet Union.[54]

NOTES TO CHAPTER 9

1. Bruce Page, David Leitch, and Phillip Knightley, *The Philby Conspiracy* (New York: Signet, 1969), pp. 66, 73.
2. Ibid., pp. 74–102.
3. Ibid., pp. 139–42.
4. Ibid., pp. 168–76.
5. Ibid., pp. 177–89.
6. Ibid.
7. E.H. Cookridge, *George Blake: Double Agent* (New York: Ballantine, 1982), pp. 32–33.
8. Ibid., pp. 79–86.
9. David Martin, *Wilderness of Mirrors* (New York: Harper & Row, 1980), p. 100.
10. Chapman Pincher, *Their Trade Is Treachery* (London: Sidgwick & Jackson, 1982), pp. 150–51.
11. Cookridge, *George Blake*, pp. 213–17.
12. William Hood, *Mole* (New York: Norton, 1981), pp. 265–66.
13. Cookridge, *George Blake*, pp. 163–64.
14. Pincher, *Their Trade is Treachery*, pp. 126, 147, 187.
15. Ibid., pp. 161, 164, 166.

16. Ibid., *Their Trade is Treachery*, pp. 90, 93.
17. Chapman Pincher, *Too Secret Too Long* (London: Sidgwick & Jackson, 1984).
18. "The Treason of Geoffrey Prime," *The Economist*, November 13, 1982, pp. 63–64.
19. Ibid.
20. Ibid.
21. Heinz Hohne and Hermann Zolling, *The General Was a Spy* (New York: Coward, McCann and Geohagen, 1971), pp. xix–xx.
22. Ibid., pp. 245–73, 277–80.
23. Ibid.
24. Ibid.
25. Ibid.
26. Ibid., pp. 192–96.
27. Ibid.
28. James Bamford, *The Puzzle Palace: A Report on NSA, America's Most Secret Agency* (Boston: Houghton Mifflin, 1982), pp. 149–53.
29. Ibid., pp. 153–54.
30. "An FBI 'Rotten Apple'," *Newsweek*, October 15, 1984, pp. 48–49.
31. William Sullivan with Bill Brown, *The Bureau: My Thirty Years in Hoover's FBI* (New York: W. W. Norton, 1979), pp. 188–89.
32. Ibid.
33. Ibid., p. 190.
34. Affadavit, United States of America vs. David Henry Barnett, October 24, 1980.
35. Ibid.
36. John Sawatsky, *For Services Rendered: Leslie James Bennett and the RCMP Security Service* (Garden City, N.Y.: Doubleday, 1982), pp. 64–73.
37. Ibid., pp. 23–32.
38. Martin, *Wilderness of Mirrors*, pp. 190–214.
39. Robert Lindsey, *The Falcon and the Snowman* (New York: Simon & Schuster, 1979), p. 49.
40. Ibid.
41. Ibid.
42. Ibid.
43. Curtis Peebles, "Satellite Photograph Interpretation," *Spaceflight*, October 1982, pp. 161-63.
44. Jeffrey Richelson, "The Keyhole Satellite Program," *Journal of Strategic Studies* 7, no. 2 (1984): 121–53.
45. "The Keyhole Caper," *Newsweek*, September 4, 1978, p. 19.
46. Samuel Cohen and Joseph D. Douglass, Jr., "Selective Targeting and Soviet Deception," *Armed Forces Journal International*, September 1983, pp. 95–101.

47. Viktov Suvorov, *Inside the Soviet Army* (New York: Macmillan, 1982), p. 106.
48. Thomas Powers, *The Man Who Kept the Secrets: Richard Helms and the CIA* (New York: Knopf, 1979), pp. 41–43, 45, 48.
49. Ibid.
50. Martin, *Wilderness of Mirrors.*
51. Ibid., pp. 110–12.
52. Ibid., pp. 112–13.
53. Powers, *The Man Who Kept the Secrets.*
54. "Tale of a Double Agent," *Newsweek*, September 14, 1981, p. 25.

10 THE WARSAW PACT AND CUBAN SERVICES

Soviet use of the Warsaw Pact and Cuban intelligence services to augment the activities of the KGB and GRU is consistent both with Soviet practices for augmenting defense capabilities and the worldwide practice of intelligence liaison and exchange. Thus, the Soviet Union uses the military forces of its Warsaw Pact and Cuban allies to augment its military capability. Use of these forces creates an extended Soviet collective security network.[1] Intelligence liaison and exchange relationships exist between and among large groups of countries, the UKUSA Agreement that involves the United States, United Kingdom, Canada, Australia, and New Zealand being a prominent example.[2]

Soviet use of the Warsaw Pact and Cuban intelligence services has numerous aspects that distinguish it from other intelligence liaison and cooperative relationships. The Soviet role in the creation of the Warsaw Pact services emanates from Soviet movement into Eastern Europe during and after World War II. The intelligence and security services of the East European nations were not created with Soviet advice and counsel but at Soviet direction, which is reflected in the structure, organization, and operations of those services.

In addition to allowing the Soviet Union to increase the resources devoted to intelligence collection and active measures, use of the Warsaw Pact and Cuban services allows penetration by Soviet surrogates into areas or countries off limits, in law or practice, to the KGB. In some countries, East German or Cuban intelligence advisers might be welcomed while the prospect of KGB advisers would be treated with apprehension. In other cases, the travel restrictions placed on Soviet "diplomats" do not apply to Hungarian or Polish "diplomats." Third, approaches to potential Western human sources might be easier through a Polish "trade official" than a Soviet official; the potential source may be far more receptive. Finally, use of other services to perform tasks such as assassination might reduce the risk of exposing the Soviet role, either through investigation or defection of the agent who is assigned the task.

WARSAW PACT SERVICES

The Warsaw Pact intelligence services are essentially mirror images of the Soviet intelligence structure in the early 1940s. Each Warsaw Pact nation generally has a civilian intelligence and security service, with internal and external functions, that is subordinate to the Communist party. The intelligence and security service is usually part of the Ministry of the Interior, as was the case in the Soviet Union in the early 1940s. Additionally, each nation has a military intelligence service subordinate to the General Staff—again, following the Soviet model. Further, the internal structure of the civilian intelligence and security services tends to be quite similar to the structure of the KGB, with directorates for foreign intelligence, counterintelligence, and military counterintelligence, and a department for active measures.

The intelligence and security services of the German Democratic Republic are the Ministry for State Security (MfS—*Ministerium für Staatssicherheit*) and the Military Intelligence Service (MND—*Militairsche Nachrictendienst*). The MfS has responsibilities in the areas of foreign intelligence, military counterintelligence, internal security, and political police work. The foreign intelligence activities of the MfS are conducted by the ministry's Main Administration for Intelligence (HVA—*Hauptverwaltung Aufklaerung*), headed for over twenty years by General Markus Wolf.[3] The HVA employs approximately 1,200 operatives distributed among eight different departments:

1. West German government
2. West German political parties and organizations

3. West German and NATO political links
4. NATO forces and military establishments in West Germany
5. Technical and scientific espionage
6. Agent infiltration of Western countries
7. Analysis and assessment
8. Communications in the agent networks

Department 4 has a small contingent of intelligence collection ships that monitor NATO naval activities in the Baltic and the North Sea.[4]

Domestic functions of the MfS are performed by the State Security Service (SSD). The military counterintelligence department of the SSD has about 1,200 officials and is responsible for detecting espionage and dissidence within the armed forces. About 900 officials are distributed among the command and staffs of the military services and throughout all levels of the military—regiment, division, battalion, and company. These officers wear the uniform and insignia of the service to which they are attached.[5]

Another department is responsible for the surveillance of all economic activities in East Germany. Its agents, located in every large industrial and commercial concern, spy on managers and employees as well as watching productivity. The SSD's counterespionage service has a special tourist section to watch over foreign visitors and provides "guides" to accompany businessmen, visitors to the Leipzig Fairs, and newspaper correspondents. Another department focuses on political, scientific, and cultural organizations. Its activities include censorship of the mail and telecommunications and the advising of the editors and publishers of newspapers, journals, and books. One section looks for deviationist tendencies among university lecturers and students.[6] Protection of heavy industry (including armaments) against industrial espionage is yet another SSD responsibility.

Very little is known about the MND. In fact, its very existence was in doubt until the defection of an MfS officer in 1979.

In Hungary the III Main Group Directorate (III *Foescoe Portfoenocksey*) or State Security Authority (AVH—*Allavedelmi Hatosag*) is the civilian intelligence and security organization.[7] It is responsible for both internal and external intelligence and is subordinate to the Ministry of the Interior. The original nucleus of the AVH was set up in December 1944 by special units of the NKVD which accompanied Soviet occupation forces into Hungary.[8] Military intelligence is the responsibility of General Staff Directorate II (VKF/II).[9]

Intelligence and security functions in Bulgaria are divided between two organizations, known by the initials DS and RUMNO. DS stands for *Durzhavna Sigurnost*, Bulgarian for State Security. It was previously known as the KDS—Committee for State Security—a rather accurate reflection of DS's subservience to the KGB. As the civilian intelligence and security service, the DS is formally subordinate to the Ministry of the Interior, its operations being directed by the First Deputy Minister. It has 700 officers, approximately 350 of whom are abroad; 9,000 agents; and 18,000 domestic informants.[10]

The DS is divided into seven departments. The Department of Foreign Intelligence is responsible both for clandestine intelligence collection and active measures (which may include assassinations) abroad. The Department of Counterintelligence also operates abroad. In addition to monitoring dissidents in Bulgaria, it monitors the activities of exiles. The Department of Military Counterintelligence, like the KGB's Third Directorate, infiltrates the armed forces looking for signs of espionage or subversion.[11]

The Department of Technical Support provides electronic surveillance equipment, such as listening devices and tapping equipment, as well as other devices. It is also responsible for trying to jam the broadcasts of Radio Free Europe. Guarding the major officials of the government and Party is the responsibility of the Department of Security and Vigilance. The Department of Propaganda is responsible for white, grey, and black propaganda operations; the Department of Information and Analysis gathers statistics and analyzes internal matters.[12]

RUMNO is the acronym for Intelligence Division, Ministry of National Defense.[13] As with the East German MND, little information exists in the public domain.

Czechoslovakia and Poland depart from the Soviet model in one way or another. In Poland the civilian security and intelligence organization is known as the SB (*Sluzba Bezpiecezenstwa*) or Security Service.[14] As with other Warsaw Pact services, it has both domestic and foreign functions and is subordinate to the Ministry of the Interior. SB directorates are responsible for foreign intelligence, counterintelligence, political police work, and religious affairs—the separate directorate for religious affairs reflecting the major role of the Church in Polish society.

The SB does not have a directorate, however, for military counterintelligence and countersubversion as does the KGB and other Warsaw Pact civilian security services. Rather, the military counter-intelligence/countersubversion role is performed by an organization established in 1957, the Military Internal Service (WSW—*Wojska Sluzby Wewnetrznej*) of the Ministry of Defense.[15] Whether this location of the military countersubversion function within the Ministry of Defense had a significant, or any, impact on General Jaruzleski's ability to seize power in 1981 is not known. In any case, it might serve to reinforce the location of military countersubversion functions within the Party-dominated civilian intelligence and security services of the other Warsaw Pact nations.

Polish military intelligence is the responsibility of ZARZAD-II (Z-II)—the Second Directorate of the General Staff.

Czechoslovakia also departs from the Soviet model but in a different way than does Poland. Civilian intelligence and security service operations are directed from the Czech Ministry of the Interior. However, no security and intelligence service superstructure exists. Rather, the functions are performed by a variety of independent directorates within the ministry, foreign intelligence being the responsibility of the Main Directorate of Intelligence (HSR—*Hlavni Sprava Rozvedky*).

As of 1969 the HSR was divided into five directorates and a secretariat. Directorate A (Political Intelligence) was subdivided into four departments covering West Germany and German-speaking countries (First Department); Europe (Second Department); Africa-Asia (Third); and the United States, Canada, and Latin America (Fourth).[16] The directorate collects not only political but also economic and sociological intelligence.

Directorate B, Foreign Counterintelligence, had three departments. The First Department or Inspectorate was responsible for the HSR's internal security; the Second Department (Foreign Counterintelligence) actually performed foreign counterintelligence functions—analysis of hostile intelligence services and operations to penetrate and disrupt those services. Directorate B also was responsible for Active Measures and Special Operations, its Third Department being so titled.[17]

The Secretariat of the HSR was divided into four departments: Mobilization, Cadre, Information, and Analytical. Directorate C, Scientific Intelligence, was divided into only two departments—one for the United States (First Department), the other for the rest of the world (Second). Illegals were under the control of the Illegals

Directorate (D), which consisted of four departments. Finally, Directorate E, Rear Units, performed a variety of support services, as indicated by the titles of its four departments: First Department, Records; Second Department, Rear Services; Third Department, Radio & Codes; Fourth Department, Diplomatic Couriers.[18]

The HSR apparently underwent some reorganization as a result of the defection of Joseph Frolik and others after the Soviet invasion in 1968. However, it appears that this reorganization was not extensive.[19]

Internal security and political police activities are the responsibility of the Federal Directorate of Intelligence Services (FSZS), under which there are seven directorates and three special departments. The directorates are: Second (Counterintelligence), Third (Military Counterintelligence), Fourth (Surveillance), Fifth (Protection of Government), Sixth (Technical), Interrogation, and Passport and Visa. The departments are: First Special Department (Records), Second Special Department (Radio Counterintelligence), and Third Special Department (Code Breaking).[20] Whereas responsibility for the HSR lies with the minister himself, the First Deputy Minister supervises the FSZS. Yet another deputy minister is responsible for border protection, supervising the Main Directorate for Protection of Borders.[21]

Military intelligence is the responsibility of the ZSGS (*Zpravodajska Sprava Generalniko Stabu*), the Intelligence Directorate of the General Staff.

Although part of the Warsaw Pact, Romania's intelligence services do not maintain liaison with the KGB and GRU, having broken off liaison relations in 1964.

CUBAN SERVICES

Whatever the present extent of Soviet control over Cuban intelligence operations, the structure of the Cuban intelligence and security community is sharply different from the Soviet model, having emerged, in part, in the early 1960s from the intelligence services of dictator Fulencio Batista.

Organizations concerned with intelligence and security operations include three within the Ministry of the Interior:

- the Directorate General of Intelligence (DGI—*Direccion General de Inteligencia*)

- the Department of State Security (DSE—*Departmento de Sequridad del Estado*)
- the Directorate of Special Operations (DOE—*Direccion de Operaciones Especiales*)

one within the Ministry of Revolutionary Armed Forces:

- the Military Counterintelligence Department

and two subordinate to the Cuban Communist Party's Central Committee:

- the Americas Department (DA—*Departmento America*)
- the Department of Foreign Relations (DGRE—*Departmento General de Relaciones Exteriores*).[22]

Foreign intelligence collection is the responsibility of the DGI. In 1971 the Soviet Union substantially increased its influence and control over the DGI, resulting in the replacement of Manuel Pinero Losada as DGI chief by Jose Mendez Cominches and the entire reorganization of the DGI.[23]

According to a 1976 Air Force report, the DGI's six divisions can be divided into two categories of equal size: the Operational Divisions category and the Support Divisions category. The former category consists of the Political/Economic Intelligence Division, the External Counterintelligence Division, and the Military Intelligence Division; the latter category consists of the Technical Support (M-1) Division, the Information Division, and the Preparation Division.[24]

Other sources indicated that the Political/Economic Intelligence Division consists of four sections: Eastern Europe, U.S. (which operates in Mexico and Canada as well), Western Europe, and Africa-Asia-Latin America.[25] The External Counterintelligence Division operates against foreign intelligence services and exiles. The operations of the Military Intelligence Division are directed mainly at U.S. armed forces. Division representatives are also stationed in Cuban embassies in Western Europe to collect information on NATO and the armed forces of Britain, France, and Italy.[26]

The Technical Support Divison is responsible for secret writing, false passports and other documents, transmission and receipt of coded messages, and devices for carrying concealed microfilm. The Information Division is responsible for analysis and maintaining the files of the DGI.[27] The functions of the Preparation Division are not apparent.

DSE replaced what was called G-2 in the early years of the Castro regime. Headed by the First Vice Minister, Gen. Jose Abrahantes, DSE is responsible for detecting and eliminating dissent as well as for conducting counterespionage activities. In this latter capacity, its prime target is the CIA. DSE also maintains an overseas presence in areas where exiles operate against the Castro regime—for example, Miami. The DOE is an elite special forces detachment used to train guerillas of other countries and is involved in the clandestine transportation of men and materials. DOE troops were the first Cuban troops to enter Angola.[28]

The DA was previously known as the Liberation Department of the Central Committee and prior to that it was subordinate to the DGI. During that period it trained African revolutionaries and provided money and training for those who overthrew the government of Zanzibar in 1963.[29]

The DGRE is headed by an alternate member of the Politburo, Jesus Montane Oropesa, and the DA is headed by former DGI chief, Manuel Pineiro Losada. Both engage in covert activities—the DGRE in Europe, Asia, Africa, and the Middle East, the DA in the Western Hemisphere. These activities may involve support to dissident (guerilla) groups or aid in facilitating a coup.[30]

THE NATURE OF THE RELATIONSHIP

The relationship between the Soviet intelligence and security services and those of the Warsaw Pact nations and Cuba vary with the particular service, the Bulgarians and Cubans being the most and the Romanians the least tightly tied. With the exception of the Romanians, the KGB and GRU exert substantial influence and control over the operations of those services.

The exact nature of the relationship depends on a variety of factors: historical evolution, the internal events in a particular country, Soviet needs, and the ways in which those needs can be satisfied by a particular service. In general, the degree of Soviet control has lessened since the late 1940s and early 1950s. However, situations such as the Czechoslovak Prague Spring and the rise of Solidarity in Poland almost inevitably result in tightened controls in the end.

Thus, when the Warsaw Pact services were initially formed it was Soviet force of arms that backed up NKVD pronouncements concerning the organization and personnel of the new services. Not only were high officials installed at the direction or with the approval of the NKVD but, in some cases, NKVD personnel occupied major positions in the new services. Additionally, Soviet advisers were provided not only to the services as a whole but also to individual departments.[31] The East European services were thus under the tight control of the Soviet Union.

Over time, the Warsaw Pact services became a highly effective and integrated component of the Soviet intelligence network. Their initial purpose was to perform internal security work against Western agents: The Soviet Union staffed and trained them to help keep Eastern Europe under Communist control. With Eastern Europe relatively safely in the Soviet sphere, the services then began to carry out ad hoc assignments for the KGB abroad. Each service focused on its own natural targets.

In these early years Soviet advisers directed these operations, sifted through the intelligence collected for items of interest, and took over the handling of any agent they chose. The agent might be a British diplomat recruited by the Poles or a German parliamentarian recruited by East Germany. Likewise, structural changes, such as the creation of disinformation departments in 1958, could be mandated by the KGB.[32]

Within ten years—that is, by the 1956–57 period—the KGB had established an extended strategic intelligence system with basic missions in support of the KGB assigned to each service. The missions were directed against both European and global targets. By the early 1960s each Warsaw Pact service had its tasks spelled out in a separate formal understanding with the KGB.[33]

This has generally resulted in a loosening of the KGB's leaden hand, but influence is still exerted in a variety of ways—via training, technical assistance, intelligence exchanges, subsidies for special operations, and liaison. These liaison officers have replaced the advisers in most countries; however, they exert considerably more influence than common liaison officers. They can still impose intelligence and operational requirements on each service and have direct access to the intelligence produced. Further, it is via these officers that the East European services submit a yearly account of their activities to Moscow.[34]

In the case of the Warsaw Pact military intelligence services, their subordination to the Soviet Ministry of Defense is established, indirectly, by treaty. The military intelligence directorate of each Warsaw Pact country is subordinate to its Chief of the General Staff, who is in turn subordinate to the Chief of Staff of the Warsaw Pact, who is always a Soviet and simultaneously a First Deputy Minister of Defense.[35]

Not surprisingly, then, the intelligence priorities of the satellite services reflect the concerns of the KGB and GRU, the civilian services being primarily concerned with political, scientific, and economic intelligence on the United States and West European countries and the military services focusing on U.S. and NATO military affairs.[36]

The geographical focus of the services is the product of both their natural targets and KGB input. Hence, 75 percent of the work of the MfS and MND (the East German services) is directed against West Germany, the remaining 25 percent involving Middle East and African targets. Much of the Polish SB's European work is directed against Scandinavia. Bulgarian targets include Turkey, Greece, and Hungary, and prime Czech targets are Austria and West Germany.[37]

Not only is there a geographic division of responsibility but, there is also a substantive one. East Germany's MfS and the Czechoslovak HSR are employed extensively for active measures and training in addition to collection. The Polish and Hungarian services focus mainly on collection, the Bulgarians on collection and assassination. Thus, the MfS has set up and trained personnel for intelligence organizations in Mozambique, Guinea-Bissau, and Angola—the latter at the specific request of the KGB.[38] All can be employed to infiltrate false refugees into Western nations and exploit former citizens who emigrated to the West.

The Warsaw Pact service that is most tightly linked to the KGB, the Bulgarian DS, is the one that since 1964 has been assigned responsibility for "wet affairs"—assassinations.[39] In addition, there are several other strong links between the KGB and DS. KGB advisers oversee its operation and recruit local agents. Further, most DS personnel are graduates of Moscow's Institute for International Relations and spend six to seven years in the Soviet Union.[40] Finally, there is at least one officer in every embassy that reports to the KGB.[41]

As noted above, the relationship between the Czech, Polish, and Hungarian services and the KGB has changed with time. Until the mid-1960s the Czech services had numerous KGB advisers who were informed of all operations from their initial planning stages. After that time and until the 1968 invasion, there was a relative degree of independence. By early 1969 KGB advisers were once again installed at headquarters department level and in regional and district offices.[42]

In the early 1950s the MGB (and then the KGB) exercised strict supervision over the Polish civilian intelligence and security service, then known as the UB (*Uzrad Bezpiecezenstwa*-Security Forces). Each branch of the UB had to inform its Soviet adviser of its activities. In some instances, the Soviet adviser ordered a case dropped. In other instances, the UB was instructed to recruit an individual of Polish origin. Documents collected or produced by the UB were translated into Russian and sent to Moscow.[43]

During the 1956 uprising that restored Gomulka to power, the Soviet advisers were kicked out of UB headquarters. They soon set up an alternative headquarters and by the end of 1956 and the revolution in Hungary were regulating UB contact with other Warsaw Pact services.[44] In Hungary Soviet advisers first arrived in 1949 and after 1956 were renamed "collaborators," with their number being reduced. However, the Hungarian services pass all significant intelligence to the KGB and consult it about prospective agents. The KGB provides technical assistance and might finance operations of special interest.[45]

In the case of Cuba, the intelligence relationship dates back to 1959, 1968–1971 being the most important years in determining the nature of the relationship. In 1968 a committee consisting of the chiefs of Cuba's intelligence services went to the Soviet Union to offer intelligence gathered in the United States.[46] The Soviets accepted the intelligence and proceeded to turn the DGI into a KGB subsidiary.

By 1969 the Soviet Union and Cuba had developed an involved relationship with the Soviets, providing massive economic support to Castro's regime. The Soviets employed this economic lever to pressure the Cubans to follow the Soviet line more directly. The pressure was successful in producing a Cuban surrender during Raul Castro's visit to the Soviet Union in April and May 1970.[47]

The anti-Soviet chief of the DGI was replaced by a pro-Soviet chief, as noted earlier. Prior to 1970 intelligence plans had been approved by the head of the DGI. After Raul Castro's visit a Soviet adviser, General Semenev, was installed in a suite next to the director and given initial approval authority for their development. The plans were then sent to the Soviet Union for final approval.[48]

Under this new arrangement the DGI also had to send the KGB the names of all their agents working in the United States. Previously, the DGI only sent pseudonyms. The DGI also altered the focus of its activities, as the Soviets had never been favorable toward Castro's attempts to export revolution. Thus, DGI activities in New York were switched from support of a Puerto Rican liberation group to the collection of information about the United States.[49]

Presently, twenty Cuban agents work out of the Cuban Interest Section in the Czechoslovak embassy in Washington, and about forty Cuban agents work at the Cuban mission to the United Nations, including employees of the Americas Department and the Cuban Institute for the Friendship with People (ICAP).[50]

The relationship has proved to be extremely valuable for the Soviet Union. In 1971 the Cuban agents in London took over control of Soviet agents when 107 Soviets were expelled.[51] In the past decade Cuban intelligence has also developed a good reputation in more distant areas, especially in the Far East, where its officers seek to develop agents with access to government officials in the Philippines, Tokyo, and Indonesia.[52]

According to Harry Rositzke,

> the usefulness to the KGB of Cuban intelligence cannot be underrated. In Latin America itself it has natural advantages over the KGB—the absence of a language barrier (outside Brazil) as well as the increasingly benign image of Havana in many Latin American countries. All of these open many doors for the Cubans that are closed to the Russians. Cuban intelligence now has a working liaison with some security services, for example in Panama and Venezuela.[53]

HUMAN SOURCES

Soviet use of the intelligence services of the Warsaw Pact countries for human collection began once those services were firmly established and the situation in each country stabilized. It is estimated that 30 to 40 percent of all East Bloc officials in the United States—diplomats, correspondents, and trade officials—are intelligence officers. This gives the Soviet extended intelligence network a strength of 180 to 240—an increase of about 50 percent over the estimated number of Soviet intelligence officials.[54]

And as noted earlier the officers are not subject to the same travel restrictions in the United States as Soviet officials. The United States imposes such restrictions only when areas of foreign countries are specifically closed to U.S. diplomats. Since the East European countries do not impose such restrictions on U.S. diplomats, the United States imposes no such restrictions on East European diplomats (this excludes sensitive areas declared off limits to all but authorized personnel).[55]

Restrictions placed on Soviet diplomats are determined only partly by security concerns. In other cases, areas are designated off limits to Soviet officials for no particular reason other than the need to implement the official policy of reciprocity. Areas denied to Soviet officials include Silicon Valley, Houston (because of its being the center of oil technology), and areas of Los Angeles County that include the RAND Corporation, TRW, and Lockheed. Even travel to "open" areas requires advance notification except when the travel is within a twenty-five-mile radius of a Soviet mission. There are three such missions in the United States: the San Francisco consulate, the U.N. mission in New York, and the Washington, D.C. embassy.[56] Hence, the lack of travel restrictions on Polish and other officials has allowed the Soviet Union to productively employ surrogates in sensitive areas of the United States, as demonstrated below.

Outside of the United States the relationship has also been fruitful. The East German MfS ran an agent for twenty years. When finally detected and arrested in 1979 this agent, Gunter Guillaume, had completed several years of service as a high-ranking aide to West German Chancellor Willy Brandt. The arrest resulted in Brandt's resignation from office.[57]

Czechoslovak intelligence ran agents in both the British and West German parliaments. The German agent was Alfred Frenzel, a member of the Bundestag's NATO Defense Committee. Frenzel was recruited in 1956 and, until his arrest in 1960, passed NATO weaponry information to his Czech contact, who met Frenzel on twenty-two different occasions inside the Bundestag itself.[58]

In the 1950s the Polish UB recruited a British clerk in Moscow, Henry Houghton. Houghton was transferred back to London, where he worked for the British naval establishment and the KGB—the latter took him over from the UB.[59] More recently in the United States Polish agents have acquired a variety of military and technological secrets from two employees of defense contractors.

William Bell, a Hughes engineer, passed substantial amounts of information to a Polish agent. Beginning in 1979 Bell delivered a variety of documents to a Polish agent who was operating under cover of a Polish trade firm with offices in southern California. The documents concern the F–15 look-down, shoot-down radar system, the quiet radar system for the B-1 and Stealth bomber, an all-weather radar system for tanks, an experimental radar system for the U.S. Navy, the Phoenix air-to-air missile, a shipborne surveillance radar, the Patriot surface-to-air missile, and a NATO air defense system. The documents might make possible the design of effective countermeasures as well as save the Soviet Union millions in R&D costs.[60]

A subsequent case involving the sale beginning in 1980 of classified documents to Polish agents involves James D. Harper, a Silicon Valley electrical engineer. Harper, via his wife, who worked for a southern California defense contractor, obtained copies of well over a hundred pounds of classified reports which he sold to the SB for over $250,000. Most of the documents pertained to the U.S. Minuteman missile and ballistic missile defense programs and were classified either Confidential or Secret. According to the affidavit of FBI agent Allan Power, the documents "describe extremely sensitive research and development efforts undertaken by the Department of Defense which would enable the Minuteman missile and other strategic forces of the United States to survive a preemptive nuclear attack by the Soviet Union."[61] The documents sold to the SB included the 1978 *Minuteman Defense Study (Final Report)*, the 1981 *Report on the Task Force on U.S. Ballistic Missile Defense*, and a 1978 Martin Marietta Corporation study entitled *Endoatmospheric Nonnuclear Kill Technology Requirements and Definition Study.*[62]

The Harper case is a particularly good illustration of an East Bloc intelligence service acting on behalf of the KGB. When Harper first brought some of his documents to Warsaw in June 1980, a team of twenty KGB scientists and engineers flew in to examine them. Subsequently, the SB officers running Harper received a letter of commendation signed by then KGB Chairman, Yuri Andropov.[63] Harper was detected by a CIA mole in the SB. When arrested he was preparing to deliver an additional 150 to 200 pounds of documents.[64]

The Czechoslovak civilian foreign intelligence service, the HSR, operates in the United States through the Czechoslovak embassy and U.N. mission as well as through CSA (Czechoslovak Airlines), CTK (press office), CEDOK (travel office), and the various commercial organizations (e.g., Jawa and Juzek) located in a number of U.S. cities. There are four basic areas of concentration: politics, counterintelligence, science and technology, and economics. The primary political targets include the Pentagon, White House, State Department, National Security Council, and State Department; lesser targets include the Congress, the major political parties, and mass organizations such as the AFL–CIO and National Association for the Advancement of Colored People (NAACP).[65]

The scientific and intelligence targets of the HSR in the United States include government research organizations and research organizations of private companies oriented toward military research of all varieties, chemistry, and computers. Economic targets include the Departments of Commerce, Treasury, and Agriculture. The main information sought concerns economic relations between the United States and the Common Market, the United States and developing countries, and the United States and the socialist bloc.[66]

The Czech military intelligence service in the United States also operates through the embassy's attachés (air and military), 30 percent of its diplomatic personnel, and 10 percent of its commercial section's personnel. Its targets include naval air and ground bases, troop movements, troop morale, and new types of weapons.[67]

Other recent attempts to acquire information for eventual transmittal to Moscow have involved the Mfs and DS. Thus, an East German physicist affiliated with the MfS was arrested on charges of attempting to obtain classified information on military technology from a civilian Navy employee. The physicist had met the Navy employee, who worked for the Naval Electronics System Engineering Center in Charleston, South Carolina, in Mexico City in October 1982. The physicist requested that the employee obtain classified documents and manuals dealing with military technology.[68] Similarly, the assistant counselor of the Bulgarian Commercial Office in New York was arrested in September 1983 for attempting to purchase secret documents on security procedures for U.S. nuclear weapons, including one document entitled *Report on Inspection of Nevada Operations Office.*[69]

TECHNICAL COLLECTION

Although the primary utility to the Soviet Union of the Cuban and Warsaw Pact nations' intelligence service is with respect to human source collection and active measures, they also augment Soviet technical collection activities. In July 1982 two Cuban U.N. delegates were expelled for attempting to set a telecommunications monitoring system for eavesdropping on U.S. satellite relays.[70] On April 8 of the previous year—two days before the first space shuttle launch from Cape Canaveral was to occur—CSA requested a "special flight" through U.S. airspace which would overfly Cape Canaveral. When the launch was postponed CSA requested new flight dates that coincided with the shuttle launch schedule.[71]

As noted above, the MfS maintains a small fleet of ships that collect signals intelligence. Cuba also maintains intelligence-gathering ships. The Cuban Navy converted a large trawler into an intelligence-gathering ship, the *Balzan*, to shadow U.S. naval activities in the Caribbean.[72] In 1983 U.S. intelligence received information that Soviet signals intelligence equipment had been mounted on a Cuban merchant ship, the *Isla de la Juventud.* The equipment will enhance Cuban capability to collect intelligence within the Caribbean area against the United States as well as other Caribbean countries.[73]

Cuba has also conducted airborne ocean surveillance operations. In 1983 six Cuban Bear aircraft followed the initial stages of the naval exercise of the United States Second Fleet with British and Dutch units.[74]

COUNTERINTELLIGENCE

The KGB has also exploited East Bloc services for counterintelligence purposes. One particular case occurred in the mid-1960s when the Czechoslovak government decided to allow Germans living in Czechoslovakia to resettle in West Germany if they chose. Seventy thousand requests were received from the 170,000 Germans then living in Czechoslovakia.[75]

In numerous cases, the applicants were told they could emigrate provided they would agree to become agents of the HSR. The expectation was that they would agree and then report their "recruitment" to West German authorities. To make their recruitment more plausible they were given rudimentary training in tradecraft and communications. Thus, they learned techniques such as invisible ink writing and cover addresses. They were also given targets to investigate and report on.[76]

The HSR had no expectation that their new "recruits" would ever become operative. The entire operation, Operation Transfer, was a counterintelligence operation with two objectives. The first was to divert West German intelligence and counterintelligence resources by causing lengthy and numerous interviews. The expected consequence was an easier environment for true Soviet Bloc agents. The second objective was to, by purposely giving the emigrés false or nonpriority targets, divert West German attention from the real targets as well as mislead them concerning the state of Czech knowledge concerning the target base.[77]

According to the FBI, Czech intelligence also helped the KGB achieve a low-level penetration of the CIA. According to an FBI account, Karl F. Koecher was trained by the HSR as an intelligence officer from 1963 to 1965 and entered the United States legally in 1965. Subsequently, Koecher became a naturalized American citizen and obtained employment with the CIA. From February 1973 to August 1975 Koecher was a Washington-based employed as a support or contract employee and had access to classified information. In 1975 he was transferred to New York, where he served until he left the agency in 1977.[78]

ACTIVE MEASURES

The intelligence services of Cuba and of several Warsaw Pact nations have been used extensively for the conduct of active measures operations. In some cases, there was clearly no direct German or Czechoslovak interest but a definite Soviet interest.

Recently, the East Germans began financing a Communist newspaper in Greece.[79] Among previous East German operations have been several forgeries and a book allegedly listing CIA agents. The forgeries date back to 1958 and include an alleged report by Secretary of State John Foster Dulles on how to sabotage an upcoming summit conference.

In 1968 the East Germans were responsible for the publication of *Who's Who in the C.I.A.* by Julius Mader. The book purported to be a listing of CIA personnel. It includes not only CIA personnel but a large number of U.S. diplomats, politicians, newsmen, public officials, Peace Corps Volunteers, and United States Information Agency (USIA) employees. The objective was not so much to impede the work of the CIA personnel named but rather to tarnish and impede the work of non-CIA personnel—such as Peace Corps volunteers—who dealt with the public or public officials abroad.

Czech active measures operations have included a 1956 operation to damage the workings of a right-wing German organization as well as Operation Neptune and Operation Thomas Mann. In 1956 the Czech intelligence organization sent out hundreds of letters to important foreigners thanking them for support of the Sudeten movement, when in fact those individuals were opposed to its activities. In addition to deluging the organization with complaints, it further damaged its reputation.[80]

Two major operations were conducted in 1964—one close to home, one far away. Operation Thomas Mann was intended to demonstrate that U.S. foreign policy toward Latin America had undergone a fundamental reevaluation since the death of John Kennedy. The "change" was to increase economic exploitation and political interference in the domestic affairs of Latin American countries. The "author" of this new policy was to be identified as Assistant Secretary of State Thomas Mann.[81]

The operation involved the dissemination of a series of forgeries. First, a counterfeit USIA press release was produced that contained a statement of the principles of the "new" U.S. foreign policy. Second, a series of circulars was published in the name of the nonexistent "Committee for the Struggle Against Yankee Imperialism" which named hundreds of CIA, Pentagon, and FBI agents. Third, a forged letter attributed to J. Edgar Hoover gave credit to the FBI and CIA for the Brazilian military's coup d'état of April 1964.[82] The campaign was successful in drawing press attention to the charges over a period of months. One newspaper ran the USIA memo story under the headline "MANN FIXES HARDLINE FOR THE USA," and numerous papers picked up the Hoover letter story.[83]

The operation that took place closer to home was Operation Neptune. In the last days of May 1964 members of Czech intelligence lowered four large, asphalt-coated cases into the Bohemian Black Lake. Several weeks later the cases were "discovered" by a Czech television crew while shooting a documentary film. The discovery represented one part of Operation Neptune. The documents were Nazi documents, the discovery and distribution of which was intended to aid Soviet/Czech propaganda and political objectives with respect to West Germany.[84]

The specific goals were to:

1. develop a campaign against the lapse of the statute of limitations for war crimes in West Germany, the statute being due to expire in May 1965;
2. exploit the war crimes question in an anti-German political campaign in order to revive anti-German feelings; and
3. limit the activities of the West German Federal Intelligence Service (BND) on Czech soil.[85]

The documents were authentic and were drawn from both Czech and Soviet archives. Included were materials on the activities of the Nazi party's Security Service (SD) in Italy during World War II. The documents indicated extensive SD espionage directed against their Italian allies. Also included were documents concerning the operations of German military intelligence (the Abwehr) in France after the June 1944 Allied invasion as well as documents on the treatment of Allied POWs. In addition to producing an extension of the statute of limitations for war crimes, the operation also had success in stimulating anti-German feelings in France and Italy.[86]

The extent to which the Warsaw Pact and Cuban services have been employed by the Soviet Union to support terrorism and assassinations have been subjects that have generated much controversy. It is well known that the Soviet Union and the rest of the Soviet Bloc provide training and aid to national liberation movements, including aid to liberation movements that have employed terrorist tactics. The most prominent recipient of such aid has been the Palestine Liberation Organization (PLO), as noted in Chapter 7. According to one account, East Germany's MfS supplied the PLO with important information required for carrying out an attack against industrial installations in West Berlin, and Czechoslovakia provided a training base for those who in 1973 took over a train in Austria that was carrying immigrants from the Soviet Union. In 1977 approximately 300 Palestinians were reported to be training in Cuba.[87]

It has also been alleged that the KGB and the East European services operate training camps in the vicinity of Pankow and Finsterwalde in East Germany, and at Varna in Bulgaria, Karlovy Vary and Ostrava in Czechoslovakia, and Lake Balaton in Hungary.[88] Among the groups—some of whose members allegedly have been trained at such bases as well as bases in Algeria (by Cuban instructors) and Soviet Yemen (by Cuban and East German instructors)—are the Irish Republican Army, ETA (Basque Separatists), and Red Brigades.[89] One report stated that East Germany ran a life support system for the Baader-Meinhof Gang since 1970, when that organization's first safe house was set up in East Berlin. The MfS allegedly furnished false documents, money, paramilitary training, and weapons storage.[90]

Most recently, in addition to charges of Bulgarian complicity in the attempted assassination of Pope John Paul II, it has been asserted that the Soviet Union and Bulgaria, via the DS, have been involved in drug smuggling and support of Turkish terrorist groups.[91] The support to the Turkish left-wing groups is said to involve a "massive arms-smuggling operation."[92] It is safe to assume that any East European and Cuban support of such groups has received at least a nod of approval from the KGB. However, the extent of support (if any) that there presently is for groups like Baader-Meinhof, the Red Brigades, and the Japanese Red Army is not clear. As noted earlier, according to some intelligence officials, information alleging such links dates back to the late 1960s.[93]

It is beyond the scope of this book to discuss in any detail the charges of Soviet and Bulgarian complicity in the attempted assassination of Pope John Paul II.[94] If such complicity exists it will be the first time since the early 1960s that individuals other than defectors and emigrés were targeted by the Soviet Union for assassination. It should be noted that Bulgaria does hold the KGB "franchise" for "wet work." As mentioned earlier, in 1964 the KGB and DS signed a protocol under which the DS would carry out any assassinations that the KGB considered necessary. Of course, that does not mean that the franchise was exercised in the case of Pope John Paul II. Indeed, it seems that the "Bulgarian connection" may well be the creation of elements of the Italian military intelligence service.[95]

NOTES TO CHAPTER 10

1. Avigdor Haselkorn, "The Expanding Soviet Collective Security Network." *Strategic Review* 6, no. 3 (1978): 62–73.
2. Jeffrey Richelson and Desmond Ball, *Ties that Bind* (London: Allen & Unwin, 1985).
3. E. H. Cookridge, *Gehlen: Spy of the Century* (New York: Random House, 1972), pp. 268–69.
4. Ibid., pp. 269–70; "More on Misha," *Foreign Report*, November 8, 1984: 1–4.
5. Cookridge, *Gehlen*, p. 269; A. Ross Johnson, Robert W. Dean, and Alexander Alexiev, *East European Military Establishments: The Warsaw Pact Northern Tier* (New York: Crane & Russak, 1982), p. 78.
6. Cookridge, *Gehlen*, pp. 269–70.
7. Air Force Office of Special Investigations, *Special Report: Hungarian Intelligence Services (U)* (Washington, D.C.: AFOSI, 1975), p. i.
8. Paul Ignotus, "The AVH: Symbol of Terror," *Problems of Communism* 6, no. 5 (September 1957): 19–25.
9. Air Force Office of Special Investigations, *Special Report: Hungarian Intelligence Services (U)*, p. i.
10. Nicholas Gage, "Bulgarian Agents Described as Ready to Do Moscow's Bidding," *New York Times*, March 23, 1983, p. 12.
11. Ibid.
12. Ibid.
13. Air Force Office of Special Investigations, *Special Report: Bulgarian Intelligence Services (U)* (Washington, D.C.: AFOSI, 1975), p. i.
14. David Wise, "How Our Spy Spied Their Spy," *Los Angeles Times*, October 23, 1983, p. 6 (Part IV).
15. Johnson, Dean, and Alexiev, *East European Military Establishments*, pp. 37–38.
16. U.S. Congress, Senate Committee on the Judiciary, *Communist Bloc Intelligence Activities in the United States* (Washington, D.C.: U.S. Government Printing Office, 1975), p. 30.
17. Ibid.
18. Ibid.
19. Ibid., p. 57.
20. Ibid., p. 31.
21. Ibid.
22. Jay Mallin, "How Cuban Agents Deliver Arms to Leftist Guerrillas in El Salvador," *Washington Times*, August 22, 1983, pp. 1A, 5A.
23. Brian Crozier, "Soviet Pressures in the Caribbean: The Satellisation of Cuba," *Conflict Studies* 35 (May 1973).

24. Air Force Office of Special Investigations, *Special Report: The Cuban Intelligence Service* (Washington, D.C.: AFOSI, 1976), p. i.

25. Crozier, "Soviet Pressures in the Caribbean."

26. Ibid.

27. Ibid.

28. Mallin, "How Cuban Agents Deliver Arms. . . . "

29. Crozier, "Soviet Pressures in the Caribbean."

30. Mallin, "How Cuban Agents Deliver Arms. . . ."

31. See Mr. X with Bruce E. Henderson and C. C. Cyr, *Double Eagle* (New York: Ballantine, 1979), pp. 110–115.

32. Ladislav Bittman, *The Deception Game: Czechoslovak Intelligence in Soviet Political Warfare* (Syracuse, N.Y.: Syracuse University Research Corporation, 1972), ch. 4.

33. Harry Rositzke, *KGB: The Eyes of Russia* (Garden City, N.Y.: Doubleday, 1981), p. 142.

34. "Bulgaria's Spy Masters," *Newsweek*, January 3, 1983, p. 27.

35. Viktor Suvorov, *Soviet Military Intelligence* (London: Hamish Hamilton, 1984), p. 42.

36. Brian Crozier, "The Surrogate Forces of the Soviet Union," *Conflict Studies* No. 92, 1978.

37. Ibid.; John Vinocur, "The KGB Goes on the Offensive and the West Begins Striking Back," *New York Times*, July 24, 1983, pp. 1ff.

38. Crozier, "The Surrogate Forces of the Soviet Union."

39. Nicholas Gage, "Bulgarian Agents Described as Ready to Do Moscow's Bidding."

40. "Bulgaria's Spy Masters."

41. Gage, "Bulgarian Agents Described as Ready to Do Moscow's Bidding."

42. Crozier, "The Surrogate Forces of the Soviet Union."

43. Mr. X., *Double Eagle*, pp. 110–115.

44. Ibid.

45. Ignotus, "The AVH."

46. U.S. Congress, Senate Committee on the Judiciary, *The Role of Cuba in International Terrorism and Subversion* (Washington, D.C.: U.S. Government Printing Office, 1982), p. 11.

47. Crozier, "Soviet Pressures in the Caribbean."

48. U.S. Congress, Senate Committee on the Judiciary, *The Role of Cuba in International Terrorism and Subversion*, p. 24.

49. Ibid., p. 12.

50. Ibid.; David Atlee Phillips, "Castro's Spies Are No Longer Teenagers," *Retired Officer*, January 1982, pp. 16–19.

51. Phillips, "Castro's Spies Are No Longer Teenagers."

52. Rositzke, *The KGB*, p. 225.

53. Ibid., pp. 225–26.

54. U.S. Congress, House Committee on the Judiciary, *Communist Bloc Intelligence Gathering Activities on Capitol Hill* (Washington, D.C.: U.S. Government Printing Office, 1982), p. 13.

55. Bernard Gwertzman, "State Department Alters the Rules for Russians' Travel in U.S.," *New York Times*, November 20, 1983, pp. 1, 17; Steve Harvay, "Ban on Soviet Travel is Map of Curiosities," *Los Angeles Times*, December 9, 1983, pp. 1, 2 (Metro).

56. Ibid.

57. Rositzke, *The KGB*, pp. 149–50.

58. Joseph Frolik, *The Frolik Defection* (London: Leo Cooper, 1975), p. 160.

59. Rositzke, *The KGB*, p. 144.

60. John Barron, *The KGB Today: The Hidden Hand* (New York: Reader's Digest Press, 1983), pp. 196–204.

61. Affadavit of Allan M. Power, Federal Bureau of Investigation, submitted to State and Northern District of California, City and County of San Francisco, October 16, 1983, pp. 1–2.

62. "Partners in Espionage," *Security Awareness Bulletin*, August 1984, 4–84, pp. 1–8; Linda Melvern, David Hebditch, and Nick Anning, *Techno-Bandits; How the Soviets Are Stealing America's High Tech Future* (Boston: Houghton Mifflin, 1984), p. 242.

63. Affadavit of Allan M. Power; "For Love of Money and Adventure," *Time*, October 31, 1983, pp. 39–40. On the Harper case, see also Wallace Turner, "American Is Arrested on Charges of Selling Poland Missile Secrets," *New York Times*, October 18, 1983, pp. A1, A25; Howard Kurtz, "California Man Charged with Spying," *Washington Post*, October 18, 1983, pp. A1, A4.

64. Affadavit of Allan M. Power; Howard Kurtz, "Spy Suspect Said to Possess More Missile Documents," *Washington Post*, October 19, 1983, p. A20.

65. U.S. Congress, Senate Committee on the Judiciary, *Communist Bloc Intelligence Activities in the United States*, p. 4.

66. Ibid., p. 5.

67. Ibid.

68. Leslie Maitland Werner, "East German Held in Espionage Case," *New York Times*, November 4, 1983, p. A20; Colin Norman, "To Catch a Spy," *Science* 222 (November 1983): 904–5.

69. Robert D. McFadden, "U.S. Says Bulgarian Suspect Bought Data on Atom Arms," *New York Times*, September 25, 1983, pp. 1, 6.

70. Michael J. Berlin, "U.S. Expels 2 Cubans at U.N. for Spying," *Washington Post*, April 20, 1983, p. A17.

71. "CSA's April 10–12 'Special Flights' and the Space Shuttle Launch," *Armed Forces Journal International*, May 1981, p. 56.

72. Drew Middleton, "U.S. Officers Report a Buildup by Cuba," *New York Times*, March 28, 1983, p. A3.

73. Department of Defense, *Soviet Military Power 1984* (Washington, D.C.: U.S. Government Printing Office, 1984), p. 126.
74. Middleton. "U.S. Officers Report a Buildup by Cuba."
75. Ladislav Bittman, *The Deception Game, Czechoslovak Intelligence in Soviet Political Warfare* (Syracuse, N.Y.: Syracuse University Research Corporation, 1972), pp. 75-78.
76. Ibid.
77. Ibid.
78. "Ex-C.I.A. Employee Held as Czech Spy," *New York Times*, November 28, 1984, pp. A1, A13; Selwyn Raab, "Intrigue and Countercharges Mark Case of Purported Spies," *New York Times*, January 13, 1985, pp. 1, 20.
79. Paul Anastasi, "East Germany Helps Party in Greece Publish," *New York Times*, October 7, 1983, p. A15.
80. Bittman, *The Deception Game*, pp. 72-78.
81. Ibid., pp. 102-6.
82. Ibid., pp. 39-72.
83. Ibid.
84. Ibid.
85. Ibid.
86. Ibid.
87. Ray S. Cline and Yonah Alexander, *Terrorism: The Soviet Connection* (New York: Crane & Russak, 1983), pp. 45, 71.
88. Ibid.
89. Ibid., p. 71; Claire Sterling, *The Terror Network* (New York: Berkley Books, 1982), p. 155.
90. Sterling, *The Terror Network*, p. 270.
91. Henry Kamm, "Bonn is Fearful of Bulgaria Tie with Terrorists," *New York Times*, December 12, 1982, p. 18; "Testimony of Robert Moss," in U.S. Congress, Senate Committee on the Judiciary, *Terrorism: The Role of Moscow and Its Subcontractors* (Washington, D.C.: U.S. Government Printing Office, 1981), p. 43.
92. "Testimony of Robert Moss."
93. Leslie Gelb, "Soviet-Terror Ties Called Outdated," *New York Times*, October 18, 1981, p. 9.
94. The two major works charging complicity are Claire Sterling, *The Time of the Assassins* (New York: Holt, Reinhart and Winston, 1983) and Paul Henze, *The Plot to Kill the Pope* (New York: Charles Scribner's Sons, 1983). For a skeptical review, see William Hood, "Unlikely Conspiracy," *Problems of Communism* (March–April 1984): 67-70. Also see, Frank Brodhead, Howard Friel, and Edward S. Herman, "The 'Bulgarian Connection' Revisited," *Covert Action Information Bulletin* 23 (Spring 1985): 3-38.
95. See Alexander Cockburn, "The Gospel According to Ali Agca," *The Nation*, July 6/13, 1985, pp. 1, 6-7.

11 INTERNAL SECURITY

Although it is the external aspects of the KGB's activities that attract the most attention throughout the world, it is the domestic side of its activities that represents the major expenditure of resources and utilization of manpower. KGB domestic activities can be subdivided, albeit not perfectly, into internal security and political police activities.

Internal security operations are the responsibility of the Second Chief Directorate (Counterintelligence), the Third Directorate (Armed Forces Directorate or Directorate of Special Departments), the Seventh (Surveillance) Directorate, the Ninth (Guards) Directorate, the Border Guards Directorate, and the Government Signal Troops. Well over 300,000 individuals are involved in this aspect of KGB activity.

With the exception of the Second Chief Directorate, all of the above-mentioned units operate, on various occasions, outside Soviet borders. Their primary activities, however, take place within Soviet territory.

COUNTERINTELLIGENCE AND SECURITY

The primary mission of the Second Chief Directorate is to prevent hostile intelligence services—particularly those of the United States and Britain—from acquiring information that the Soviet leadership wishes to deny them. A KGB manual entitled *Fundamentals of Counter-Espionage Activities of KGB Organs* specified that the counterintelligence functions were:

- to discover the agents of foreign espionage organizations;
- to keep a check on everything dispatched abroad;
- to check postal dispatches for the presence of secret writing and other forms of conspiratorial communication; and
- to keep a check on the internal correspondence from persons working and residing in areas where special security regulations are in force.[1]

In seeking to perform these functions, the KGB carries out a variety of human and technical surveillance operations. These activities include the trailing of embassy personnel and Soviet citizens under suspicion, human and technical monitoring of particular locations or establishments (the latter via cameras and audio devices), and the interception of embassy and individual communications—whether by phone or radio transmission.

Specific locations that are the subject of surveillance obviously include foreign embassies as the priority target. Also included are the hotels and restaurants to which tourists are guided as well as motels, campsites, gasoline stations, and garages along highways traveled by tourists.[2] Surveillance in hotels involves that performed by informers as well as by audio and video devices installed in some rooms.

Several KGB activities performed by the Second Chief Directorate simultaneously serve counterintelligence, political police, and recruitment purposes. These activities include control of Intourist, through which unofficial visitors must make their travel plans, and Sputnik, a travel agency that offers economy trips for foreign youth. Additionally, authorized contacts between tourists and Soviet citizens are planned, and unplanned contacts are investigated.[3]

Surveillance of U.S. diplomats has produced at least two expulsions for espionage activities in recent years. On March 10, 1983 Richard Osborne, a first secretary at the embassy, was expelled. According to the Soviet account, Osborne was caught "red-handed" working with portable satellite communications gear and other espionage equipment.[4] Previous to that the Soviets expelled U.S. diplomat Martha Petersen in 1977, charging that she had been servicing a dead drop. Petersen was apparently detected as a consequence of the Soviets' uncovering a U.S. agent, codenamed Trigon, operating in the Soviet Foreign Ministry.[5]

In addition to counterintelligence, industrial security is an important aspect of domestic KGB activities, particularly with regard to weapons-related industry. Thus, the KGB, through the Second Chief Directorate, monitors the situation in heavy industry, arms production factories, nuclear research, and nuclear production facilities. Each such facility has a First Department staffed by KGB personnel to perform countersubversion, counterintelligence, and security functions.[6]

To further restrict the acquisition of information by foreigners (and further curb unauthorized contacts between foreigners and Russians), the Soviet Union in 1984 promulgated a new law providing prison terms for anyone passing economic, scientific, technical, or other "official" secrets to foreigners. Thus, Article 13-1 of the Soviet legal code, titled "Passing Information Comprising Official Secrets to Foreign Organizations," stated that

> Passing and gathering with the intention of passing to foreign organizations or their representatives economic, scientific-technological or other information comprising official secrets, by a person to whom this information was entrusted through service or work or became known by other means, will be punished by deprivation of freedom for up to three years or corrective work for up to two years.

The law would seem to cover not only state secrets, which are already covered by a multitude of laws, but also information received at work—whether classified or not.[7]

MONITORING THE ARMED FORCES

There are two very interesting general points to be made concerning Soviet monitoring of their armed forces. First, it is a case where the security, counterintelligence, and "countersubversion" functions merge; indeed, the latter may be the most important of the three in Soviet eyes. The Soviet leadership may feel more threatened by some of its own troops than by foreign agents. Second, it represents, with regard to the countersubversion function, a perfect example of a dual system at work, with the covert activities of the KGB's Third Directorate complementing and reinforcing the overt activities of the Main Political Administration of the Soviet Army and Navy (MPA).

In regard to the first point, it might be noted that, according to John Barron, the Third Directorate is organized not along functional lines (i.e., counterespionage, countersubversion) but by the targeted portion of the military. Thus, it is allegedly broken down into twelve departments: Ministry of Defense/General Staff, GRU, conventional ground forces, naval forces, air forces, border troops, military and internal troops under the MVD, missile forces, nuclear forces, civil aviation, and the Moscow military district.[8]

The organization officially responsible for the overt political education of the armed forces and ensuring continued political reliability of both officers and noncommissioned personnel is the MPA. The MPA political officers in each unit are identified to the other military personnel and hold open discussions, lectures, and meetings. The MPA also aids in the combat preparation of troops; controls the ideological content of military newspapers, journals, and publishing houses; and takes part in the selection and placement of officers.[9]

Military Counter–Intelligence Regulation No. 00270 of September 8, 1961 specified the duties of the armed forces special departments to include:

1. preventing enemy agent networks from penetrating into units and establishments of the Soviet Army, Navy, KGB, and MVD forces;
2. identifying and unmasking agents and others who have penetrated the armed forces;
3. searching for imperialist agents among the armed forces and their immediate surroundings;
4. averting cases of treason to the motherland by individual servicemen, workers, and employees of units and establishments;
5. ensuring the preservation of state military secrets and severing channels of leakage of secret information abroad;
6. counterintelligence work on special and particularly important targets and on transport, and
7. suppressing hostile actions of anti-Soviet and nationalist elements within the country.[10]

The emphasis in the regulation is on counterintelligence, but the countersubversion or political police functions that are implicit are at least as important—since in the Soviet Union treason involves not only the disclosure of classified information to a foreign power, but also political activities, even thoughts, that might "undermine" the Soviet state.

As a result of being assigned the responsibility of preserving state secrets, the special departments are responsible for all security clearances of military personnel and investigation of violations of security regulations.[11] According to one Soviet account, the importance of maintaining security has increased with the advent of nuclear weapons: "The reliable defense of Soviet forces from all types of espionage took on special significance when the basic defensive strength of the country came to consist of the most contemporary weapons systems, especially ballistic-nuclear weapons."[12]

As a result of their role in supervising security arrangements and issuing clearances, the special departments have control over or access to military personnel files and all information relating to the political reliability of members of the armed forces. In addition to examining such files for signs of treason or potential treason, the special departments engage in a massive active surveillance campaign. The campaign includes human and electronic surveillance of all categories of military personnel; study of the morale and stability of individual officers and men or of groups; discovery of dissatisfaction with the regime and of actions hostile to it; and the uncovering of abuses, negligence, and any other undesirable manifestations among officers and men.[13]

Occasionally, Third Directorate arrests for political crimes come to light. In May 1969 three Soviet naval officers were arrested for founding a group that called itself a Union to Struggle for Political Rights. The KGB discovered copies of the United Nations Declaration on Human Rights and two poems—one entitled "Dream on Freedom," the other "On the Death of Kennedy." A few months later, during the summer of 1969, the KGB arrested thirty-one additional naval personnel. The personnel, stationed in Estonia, were possibly arrested for criticism of the Soviet invasion of Czechoslovakia.[14]

In order to prevent such occurrences, the Third Directorate works closely with the MPA. Representatives of the special departments attend monthly meetings at MPA headquarters in military districts to discuss the level of discipline among the troops. Indeed, the special departments may be taking on a portion of the educative, indoctrination function usually considered the responsibility of the MPA. Amy

Knight cites the following incident described in a Soviet book on the special departments:

> News reached the 00 [Special Department] that in a small, distant garrison two young soldiers were discussing Soviet foreign policy and taking the wrong position. The 00 conducted several talks with these soldiers and their behavior became the subject of a stern, critical examination by their comrades at a meeting of soldiers.[15]

To carry out their surveillance functions, the Third Directorate has planted informers "in every military subdivision, in every class in intermediate and higher military educational institutions, in personnel departments, directorates, and orderly rooms, at bases, depots, shops, hospitals, cultural-educational organizations, post exchanges, and other military trade establishments."[16] The proportion of informers among military personnel during World War II was approximately 12 percent, but figures probably vary from 1 to 3 percent depending on the branch of the service.[17]

These informers are drawn from all categories of military personnel including general officers as well as from civilians employed by the military. Informers are not paid for their work but work on a "voluntary" basis due to their "political conscientiousness." At the company level informers usually focus on drunkenness, arguments, fights, insulting subordinates, poor work attitudes, violation of military orders or regulations, religious or anti-Soviet statements, criticism of Party or government policy, or any other manifestation of discontent. Sometimes informers or agents serve a provocateurs. The provocateur will start a discussion of an "anti-Soviet" nature in the presence of a targeted individual and observe how the individual reacts. Likewise, the provocateur might steal weapons or classified documents and then forward them to the Third Directorate in order to check security procedures.[18]

At higher levels more attention may be paid to counterespionage duties, particularly with regard to surveillance of the GRU. There are at least three cases of GRU officers serving as agents of the CIA and/or British Secret Intelligence Service: Colonel Peter Popov and Colonel Oleg Penkovskiy in the late 1950s and early 1960s and Colonel Anatoli Filatov in the 1970s. These agents provided the United States with hundreds of sensitive documents concerning intelligence operations, weapons systems capabilities, and nuclear targeting policy—in some cases at critical times. Thus, much of

Penkovskiy's material, including a medium range ballistic missile (MRBM) manual, was passed to the United States at the time of the Cuban missile crisis.[19]

Under task number 11 of Military Counter-intelligence Order 00270, the special departments are responsible for operations in the areas in the immediate vicinity of military installations. In support of these functions the special departments regularly receive operational-political surveys of such areas from the KGB. The documents contain a political description of those administrative areas of the Soviet Union from which given military formations receive new recruits.[20]

The surveys provide information concerning the local population and its ethnic composition as well as possible causes for hostility toward the regime. Such surveys may consider a variety of factors: whether the population lived under German occupation during the war, whether the population of the area includes a large number of prisoners serving out their sentences, and whether there had been Soviet deportations of the population due to a lack of political reliability.[21]

Inasmuch as Soviet forces are stationed on the Soviet border and in foreign countries, the functions of the Third Directorate have a foreign dimension. There are several hundred representatives of the Third Directorate in East Germany, their main task being the security of the Group of Soviet Forces in Germany (GSFG) and counter-espionage directed against the U.S., British, French, and West German intelligence services. Aleksei Myagkov, when assigned to the Third Directorate unit attached to the GSFG, was told that his tasks included:

1. first, to prevent in the battalions assigned to you, Western espionage agencies from recruiting any Soviet citizen whatsoever, military or civilian;
2. second, if the Western agencies have already recruited someone then it is your business to find that person and render him harmless;
3. third, seeking out anti-Soviets, the enemies of Soviet power; and
4. fourth, seeking out Western espionage agency agents among East German nationals residing near your charges.[22]

He was further instructed that to carry out these tasks he should plan to recruit "agents, agents, and more agents."

In one counterespionage operation one of Myagkov's informers reported that an East German citizen who then lived in Bernau kept certain "mysterious" chemical substances at his home. She was instructed to steal some of these substances. When analyzed, it was discovered that they could be used to prepare secret texts. The suspect was put under close observation and it was soon established that, under various pretexts, he often turned up near military emplacements and sometimes, under the pretext of buying goods, even in Soviet shops. Further investigation established his involvement in collecting information on Soviet units. After his arrest and during his interrogation he confessed that he had been working for the French for about fourteen years.[23]

BORDER TROOPS

The Soviet border troops represent the largest single component of the KGB. The Chief Directorate of Border Troops consists of between 200,000 and 250,000 personnel.[24] The border troop organization consists at the Moscow main headquarters of a chief of staff responsible for intelligence, operations, communications, and training; a chief of the political directorate; and the chief of the rear, responsible for logistics and procurement. The Moscow headquarters may be an operational one with day-to-day activity along the 37,500 miles Soviet frontier being controlled and coordinated or closely watched from headquarters.[25]

Soviet border troops are distributed around the perimeter of the Soviet Union in about nine border districts adjacent and parallel to the national border. Some of the individual district areas are thought to extend along the border from 600 to more than 1,800 miles and to stretch 185 to 375 miles into the interior.[26] Figure 11–1 shows the concentration of border troops, the greatest concentrations being on the Southwest Asian/Chinese border, and the northeastern Siberian border.

Subordinate to the district are a number of border detachments. The districts are thought to have at least six detachments, each detachment being responsible for land areas from 30 to 300 miles in length and 30 to 60 miles in depth. Each detachment has from three to five line commands, each command consisting of three to seven line outposts, a reserve outpost, and a support outpost. The outposts

Figure 11-1. Soviet Border Guard Concentration.

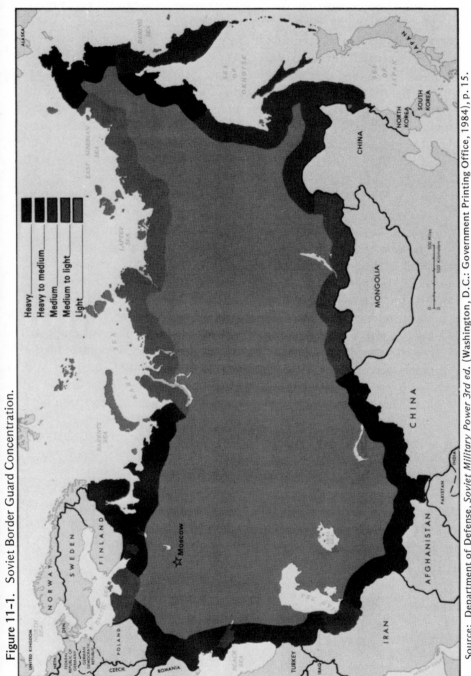

Source: Department of Defense, *Soviet Military Power 3rd ed.* (Washington, D.C.: Government Printing Office, 1984), p. 15.

consist of approximately fifty men and cover an area as small as three miles by two miles to one as large as twelve miles by ten miles.[27]

The primary function of the border troops is to seal off the border—to prevent Soviet citizens from exiting.[28] The secondary function is to defend Soviet borders from incursions by foreign troops. In the case of a full-scale onslaught, the border troops would be responsible for delaying the invading troops until regular military forces could arrive.

The border troops are equipped with small arms including light and heavy machine guns as well as some armored personnel carriers. Some units might be equipped with light tanks, light artillery, and mortars. The border troops have been described as being completely motorized and possessing whatever transportation is required by a particular terrain, including horse-mounted and ski patrols.[29]

In seeking to maintain the physical security of Soviet borders, the border troops employ a vast combination of security procedures and checks. Included are pass controls, hidden and open chemical and electronic barriers, searchlights, infrared devices, telescopes, dogs, mines, fences, wire, ploughed areas, fixed and roving patrols, detection and alarm devices, explosives, trip wires, and observation posts. This elaborate network is reinforced by the human watchmen of the border troops. Additionally, the air elements employ airplanes and helicopters to patrol border areas that are not otherwise easily accessible. These aircrafts are used for reconnaissance, transportation of supplies, and operations.[30]

The pass control system tightens by degree by zones as distance from the border decreases. The system limits the number and type of people living in the border zones. In the immediate border area inhabitants and traffic is completely forbidden. Border troop units are stationed at the small number of legal entry-exit road and rail crossing points as well as international entry points at Soviet airports and seaports. Legal travelers, whether entering or exiting, are subjected to strict scrutiny, all vehicles being searched for illegal crossers.[31]

In addition its ground and air elements, the border troops also maintain significant numbers of maritime troops. Maritime units are thought to be assigned directly to the headquarters of districts with water areas. Most units are equipped with light, fast, armed cutters, many on hydrofoils. These units are responsible for enforcing the twelve-mile territorial waters limit along the Soviet sea frontiers.[32]

Maritime units are also found at the major border lake and river areas. Shore elements of the maritime units also conduct shore and port security watches, employing towers and searchlights. In some instances they maintain wharfside guards or guards on a ship under surveillance. A *Red Star* article claimed that the maritime border troops vessels travel more than 2.5 million miles each year along the Soviet frontiers.[33]

In some instances, the border troops may operate on foreign soil. Thus, in border areas that are adjacent to hostile Communist or any non-Communist country, the border troops employ undercover operatives for counterintelligence and intelligence purposes. These operatives are active on both sides of the border, gathering tactical intelligence to a considerable depth into foreign territory. During the occupation of Germany the border troops played a role in guarding the critical German atomic research facilities. Additionally, according to Soviet sources, they guarded important installations (such as the site of the surrender negotiations) as well as war criminals. More recently, Polish and Soviet border troops have engaged in joint operations, and the Soviet troops helped North Vietnam set up a border troop system.[34]

As a result of its variety of roles that overlap with other intelligence and military organizations, the border troops apparently coordinate some of their activities with organizations outside the KGB. Thus, cross-border intelligence operations are probably coordinated with intelligence directorates of the military districts on the Soviet border. The border troops also coordinate with the army and Ministry of Internal Affairs (MVD) with regard to actions in the event of war. Border Troop commanders have the responsibility of drafting and maintaining an up-to-date local defense plan with their opposite numbers in the army and Ministry of Internal Affairs. The plan details actions to be taken in case of an armed attack and usually calls for an initial dispatch of ground forces or internal troops. These troops come under the operational command of the local border troop units until major army reinforcements arrive. Upon the latter's arrival, the border troops assume a rear security role, providing road, rail, and transportation protection as well as aiding antipartisan operations.[35]

GUARDS DIRECTORATE

Probably the most sensitive directorate in the KGB, at least to the Soviet leadership, is the Guards Directorate. The directorate, the primary responsibility of which is guarding the members of the Politburo and military leadership, is virtually an all-Russian ethnic organization. Only three nationalities are represented in the entire corps: Russian, Ukranian, and Byelorussian.[36]

The view of the Guards Directorate presented to the public is in the form of directorate personnel who make up the Special Guard battalion posted at almost every door and hallway in official buildings. The battalion consists entirely of officers. Entrance standards are the highest and strictest of any Soviet military organization. There are also thousands of directorate officers who keep a twenty-four-hour watch over particular stretches of roads and streets in the Kremlin.[37]

At Party meetings—whether congresses or Supreme Soviet meetings—an armed Guards officer sits at every table of fifteen or twenty delegates. In addition to a protective role, the officer serves to discourage any sudden subversive actions by any of the delegates. At larger functions, including Red Square parades and Moscow official government functions, the Guards are responsible for listing suspects in advance and ensuring that they are kept under strict surveillance for the duration of the event.[38]

At parades or demonstrations a significant proportion of those on the reviewing stand are members of the Guards Directorate armed with concealed weapons. In the late 1950s the rightmost individual in each row was a state security officer or agent or Party member given special clearance so as to lessen the chance of assassination attempts.[39]

During military parades a principal responsibility is to ensure that no troops carry live ammunition. Failure can bring a penalty of twenty-five years at hard labor for the soldier carrying the ammunition, his officers, and all Guards or other state security personnel involved in his clearance. Additionally, a full battalion of troops equipped with automatic weapons is stationed in the basement of the Lenin mausoleum, and machine gun posts are set upon the wall of the Kremlin and on the roofs of some of the nearby buildings.[40]

There is a certain degree of variation in the number and identity of officials who receive individual protection from the Guards. Generally, in addition to the members of the Politburo, the Chairman of the Council of Ministers and his deputies; the chairmen of the Council of Ministers of the component unit republics; and officials heading the Party committees in the republics, oblasts, and Krays are under protection of the Guards. Guards are also provided for visiting foreign officials.[41] In addition, some leading scientists and technicians receive individual protection beyond that afforded their installations.[42]

The total number of personnel assigned to the directorate is probably well over 20,000; a 1959 estimate put the number at 15,000.[43] The protection scheme developed gradually. Until 1943 the Guards consisted of one section of a directorate inside the state security service when it became an independent directorate. Its power and scope increased regularly until 1947, when it was consolidated with a separate directorate for guarding the Kremlin.[44]

There have been very few recorded assassination attempts against the Soviet leadership. During the twenty-five years of Stalin's rule, only two definite assassination attempts or plots were uncovered. The first was a shooting by a potential assassin near Adler, in the Caucasus, in 1930. The second plan was due to German military intelligence (the Abwehr), in 1942, but it was uncovered by a Soviet agent who had penetrated the Abwehr. The would-be assassin, who was to hurl a bomb into Stalin's car as he passed on the route Stalin took between his dacha and the Kremlin, was captured when he parachuted into the woods near Moscow.[45]

More recently, in January 1969 an assailant took several shots at the motorcade of then General Secretary Leonid Brezhnev. Although Brezhnev was unhurt, one bodyguard was killed and others wounded. Apparently, Brezhnev escaped solely due to the gunman's mistake. Possibly due to fear of military involvement in the attempt, Brezhnev beefed up the directorate, and liaison was strengthened with two standby divisions of state security troops.[46]

GOVERNMENT SIGNAL TROOPS

The Government Signal Troops, which are subordinate to the KGB, are responsible for the installation, maintenance, operation, and security of communications facilities. Additionally, they are responsible for communications between Moscow and the republic capitals as well as between the Ministry of Defense and the Groups of Soviet

Force headquarters in Eastern Europe. Within the KGB the signal troops are responsible for intra-KGB communications—communication between Moscow KGB headquarters and KGB headquarters at district, oblast, and Kray levels.[47] The present strength of the unit has been estimated at between 30 and 50,000 troops.[48]

In the event of nuclear war the signal troops would undoubtedly be responsible for attempting to maintain communications among the various components of the Soviet leadership and to vital institutions and activities. Thus, the signal troops probably have a major responsibility in planning to preserve and restore Soviet civilian and military command, control, and communications (C^3) in the event of a war and therefore probably man some of the numerous command bunkers distributed throughout the Soviet Union.

NOTES TO CHAPTER 11

1. Aleksei Myagkov, *Inside the KGB* (New York: Ballantine, 1981), p. 45.
2. John Barron, *KGB: The Secret Work of Soviet Secret Agents* (New York: Reader's Digest Press, 1974), p. 82.
3. Ibid.
4. Robert Gillette, "Soviets Outsting U.S. Diplomat as a Spy," *Los Angeles Times*, March 11, 1983, p. 4.
5. Dusko Doder, "Soviets Expel U.S. Diplomat as Spy," *Washington Post*, March 11, 1983, pp. A1, A7.
6. Barron, *KGB*, p. 83.
7. Serge Schmemann, "Moscow Issues a Law on Official Secrets," *New York Times*, February 4, 1984, p. 3.
8. Barron, *KGB*, p. 83.
9. Michael Deane, *Political Control of the Soviet Armed Forces* (New York: Crane & Russak, 1977), p. 282; Also see Timothy J. Colton, *Commissars, Commanders and Civilian Authority: The Structure of Soviet Military Politics* (Cambridge, Mass.: Harvard University Press, 1979).
10. Myagkov, *Inside the KGB*, pp. 175-76.
11. Amy W. Knight, "The KGB's Special Departments in the Soviet Armed Forces," *Orbis* 28, no. 2 (1984): 257-80.
12. Cited in Ibid., p. 275.
13. Vyacheslav P. Artemiev, "OKR: State Security in the Soviet Armed Forces," *Military Review* (September 1963): 21-31.
14. Barron, *KGB*, p. 16.
15. Knight, "The KGB's Special Departments in the Soviet Armed Forces."
16. Artemiev, "OKR: State Security in the Soviet Armed Forces."

17. Knight, "The KGB's Special Departments in the Soviet Armed Forces."
18. Artemiev, "OKR: State Security in the Soviet Armed Forces."
19. Oleg Penkovskiy, *The Penkovskiy Papers* (New York: Doubleday, 1965); William Hood, *Mole* (New York: W. W. Norton, 1982); John Prados, *The Soviet Estimate: U.S. Intelligence and Russian Military Strength* (New York: Dial Press, 1982), p. 148; Harry Rositzke, *The CIA's Secret Operations* (New York: Reader's Digest Press, 1977), pp. 68–69.
20. Artemiev, "OKR: State Security in the Soviet Armed Forces."
21. Ibid.
22. Myagkov, *Inside the KGB*, pp. 37, 80–81.
23. Ibid., pp. 102–3.
24. Department of Defense, *Soviet Military Power 1984* (Washington, D.C.: U.S. Government Printing Office, 1984), p. 14.
25. James T. Reitz, "The Soviet Security Troops—the Kremlin's Other Armies," *Soviet Armed Forces Review Annual* 6 (1982): 279–326.
26. Ibid.
27. Ibid.
28. Department of Defense, *Soviet Military Power 1984*, p. 15.
29. Reitz, "The Soviet Security Troops . . ."
30. Ibid.
31. Ibid.
32. Ibid.
33. Ibid.
34. Ibid.
35. Ibid; also see Amy W. Knight, "Soviet Politics and the KGB-MVD Relationship," *Soviet Union* 11, no. 2 (1984): 157–81.
36. Peter Deriabin and Frank Gibney, *The Secret World* (New York: Ballantine, 1982), p. 134.
37. Ibid., p. 135.
38. Ibid.
39. Ibid.
40. Ibid.
41. Ibid.
42. Ibid., p. 137.
43. Ibid., p. 134.
44. Ibid., pp. 137–38.
45. Ibid.
46. Peter Deriabin, *Watchdogs of Terror: Russian Bodyguards from the Tsars to the Commissars* (Frederick, Md.: University Publications of America, 1982), p. 349–50.
47. Reitz, "The Soviet Security Troops . . ."
48. Department of Defense, *Soviet Military Power 1984*, p. 14.

12 POLITICAL POLICE OPERATIONS

The KGB's internal functions fall into two basic categories: the internal security functions (dealt with in Chapter 11) and the political police function. It is this latter function that leads to the KGB and other such institutions being labeled secret police forces. This chapter examines the objectives of the KGB in its internal operations, the targets of its activities and the laws, institutions and techniques employed to attain its objectives.

OBJECTIVES

One can distinguish differing and increasingly stringent objectives for a political police force. The particular level that force aims for is, in part, a function of the nature of the government or society it serves and determines the extent to which it seeks to penetrate or control society and the methods employed.

At a very minimum, a political police force seeks to prevent or at least limit or control any major organized political activity. In such cases, the regime may see a value in maintaining a facade of democracy—as a means of preventing any real opposition or obtaining aid or favorable international opinion. By permitting opposition groups to exist while at the same time preventing them, via infiltration and disruption, from operating effectively, it can have the "best" of both worlds.

At the next level, the objective will be to prevent not only any major organized political activity but to prevent or strictly control even minor organized political activity. Thus, it is not surprising that the KGB immediately seeks to eliminate any organized opposition group, no matter how small. The militant Action Group for the Defense of Human Rights, for example, was established in 1969. By the end of 1973 fourteen of its fifteen members had been warned into inaction or tried and imprisoned. The small Human Rights Committee, organized in 1970 by Andrei Sakharov, became inactive by 1973.[1]

At the next level, a political police force may seek to prevent the public communication of dissenting political, social, or economic views—whether they are communicated orally or in print. Thus, the KGB devoted great effort to closing down the *Chronicle of Human Events*—a move it accomplished by threatening to punish a number of innocent hostages if another issue appeared.[2] Likewise, anyone who publicly protested, in any manner, the Soviet invasion of Czechoslovakia was subject to arrest and imprisonment.[3]

An even higher level of political control involves the secret police in attempts to prevent even the private communication of dissenting views. Such an effort involves a quantum leap in manpower requirements over that required for simply eliminating or controlling public dissent. It requires an informer network that penetrates the entire society.

Preventing even private communication of dissenting views can be an objective because it is feared that such private dissent will inevitably lead to public dissent and then to organized dissent. Preventing private dissent may also be more than a preventive measure. Total conformity may be the goal.

Conformity involves, at the very least, an outward total acceptance of the views and policies of the government and ruling party. In 1982 the then First Deputy Chairman of the KGB denounced as "western-backed subversion" reports on Soviet consumer shortages and emigrating Jews, fundamentalist Moslems, and rock music. He further indicated that any dissent, any ideological or social departure from the approved was instigated by Western subversion.[4]

In its most extreme form the conformity involves the surrender by individual citizens of their critical facilities concerning public and social matters—accepting the dictates of the regime without question and accepting the regime's statements as true. Thus, rather than follow the regime's orders reluctantly, the citizenry gives it full support and cooperation. A regime with such support and cooperation can achieve its objectives—military, economic, political, and social—far more easily.

To attain such conformity requires not only a political police force but a massive program of ideological indoctrination. The political police effort must also be massive; it must seek to prevent "disloyal" thoughts, the exchange of opinions, and all but approved contact with potentially subversive influences, whether they be foreign citizens or foreign cultures.

TARGETS

Given the objective of conformity sought by the KGB and CPSU, one can say that the entire Soviet population is the target of the KGB's political police efforts. As seen in Chapter 11, this includes the armed forces. As seen later in this chapter, it also includes the Soviet scientific elite.

In addition to the general population, there are several groups that are specific targets of KGB attention due to their "subversive" nature. Included are churches, dissidents, emigrant groups, Helsinki (human rights) monitoring groups, peace groups, national minorities, and even groups that complain about the treatment of the disabled. In addition, there are the foreign elements that might subvert "law-abiding" Soviet citizens or give aid and comfort to dissenters. Included in this latter group are foreign literature, foreign journalists, radio broadcasts, and tourists. All represent threats to conformity and unquestioned obedience to Party direction.

Religious groups tacitly represent public rejection of the Party wisdom on the pointlessness of spiritual worship. Further, such groups offer an alternative "gospel" to that of the CPSU as well as potential centers of political opposition—as underscored by the activities of the Polish church. Hence, elimination or control of such groups is an important aspect of KGB political police operations.

It is not surprising, then, that 1981 saw the arrest and trial of seventy-five Baptists and imprisonment of twenty Seventh-Day Adventists and twenty Pentecostalists.[5] When the Reverend Billy Graham preached at the Russian Orthodox Church of the Resurrection in Moscow during 1984 the churchgoers included "many well-groomed young men [standing] impassively, their attention fixed more on Western reporters and the parishioners themselves than on Mr. Graham." Additionally, "dozens more KGB agents and policemen patrolled the streets outside, quietly diverting some passers by from the street leading to the Church."[6] On another occasion in Moscow the KGB and police blockaded the streets leading to the church and prevented several dozen ticketholders, along with all the Western correspondents, from entering.[7]

Emigrant groups are also a source of annoyance to the Soviet authorities. Any substantial emigration, whether by Jews, Volga Germans, or others, would represent a substantial dissatisfaction with a regime and society that claims to be superior to all others. Second, for security reasons, the Soviets are hesitant to permit emigration by scientists who have worked in advanced scientific or military research facilities—assuming they would be debriefed by Israeli or other Western intelligence services. During 1981 at least twelve Jews campaigning for the right to emigrate to Israel or for the preservation of Jewish culture were arrested or tried. A number of Volga Germans were also arrested for seeking to emigrate.[8]

National minorities also represent a source of concern—a very large concern. The Soviet Union is only partly Russian: The Russian Soviet Federated Socialist Republic (RSFSR) is only one of sixteen republics that constitute the Soviet Union. Many of these republics are composed of individuals with different histories, languages, and cultures than the RSFR.[9] These differences represent departures from the conformity desired and roadblocks to equating loyalty to the CPSU with Russian patriotism.

Further, such disparities are of particular concern with respect to the present composition and deployment of the armed forces of the Soviet Union. Thus, troops are not stationed in their native republics for fear that their loyalty to public and culture of their native republics would outweigh their loyalty to the CPSU. Of particular concern is whether such troops, stationed in their native republics, would be willing to use force on behalf of the CPSU against their fellow citizens. In the long term, the higher birth rates for Central Asians as compared to White Russians has led to concern over the "yellowing" of the Soviet populace and the armed forces.[10]

Hence, the KGB seeks to penetrate and control national minority groups concerned with any subject—economic, cultural, or political. The authorities have arrested and imprisoned members of non-

Russian nationalities who have protested against what they consider an official policy of "Russification"—discrimination against national minorities and attempts to supplant national cultures and languages with Russian culture and language—or who have advocated political independence for their nations in accord with Article 72 of the Soviet constitution.[11]

Between February and April 1981, ten Armenians seeking political independence for Armenia by nonviolent means were arrested or tried in Erevan. All were charged with "anti-Soviet agitation and propaganda" as well as "participation in an anti-Soviet organization." Five of the ten were accused of organizing a nationalist group known as the "Union of Young Armenians." The alleged leaders were both given twelve-year sentences of imprisonment and internal exile; their colleagues received sentences of between three and eight years.[12]

Peace groups not approved (directed) by the Soviet government as well as human rights groups are also targets of surveillance, disruption, and other KGB actions. Peace groups not directed by the Soviet government, even if not opposed to Soviet policies per se, represent to the CPSU an unacceptable independent political force. Hence, the KGB harassed out of existence the founders of a citizen's committee in Moscow that opposed the arms race, despite the fact that it didn't oppose particular Soviet policies. At least one of its members was jailed, others were called in for frequent interrogations, and its founder was confined to a psychiatric hospital for more than a month.[13]

Of course, groups that monitor and report on Soviet abuses of human rights—especially those directed by the KGB—are a particularly annoying thorn in the side of the KGB and Party leadership. They offer an independent interpretation of events as well as sullying the Soviet Union's international image. Thus, in 1976 a Helsinki accords monitoring group, the Public Group to Promote the Fulfillment of the Helsinki Accords in the USSR, was formed. Of the eighty-seven self-appointed monitors, fifty-one are now in prison. Nearly all eighty-seven have been either jailed, abused in the official press, or physically attacked. Forty-four were sentenced simply for membership in the group; others were arrested and jailed for "anti-Soviet agitation and propaganda" or "anti-Soviet slander."[14]

The Soviet dissident movement has been a relatively recent phenomenon. Stalin's purges and terror tactics eliminated all open expression of dissent within and outside the Party, and even in his postwar years dissent was confined to small and secret study groups—groups consisting of liberal party intellectuals, religious, and ethnic minorities.[15]

Dissenters began to come into the open as a result of the Khrushchev thaw and the de-Stalinization that followed. The dissident movement of the last fifteen years was spurred on by events occurring in 1966 and 1968. In 1966 two Russian writers, Andrei Sinyavsky and Yuri Daniel, were put on trial for publishing abroad, under the names of Abram Terz and Nikolay Azhak. Their writings were alleged to contain "the dirtiest slanders against their country, against the Party, and against the Soviet system."[16]

In 1968 the Soviet invasion of Czechoslovakia resulted in protests—protests that were followed by arrests and secret police harassment. On August 25 a small crowd in Moscow's Red Square tried to protest with the result that five persons were arrested, including the wife of Yuri Daniel and the son of former Soviet Foreign Minister Maxim Litvinov.[17]

These events served to galvanize dissenting intellectuals and stimulate further dissident activities, in terms of meetings, unofficial publications, and communications with foreign journalists. Despite the fact that it never constituted or represented more than a tiny fraction of the population, this developing movement was extremely disturbing to the Soviet leadership. The dissident ranks, though small, included many articulate and well-known writers and scientists with ties to the West. Moreover, the movement itself represented a broad challenge to the CPSU—challenging its policies and legitimacy in a way that ethnic minorities or religious groups did not.

Since 1969 (when the KGB's Fifth Chief Directorate was formed), the KGB has devoted extensive time and energy in attempting to crush the dissident movement in the Soviet Union. The most prominent targets have been individuals such as Anatoli Scharkansky and Andrei Sakharov, who have been the victims of prison terms or external exile. The KGB has sought by such means to cut their ties with other Soviet dissidents as well as with the West.

Additionally, the suppression of *samizdat* (underground) literature has been a high priority. The literature has included individual manuscripts as well as regular publications such as *A Chronicle of Current Events* and Roy Medvedev's *Twentieth Century*.

Emigration can be another tactic employed to choke off dissent. Georgi N. Vladimov, considered one of the best Soviet postwar writers, was permitted to emigrate in January 1983; his request, however, followed a series of KGB searches, interrogations, and threats involving the seizure of manuscripts and correspondence as well as threats by the KGB to arrest his wife.[18]

Other targets were the officers of the Russian Social Fund, also known as the Solzhenitsyn Fund, a semiclandestine group that has aided thousands of Soviet political prisoners and their families over the last decade.[19] The attack on the Solzhenitsyn Fund was part of a broad onslaught, a mopping up of dissidents that included young lawyers, pacifists, right-wing Russian nationalists, consumer activists, members of religious groups, and members of SMOT, an independent and loosely knit trade union movement most of the leaders of which are imprisoned in labor camps or psychiatric institutions. Obscure political and religious groups that have had virtually no contact with the West were also purged in this sweep.[20]

This campaign also included as a major target professionals, some of whom or whose parents have held important positions. In October 1982 the KGB rounded up the leaders of an underground Socialist group in Leningrad, all of the members of which were well-educated young professionals. Referring to themselves as a "new left" opposition, they had begun a discussion journal, *Perspectives*, and were apparently planning a conference with similar groups from other cities. Despite demonstrations against the arrests by 200 students, one of the leading activists, Arkady Tsurkov, was convicted of "anti-Soviet agitation and propaganda." Tsurkov was sentenced to a total of seven years imprisonment and external exile; another dissident, Alexander Skobov, was committed to a psychiatric hospital.[21]

Another journal, *Variants*, had been appearing in Moscow since 1977. In spring of 1982 the KGB obtained leads concerning *Variants* and on April 6 conducted widespread searches and arrests in Moscow. Six men were arrested and charged with anti-Soviet agitation and propaganda. The dissidents arrested included:

- a graduate student of the Institute of World Economics and International Relations (IMEMO);

- a historian specializing in modern Latin American history, whose father was one of the Central Committee experts on Scandinavian countries;

- a senior automatic systems engineer of a research institute;

- a scientific researcher at the USSR Academy of Sciences Institute of Chemical Physics;
- a petroleum engineer; and
- a graduate student from the State Institute of Theatrical Art and son of a well-known critic.[22]

The average age of those charged was thirty.

Even a group formed to deal with the problems of the disabled was subject to KGB harassment. The KGB has conducted a four-year campaign against the Action Group to Defend the Rights of Disabled Persons in the Soviet Union, a group formed in 1978 by a small group of severely handicapped individuals who felt that their appeals for equal rights were being met with official indifference. Since its inception the group has issued a large number of documents protesting Soviet persecution of the disabled.[23] As a result, it has become a target of the KGB, its members being subjected to violent house searches, seizures of books and letters, death threats, beatings, unlawful arrests, psychiatric confinement, and deportation. In March 1981, according to the Helsinki commission, the KGB set fire to the workshop of Yuri Kiselev, an artist and founding member of the group, who has no legs and moves about on a small trolley.[24]

Foreign journalists, businessmen, and tourists also are targets. Inasmuch as they represent intelligence threats as well as providing a means by which dissidents can make their views and activities known in the West, they will be the concern of both the Second and Fifth Chief Directorates.

Expulsions of Western reporters can dramatize the risks to both Soviet citizens and reporters for unauthorized contacts. During the 1980 Moscow Olympics, foreign journalists covering the games were officially assured that they would not be harassed by the security authorities. At the same time, it was made clear that they were not free to investigate the nature of contemporary Soviet society by interviewing Soviet citizens and photographing non-Olympic scenes or arrests.[25] The KGB was particularly concerned that dissidents would take advantage of the presence of television cameras to stage a media event with worldwide impact—for example, demonstrators carrying placards ("Human Rights," "Jerusalem Now") or a man being hauled off to a jail in front of a camera.[26]

Aside from the Olympics, foreign correspondents have been harassed and expelled to discourage unauthorized contacts. In some situations, they may be set up and accused of espionage as a prelude to expulsion. The KGB also seeks to prevent the intrusion of foreign ideology by way of publications or broadcasts. In addition to routinely seizing publications ranging from *Time* to *Playboy* at border checkpoints, the KGB devotes a significant effort to the jamming of broadcasts from Radio Liberty, the BBC, and Voice of America. Complementing these activities are attempts to detect those listening to forbidden broadcasts.

LAWS, INSTITUTIONS, AND TECHNIQUES

As is clear from the discussion above, the KGB and the Soviet government employ a wide range of methods in their attempts to eliminate dissent and ensure conformity. And although the KGB would and does act in violation of the law, it also desires to eliminate dissent legally, if possible.

Two weapons in this battle are Article 70 and Article 190-1 of the Soviet constitution. Adopted in 1960, Article 70 concerns "Anti-Soviet Agitation and Propaganda" and makes slander of the Soviet political system or the distribution, preparation, or accumulation of anti-Soviet literature punishable by deprivation of freedom for from six months to seven years if carried out with the purpose of weakening or undermining Soviet power or engaging in dangerous crimes against the state.[27]

Article 190-1 was adopted in 1966 and concerns the distribution of false information that slanders the Soviet state and social system. It stipulates that the distribution in oral, handwritten, printed, or any other information of false information about the Soviet state and social system is punishable by deprivation of freedom for a period of up to three years or exile for up to five years.[28]

Beyond the laws there are several institutions that play a role in the attainment of political police objectives. Included are various councils, GLAVLIT, first departments, and special psychiatric hospitals for the criminally insane. Thus, to control the churches the Party established the Council for the Affairs of the Russian Orthodox Church and the Council for the Affairs of Religious Sects, responsible for all non-Orthodox sects. In 1966 the two councils were merged into a single Council for Religious Affairs. The first chairman of the Council for the Affairs of the Russian Orthodox Church was an NKVD general, and ever since, regulatory councils have been controlled by the KGB or its predecessors.[29]

GLAVLIT is the Chief Administration for Safeguarding State Secrets in Print. A KGB-run organization, it employs 70,000 full-time censors to screen virtually every item prior to publication. Virtually everything printed, even a bus ticket, must bear a censor's approval code mark.[30]

An important means by which the KGB maintains its pervasive network throughout Soviet society is via the first departments in every Soviet organization—whether economic, military, or political. These KGB-manned first departments function in both personnel and security roles. They provide a KGB presence at each institution that cannot be missed. This presence also provides for an on-site channel between KGB headquarters and the directors of a particular institutions—a channel via which KGB directions can be transmitted. The first departments allow on-site daily KGB supervision of activities—security, political, or production.

First departments can be found in factories, research institutes (such as the USA Institute and IMEMO), design bureaus, and so on. Indeed, the KGB watches all scientific institutions from the Academy of Sciences on down.[31] In addition, basic scientific research institutions are coordinated by the State Committee on Science and Technology (GKNT), which, as noted, is heavily staffed by GRU officers.[32]

A frequently used set of institutions in the KGB's war against dissent are the special psychiatric hospitals for the criminally insane. The most prominent of these institutions is the Moscow Central Research Institute for Forensic Psychiatry, also known as the Serbsky Institute, which treats Soviet citizens suffering from political nonconformity.[33]

The institute had a special diagnostic department, headed until his death by KGB Colonel Daniel Lunts, which collaborated closely with the KGB and political authorities in providing false diagnoses of political offenders' mental conditions.[34] Thus, Major General Petr Grigorevich Grigorenko, who was arrested on May 7, 1969 after protesting the beating of Crimean Tartars and urging withdrawal of Soviet troops from Czechoslovakia, was diagnosed by Lunts as suffering from "schizophrenia of the paranoid type."[35] Other prisoners reported to have been confined to special hospitals have included a Georgian nationalist, a worker's rights campaigners, and various Latvian Pentecostalists.[36]

Some of the chiefs of staff of the special psychiatric hospitals, which are designed for "treatment" of the especially provocative or dangerous dissidents, are MVD officials. Each special psychiatric hospital is headed by two chiefs: the director (an MVD commandant) and the chief doctor. All doctors who are heads of departments, as well as many of the treating doctors, are commissioned officers in the MVD.[37]

While the MVD is the only organization with an official role outside the psychiatric service, the KGB maintains a major presence through officers like Colonel Lunts and the directives transmitted via the First Department. The KGB has in numerous cases played a major role at various stages between confinement and release.[38] When a Leningrad engineer was confined to a psychiatric hospital in 1974 for the fourth time for his *samizdat* writings and his open protests on human rights violations to authorities, another well-known dissenter went to the deputy chief doctor of the psychiatric clinic where his friend had been diagnosed and ordered committed. "We possess the information and an evaluation from the competent authorities," the doctor told him, "officials of the KGB . . . They make a political judgment and phone us. . . . For us to make a medical diagnosis it's simply enough to know of the existence of antigovernment letters. There's no need to read them."[39] Likewise, when the wife of Georgy Feodotov, a religious activist, asked doctors at the psychiatric hospital when her husband would be discharged she was told that he could not be discharged until they received a signal.[40]

Commitment to a psychiatric hospital is one of the more extreme means of dealing with a dissident. However, this method has been used in the case of 346 individuals between 1977 and 1984. Fifty percent had engaged in sociopolitical activity, 13 percent in religious activity, 7 percent in nationalist activity, and 30 percent in emigration-related activity.[41] The "virtue" seen in commitment by the Soviet authorities lies in its being a means by which they can prevent dissidents from speaking out at trial—declaring them nonresponsible and shipping them off to an institution. Additionally, it is an attempt to discredit such dissidents, both at home and abroad, by labeling them insane. As a means of validating that image, the KGB may insti-

gate dissenting remarks from mentally ill individuals with the ultimate objective of exiling them abroad with the expectation that they
will end up in a mental institution.

Other extreme measures included prison and labor camps—
regimens from which some dissidents never return due to a combination of bad health and a harsh environment. Apparently, there has
been a growing use of torture and physical abuse of dissidents once
they reach such institutions—especially of dissidents who are well
known abroad.[42]

The main aims of this new policy are, it appears, to obtain "con-
fessions of guilt" from the victims and to intimidate their associates
and any other dissidents into submission. The simplest and most
direct means of inculcating the policy is to practice it on prominent
individuals, provoking foreign publicity, which in turn will be picked
up by Western radio stations and broadcast into the Soviet Union.[43]

For example, Anatoly Koryagin, a psychiatrist from Kharkov, was
given in 1981 up to twelve years of prison and exile for his detailed
public criticism of political abuse of psychiatry. After two years the
KGB tried to get him to recant by exerting a wide range of psychological and then physical pressures, progressing to outright torture.
Likewise, Sergei Khodorovich, for six years the publicly announced
administrator of the Russian Social Fund, was arrested and charged
with treason on the grounds that the fund is alleged to be CIA
financed. Apparently, Khodorovich was beaten up and suffered a
fractured skull. Further, he was told that he would be beaten continuously unless he confessed.[44]

A third technique for eliminating dissent is exile. Although that
does not silence dissidents with respect to the world at large, it does
remove them from activity within the Soviet Union. It also may be a
less costly means, in terms of international prestige, of silencing a dissident than jail. Solzhensitsyn does the Soviet Union less political
damage on his Maine farm than he would from inside a labor camp.

Short of incarceration or expulsion, the KGB has numerous means
of discouraging opposition political activity and encouraging political conformity. Threats and harassment provide means of letting
targets know that they are being watched and that their activities
could land them in jail. Thus, in 1981 the KGB warned a number of
Jewish scientists, who had been refused permission to emigrate,
about conducting informal scientific seminars in their apartments

and have threatened some with expulsion from the capital if they persist. The KGB was apparently intent on preventing the would-be emigrants from organizing an international gathering of scientists from the United States and Western Europe in Moscow.[45]

Beyond threats, a series of graduated pressures on active or potential dissidents is employed:

- A reprimand by the Party or by an institution like the Union of Soviet Writers puts a man on the alert.

- Expulsion from the Party, or from the Communist Youth League, curtails his career prospects and can ostracize him from professional and social life.

- A writer or artist forbidden to publish or exhibit his work is forced to take low-paid manual labor to avoid the criminal charge of being a "parasite."

- Firing one from a well-paid job in the establishment puts ones family in a tight spot in a society where all jobs are establishment jobs.[46]

Beyond such public harassment, a variety of private harassment techniques are employed, such as conducting obvious surveillance, warning colleagues against association with the dissident, or cutting off or tapping his or her telephone. Additionally, a KGB search may be conducted. Thus, one dissident had his house searched by some twenty agents armed with firearms, portable radios, mine detectors, flashlights, cameras, axes, crowbars, spades, and screwdrivers. The residents of the house were isolated in one room and placed under guard. The search lasted for almost twelve hours—beginning at 8:45 in the morning and ending at 8:15 in the evening. During the search the floors and ceilings were broken up and split, doors and walls were broken down, mattresses and pillows ripped apart. A magnetic lifting device and other electronic probes were used to examine cesspools.[47]

As can be seen, the KGB has a wide variety of means to suppress dissent and ensure political and social conformity and may use any one or a combination on a particular group depending on the specific individuals involved. In Moscow a few years ago a Western correspondent was handed a proclamation signed by seventy-two dissidents. One day a good number of them were at the Moscow Central Telephone Office picking up their mail and were seized by KGB agents and either

1. sent to psychiatric hospitals;
2. sentenced to fifteen-day prison terms;
3. expelled from Moscow under armed guard; or
4. made to sign a written promise to leave Moscow.[48]

TRENDS

As noted earlier, the dissident movement has been a relatively recent phenomenon. The natural strong KGB desire to eliminate such a movement plus the extra incentive of avoiding embarrassing incidents staged by dissidents during the Moscow Olympics has led to elimination of several human rights groups and publications in recent years. Between 1979 and 1984 roughly 1,000 dissidents have been arrested.

Having eliminated or suppressed the major dissidents—either by imprisonment, hospitalization, or internal or external exile—attention has been turned to smaller "threats," such as trade unionists, Baptists, Pentecostalists, and religious and nationalist dissidents in Lithuania and other Baltic states.

NOTES TO CHAPTER 12

1. Harry Rositzke, *The KGB: The Eyes of Russia* (Garden City, N.Y.: Doubleday, 1981), p. 261.
2. Ibid.
3. Boris Levytsky, *The Uses of Terror: The Soviet Secret Police 1917–1920* (New York: Coward, McCann and Geoghegan, 1972), p. 21.
4. Serge Schmemann, "Dissidents Routed, K.G.B. Chief Says," *New York Times*, October 7, 1981.
5. Amnesty International, *Amnesty International Report 1982* (London: Amnesty International Publications, 1982), p. 298.
6. Serge Schmemann, "Believers Flock to Graham as the KGB Watches," *New York Times*, September 17, 1984, p. A14.
7. Ibid.
8. Amnesty International, *Amnesty International Report 1982*, p. 300.
9. Helen d'Encausse, *Decline of an Empire: The Soviet Socialist Republics in Revolt* (New York: Harper & Row, 1981).

10. Enders Wimbush and Alexei Alexiev, *The Ethnic Factor in the Soviet Armed Forces* (Santa Monica, Calif.: RAND Corporation, 1982).
11. Amnesty International, *Amnesty International Report 1982*, pp. 299–300.
12. Ibid.
13. Richard Bernstein, "Andropov's KGB: Pervasive Force in Soviet Union," *New York Times* n.d.; "A Dark Tunnel of Fear," *Newsweek*, October 5, 1982, pp. 48, 53.
14. Jack Anderson, "The KGB at Work," *Washington Post*, November 14, 1982, p. C7.
15. Rositzke, *The KGB*, p. 252.
16. Levytsky, *The Uses of Terror*, p. 281.
17. Ibid., p. 293.
18. Serge Schmemann, "Writer Bids Soviet Let Him Emigrate," *New York Times*, January 13, 1983, p. 3.
19. John F. Burns, "K.G.B. Suppressing a Dissident Group," *New York Times*, May 22, 1983, p. 4.
20. Robert Gillette, "A Hidden Facet of Soviet Dissent New KGB Target," *Los Angeles Times*, August 2, 1982, pp. 1, 9–10.
21. Bohdan Nahaylo, "A New Left in Russia," *New Statesman*, n.d.
22. Ibid.
23. Walter Parchomenko and Frank G. Bowe, "Help Soviet Disabled," *New York Times*, May 30, 1984, p. A23.
24. Ibid.
25. Rositzke, *The KGB*, p. 266.
26. Ibid.
27. Zhores A. Medvedev, *Andropov* (New York: Norton, 1983), pp. 72–73.
28. Ibid.
29. John Barron, *KGB: The Secret Work of Soviet Agents* (New York: Reader's Digest Press, 1974), p. 101.
30. Ibid., p. 102.
31. Ibid.
32. Ibid.
33. Thomas Plate and Andrea Darvi, *Secret Police* (Garden City, N.Y.: Doubleday, 1984), p. 155.
34. Barron, *KGB*, p. 2; Plate and Darvi, p. 154.
35. Barron, *KGB*, p. 2.
36. Amnesty International, *Amnesty International Report 1982*, p. 301.
37. Plate and Darvi, *Secret Police*, p. 155.
38. Ibid., p. 154.
39. Ibid., p. 155.
40. Sidney Block and Peter Reddaway, *Soviet Psychiatric Abuse: The Shadow over World Psychiatry* (London: Victor Gollancz, 1984), p. 83.
41. Ibid., p. 253.

42. Peter Reddaway, "The KGB's Growing Practice of Torture," *Washington Post*, November 21, 1984, p. A17.
43. Ibid.
44. Ibid.
45. Robert Gillette, "Jewish Scientists in Moscow Warned by Police on Seminars," *Los Angeles Times*, September 29, 1981, p. 7.
46. Rositzke, *The KGB*, p. 257.
47. Plate and Darvi, *Secret Police*, p. 240.
48. Ibid.

13 CONCLUSIONS

As the most aggressive and least constrained arms of the Soviet Union in peacetime, the KGB and GRU are generally seen, on a day-to-day basis, as the most dangerous parts of the Soviet national security establishment. Concern over KGB and GRU activities tends to focus on their potential to threaten U.S. and Western military security—via intelligence and counterintelligence operations, theft of technology and active measures (particularly the alleged manipulation of peace groups), and their acquisition of information through open sources.

As demonstrated in Chapters 4 and 5, the Soviet intelligence services are certainly involved in a major effort to acquire information, often highly classified information, concerning foreign policy, defense matters, intelligence activities and economic–industrial matters, not only in the United States and Western Europe, but throughout the world. Just as obviously, the Soviet Union is attempting to acquire, by legal and illegal means, advanced technology, employing both its intelligence services and normal trade organizations. The concern in the United States over this latter activity is well demonstrated by the number of congressional hearings held over the last several years and attention the executive branch has devoted to the subject—attention demonstrated by the creation of new offices for intelligence analysis and enforcement in the Customs Service, CIA,

Department of Commerce, and Department of Defense. Likewise, the pressure that the Reagan administration has exerted on European allies and neutrals (e.g., Austria) to curb the flow of technology also vividly shows the concern in official circles.

Likewise, Soviet attempts to infiltrate or influence political groups in the West have drawn even more attention in recent years as groups in the United States and especially Europe have challenged, rather dramatically at times, the strategic nuclear policy of the United States and NATO. These challenges have come in the forms of the nuclear freeze movement and the movement opposing U.S. installation of ground-launched cruise missiles (GLCMs) and Pershing II missiles in Europe. Conservative spokesmen and journals such as *Reader's Digest* suggested that these movements were being manipulated by the KGB — a charge echoed by President Reagan.

In the area of counterintelligence, many authors have charged that United States and its Western allies have been the victims of a variety of Soviet counterintelligence, deception, and disinformation operations — and there have clearly been penetrations, at varying levels, of the U.S., British, and West German intelligence communities as well as at least one false defector in place (as detailed in Chapter 9). Beyond that, it has been charged that the Soviet Union has engaged in a massive campaign to deceive the United States concerning Soviet military, particularly strategic nuclear, capabilities by a variety of means, including feeding false data to U.S. technical collection systems.

Finally, there has been great concern over Soviet acquisition (often through the KGB and GRU) of unclassified material concerning defense and technology. Such concern is not new. During the Eisenhower administration an Office of Strategic Information was created within the Department of Commerce because of concern with Soviet acquisition of unclassified technical material. The office was to create a "prepublication awareness" of the extent to which the Soviets might be able to exploit certain types of information, such as aerial photography, in ways considered detrimental to U.S. national security.[1] More recently, the Secretary of Commerce charged that the Department of Defense and other federal agencies were permitting military and technical secrets to fall into Soviet hands by a sloppy and overly lenient declassification policy. In a letter to the Secretaries of State, Defense, and Energy as well as the administrator of NASA, the Secretary of Commerce requested help to stop "this massive giveaway program that permits the Soviets to acquire tens of thousands of scientific and technical studies as well as other strategic information."[2]

Although it is legitimate to be concerned about Soviet activities in all four areas, a case can also be made that in some cases the concern can be overdone, to the point of being counterproductive. In other cases, the concern has focused on only one of the victims. Despite Soviet acquisition of some very sensitive information via human intelligence operations, including U.S. war plans, the survival of the United States or Europe was never in danger. The damage is primarily economic—systems must be modified and countermeasures developed in response to the new knowledge the Soviets possess. If the nuclear age has brought any benefits, it is certainly that intelligence coups of whatever proportions cannot be exploited by one superpower in such a way as to eliminate the military capability of the other via surprise attack. For, whatever outcomes the computer war games might produce, such a "cosmic roll of the dice" seems to be precluded, not just by the cost of failure but even by the cost of success. Thus, while one might be concerned at possible Soviet acquisition of sensitive material it is also appropriate to be concerned that Soviet intelligence officers are seeking to obtain information not only from those only too willing to give or sell it to them but also by means of exploiting individuals' weaknesses—to the point of entrapment and blackmail.

Similarly, with regard to collection via the vast array of antennae that exist on Soviet embassies and consulates all over the world it should be noted that there are two victims. A nation as a whole or a government may be victimized by the interception of communications—whether military, political, or commercial. Additionally, the individuals whose conversations have been intercepted, whatever their position, have been victimized by an unjustified invasion of their privacy. Since the public exposure of this issue by Senator Daniel Patrick Moynihan it has received more attention, but obviously the ability of the Soviet Union to intercept and listen to unencrypted telephone conversations transmitted via microwave remains unchecked and troublesome, especially as such intelligence can be exploited for recruitment purposes.

Soviet attempts to influence the nuclear freeze and peace movements appear to have been unsuccessful, and claims of Communist subversion seem to have been analogous to the erroneous claims of Lyndon Johnson and Richard Nixon of Communist manipulation of the opposition to the war in Vietnam. Certainly, in the case of the U.S. nuclear freeze movement, the FBI's own investigation has shown Soviet influence to be negligible—in contradiction to President Reagan's claims.[3] Likewise, though U.S. intelligence officials have stated that the Soviet Union tried to capitalize on the freeze movement and that its agents were actively involved in planning a spring 1982 demonstration in the United States, they could find no evidence that those efforts had significantly influenced either U.S. policymakers or the turnout for the rally.[4] In such cases, the Soviet role is more that of follower than leader.

At the same time, the involvement of foreign covert agents, whether South Korean or Soviet, in the U.S. political process is obviously completely unacceptable. Attempts to detect and prevent such involvement, without violating the civil liberties of U.S. persons and without smearing those who oppose government policy should, of course, be pursued. Ironically, it was Ronald Reagan who stated that he believed "in the right of a country when it believes its interests are best served to conduct covert activity."[5]

Tied in with expressions of concern about Soviet active measures are often statements concerning Soviet agents of influence. Clearly, such agents do exist—witness the case of Pierre-Charles Pathé, discussed in Chapter 7. At the same time, the term "agent of influence" has been thrown around in a haphazard manner, being used to characterize—sometimes in "fictional" form—any influential person or group (e.g., the Institute of Policy Studies) that is not sufficiently "vigilant" as having, consciously or unconsciously, fallen under the Soviet spell. John Barron, in *KGB Today*, points to U.S. nuclear freeze congressmen who have talked to Soviet diplomats and participated in conferences with them in such a manner. Thus, the term agent of influence has often become the 1980s equivalent of "dupe" and "fellow traveler."

It is clear that in the area of counterintelligence the Soviet Union has achieved some major successes—for example, Kim Philby, George Blake, Heinz Felfe, William Kampiles, Geoffrey Prime. Philby and Blake, at least, were responsible for the early deaths or prolonged prison stays of large numbers of individuals. Other operations have sown confusion within the CIA and other Western intelligence services, and the material acquired from Prime, Kampiles, and Christopher Boyce gave the Soviets a detailed look at some of the most advanced technical collection systems possessed by the United States.[6]

Unfortunately, it has become an accepted truth to many that Soviet intelligence is so ubiquitous and omnipotent that the Western intelligence and security services are riddled with moles, that all defectors are false defectors, and that everything seen or heard by U.S. satellites is disinformation and deception—in other words, that the Soviet Union manages to conjure a completely false reality for the Western intelligence services while preparing in secret for its ultimate (sinister) goals. Likewise, every idle boast of a Soviet leader and every statement deploring war becomes "disinformation."[7]

Yet it should be clear that such a disinformation and deception campaign would be unmanageable; deception at the level implied would become reality since there would be little time for anything else. Military units that spend all their time undertaking deceptive maneuvers and fake missile tests would have no time for the real thing.

Beyond that, the charges of the Reagan administration concerning Soviet compliance with arms control treaties—charges based on intelligence data—refute the notion that the KGB and GRU can manipulate U.S. perceptions of reality. If the Soviet Union could so easily deceive U.S. technical and human collection systems why would it not have fed those systems data that would convince even the Reagan administration that the Soviets were in compliance with the provisions if SALT II and other arms limitation agreements?

Soviet acquisition of technology, particularly the covert acquisition, is yet another area where hyperexaggeration distorts a legitimate cause for concern. Dr. Peter Sharfman of the Office of Technology Assessment has noted that:

- Seldom, if ever, do the Soviets acquire a Western technology which they could not develop for themselves, given sufficient time and money.

- Delaying Soviet acquisition of certain technologies is attainable, denial is not.

- A significant consequence to the Soviets of relying on theft or illegal purchase is that the recipient is in a relatively poor position to capitalize fully on the acquisitions.[8]

In regard to the third, Sharfman gives the following example:

If the U.S.S.R. steals plans for an American weapon, not only must it develop its own complex system of operational support, but it will not necessarily have built the R&D base necessary if it is itself to build the next generation of the weapons. The Soviets would therefore be obliged to conduct another successful piece of espionage to gain access to the plans for the follow-on weapon.[9]

Thus, although the Soviets have made good use of the technology acquired, both legally and illegally, it does not follow that such acquisition always represents the preferred method or that if they had not acquired it from the West they would not have acquired it at all. Furthermore, according to a RAND Corporation report: "the chances of a sudden doomsday giveaway through trade are next to nil . . . the fear that the United States is unwittingly selling the rope that the Russians will shortly use to hang us is hardly credible."[10]

Part of the concern over Soviet acquisition of advanced technology has focused on their ability to acquire conference papers as well as papers appearing in academic journals. This represents an extension of concern from publications concerning cryptography to a much wider range of technical publications. Similar concern has focused on information concerning intelligence and defense matters appearing in a variety of technical or popular publications—sometimes as a result of the government releasing such information. The Reagan administration has since sharply cut back information available in several areas, including low-yield nuclear testing and the orbital parameters of certain satellites.

In the first case, there would seem to be a greater threat to U.S. security from unnecessary restrictions than from Soviet acquisition. The major reason for a U.S. technological lead is the unrestricted exchange of scientific ideas, both within and across U.S. borders. Scientific advancement is based on building on past accomplishments—theoretical and practical—and requires communication among scientists via contact and journals since it is impossible to know in advance who might be able to add the crucial piece that solves a puzzle. Restrictions that have an immediate impact on the Soviet Union today may have a more serious impact on the United States tomorrow.

In the second case, the threat is not so much to scientific advancement as to public information and the proper oversight of government activities. The Soviet Union, as detailed in Chapter 5, has an enormous system for collection of intelligence by technical means—information about nuclear testing, weapons systems performance, and space activities. "Protection" of information that the Soviet Union can easily acquire by such means deprives only the general public, who have no such collection systems but do have a need and a right to the information required to allow assessment of government claims concerning their military capabilities, Soviet capabilities, and the worth of proposed programs.

The underlying theme of this conclusion is twofold. First, the activities of the Soviet intelligence services certainly merit concern and monitoring by the U.S. and other counterintelligence authorities since their activities, if successful, are likely to be harmful both to states and individuals. Second, it is important while monitoring and counteracting those activities not to treat them as something that places Western civilization in dire and immediate peril and, as a result, lose sight of the values being protected.

NOTES TO CHAPTER 13

1. U.S. Congress, House Committee on Government Operations, *Availability of Information from Federal Departments and Agencies, Part 6* (Washington, D.C.: U.S. Government Printing Office, 1956), pp. 1671-7.

2. Stuart Auerbach, "Baldrige Warns of 'Giveaway' of Strategic Secrets to Soviets," *Washington Post*, February 21, 1985, pp. A1, A12.

3. Federal Bureau of Investigation, Intelligence Division, "Soviet Active Measures Relating to the U.S. Peace Movement," *Congressional Record*, March 24, 1983, pp. H1793-4. 1797.

4. Joanne Omang, "Soviet Effort in Nuclear Freeze Rally Cited," *Washington Post*, December 10, 1982, p. A4.

5. Tom Wicker, "A Policy of Hypocrisy," *New York Times*, October 21, 1983, p. A35.

6. For arguments that the Soviets did not gain as much as is generally believed from these disclosures, see Jeffrey Richelson, "The Keyhole Satellite Program," *Journal of Strategic Studies* 7, no. 2 (1984): 121-53 and Jeffrey Richelson and William Arkin, "Spy Satellites: 'Secret' but Much Is Known," *Washington Post*, January 6, 1985, pp. C1-C2.

7. See for example, Joseph D. Douglass, Jr., "The Growing Disinformation Problem," *International Security Review* 6, no. 3 (1981): 333-53.

8. U.S. Congress, House Armed Services Committee, *Technology Transfer* (Washington, D.C.: U.S. Government Printing Office, 1984), p. 6.

9. Ibid., p. 17.

10. Philip M. Boffey, "Assessing Technology Leaks," *New York Times*, January 2, 1985, pp. D1, D7.

INDEX

Abrahantes, Jose, 212
Academy of Sciences, 23, 24, 53
Action Group for the Defense of Human Rights, 246
Action Group to Defend the Rights of Disabled Persons in the Soviet Union, 252
active measures, 137–138, 261, 264; and agents of influence, 157–159; assassinations, 159, 162–164; by Cuban intelligence services, 221–224; forgeries, 138–146; paramilitary operations, 159–160; propaganda, 146–157; radio operations, 153–155; sabotage operations, 162; by Service A of KGB, 24, 138; terrorist operations, 160–161; by Warsaw Pact intelligence services, 221–224
activist emigrés as target for assassination, 162–164
Administration of Special Tasks, 12
Administrative Directorate of KGB, 31
Administrative Organs Department of CC, 50
Administrative/Technical Directorate of GRU, 38
Aeroflot, 81–82, 96, 98
Afghanistan, 99, 101, 158

Africa, 143, 146
Afro-Asian People's Organization, 151
agents of influence, 157–159, 264
AGI (Auxilliary-Intelligence Gathering) ships, 98–99, 106–107
aircraft, Soviet: II–18 Coot A, 98; Ram-M, 96; reconnaissance, 96, 105–107; TU–16 Badger, 106; TU–22 Blinder C, 106; TU–95D Bear, 95–96, 98, 105–106; TU–142 Bear F, 106
Albania, 53
Algeria, 224
Aliyev, Geidar, 46
All-Russian Extraordinary Commission for Combatting Counterrevolution and Sabotage. *See* Vecheka
All-Union Central Council of Trade Unions, 150
All-Union Institute of Scientific and Technical Information, 63
American Congress of Industrial Organizations, 150
American Department (Cuban), 211, 212
Amin, Hafizullah, 159, 164
Anders, Wladyslav, 200
Andropov, Yuri, 32, 46, 49, 219

269

ABOUT THE AUTHOR

Dr. Jeffrey Richelson received his Ph.D. in Political Science from the University of Rochester. He is an Assistant Professor of Government in the School of Government and Public Administration of The American University, Washington, D.C. He is the coauthor with Desmond Ball, of *Ties that Bind: Intelligence Cooperation Among Australia, Canada, New Zealand, the United Kingdom and the United States*, and author of *The U.S. Intelligence Community* (Ballinger, 1985). He lives in Alexandria, Virginia and is presently working on his next book.